THE FORSAKEN 14TH CENTURY

THE FORSAKEN 14TH CENTURY

A GLOBAL HISTORY

Mark Cartwright, Joshua J. Mark, Liana Miate, Patit Paban
Mishra, and James Blake Wiener

Edited by Ibolya Horváth
Cover design and maps by Simeon Netchev

World History Publishing

World History Publishing
UK Head Office, Brook House, Mint Street, Godalming, Surrey, GU7 1HE, United Kingdom

Copyright © 2025 World History Encyclopedia

All rights reserved.

No portion of this book may be reproduced in any form without written permission from the publisher or author(s), except as permitted by U.S. copyright law.

979-8-90148-349-7 (Hardback)

Cover design and maps by Simeon Netchev

Layout and proofreading by Joanne Taylor

Typeset in EB Garamond

While every effort has been made to provide accurate and authoritative information in regard to the subject matter covered, the publisher and authors make no representations or warranties with respect to the accuracy or completeness of the contents of this book, nor do they accept liability for any errors, omissions, or consequences arising from its use.

First Edition 2025

CONTENTS

Map of Maps	VI
List of Illustrations	VII
Timeline	IX
Preface	XVII
Map of the World in the 14th Century	XX
1. Japan	1
2. The Mongol Empire	27
3. China	57
4. India	77
5. Africa	97
6. Europe	135
7. North America	175
8. South and Mesoamerica	211
9. Oceania and Australia	245
About the Authors	269
Index	271

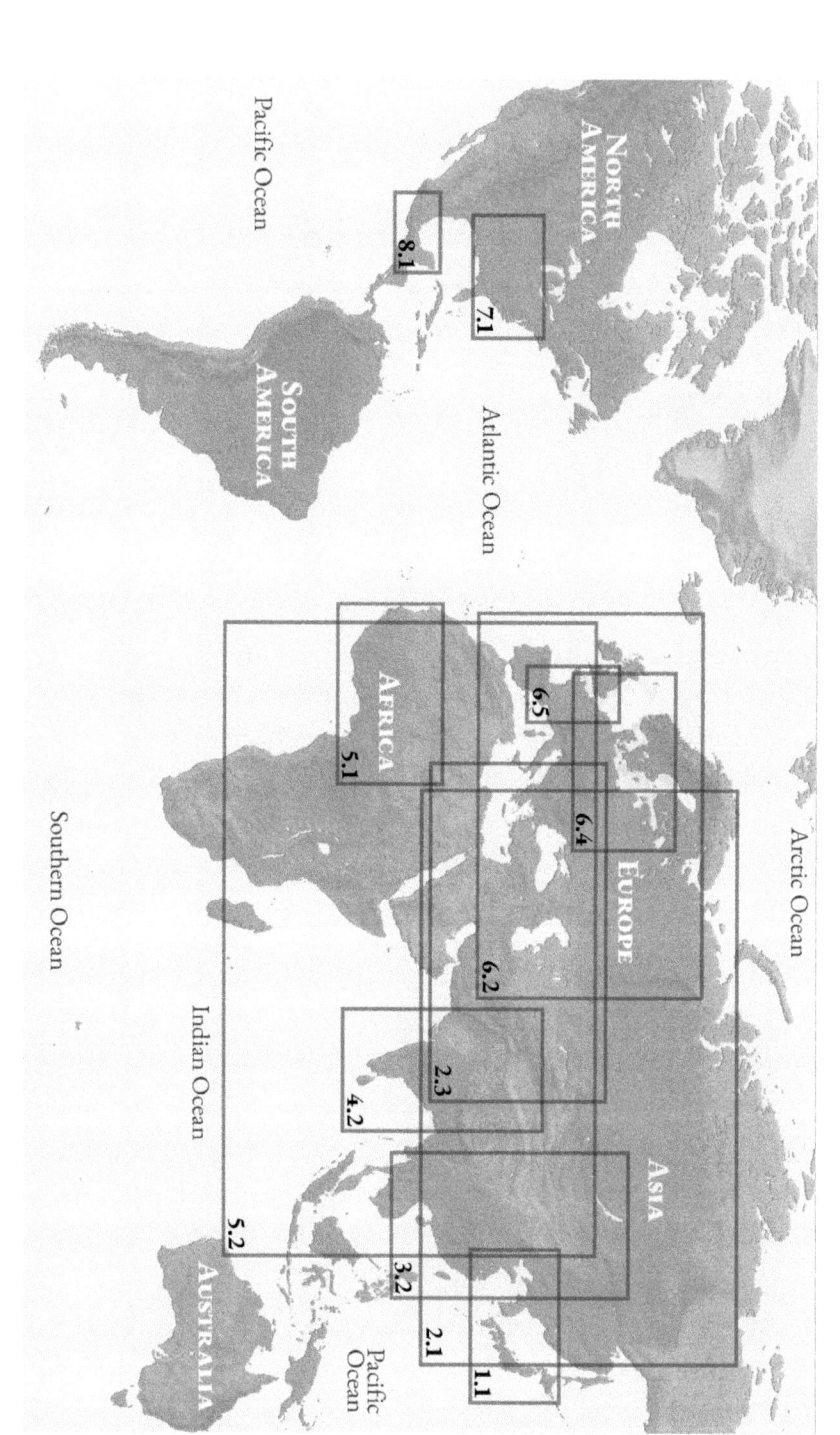

List of Illustrations

i. Map of Maps VI
ii. Map of the World in the 14th Century XX

CHAPTER 1 Japan
1.1 Map: Medieval Japan and Its Trade Relations ·7
1.2 The Great Buddha of Kamakura ·12
1.3 Kinkaku-ji Temple or the 'Golden Pavilion' ·19

CHAPTER 2 The Mongol Empire
2.1 Map: The Mongol Empire After Genghis Khan ·41
2.2 Mounted Warrior of the Mongol Empire ·43
2.3 Map: The Timurid Empire ·51

CHAPTER 3 China
3.1 Figure of a Mongol ·62
3.2 Map: The Ming Dynasty ·67
3.3 Burial Site of Ming Hongwu and Sun Zhongshan ·69
3.4 Bottle with Peony Scroll ·74

CHAPTER 4 India
4.1 Qutub Minar in Delhi ·81
4.2 Map: Medieval India ·87

CHAPTER 5 Africa

5.1 Map: The Mali Empire ·99

5.2 Map: Ibn Battuta's Travels ·107

5.3 Great Mosque of Kilwa ·118

5.4 Ife Terracotta Human Head ·123

CHAPTER 6 Europe

6.1 Infographic: Feudal Society in Medieval Europe ·137

6.2 Map: Spread of the Black Death ·143

6.3 Statue of Pope Boniface VIII ·150

6.4 Map: The Hanseatic League ·162

6.5 Map: The Hundred Years' War ·167

CHAPTER 7 North America

7.1 Map: Mississippian Cultures ·177

7.2 Etowah Statues ·181

7.3 Hopi Kachina Doll ·195

CHAPTER 8 South and Mesoamerica

8.1 Map: Mesoamerican Civilizations ·213

8.2 Turquoise Mosaic Mask of Xiuhtecuhtli ·224

8.3 Adobe Walls, Chan Chan ·236

CHAPTER 9 Oceania and Australia

9.1 Aerial View of Uluru ·247

9.2 Moa and Haast's Eagle ·254

9.3 Moai Statues, Easter Island ·259

Timeline

Circa 1300 The Ancestral Puebloan culture abandons Canyon de Chelly.

Circa 1300-1350 Ancestral Puebloans build pueblo settlements at Homolovi.

Circa 1300 to circa 1400 Kachina cult emerges in the ancient desert Southwest.

18 November 1302 Pope Boniface VIII issues the *Unam Sanctam*.

1303 The Mamluks defeat an Ilkhanate army in Syria at Marj al-Suffar.

1304-1316 Öljaitü rules the Ilkhanate.

1305-1314 Clement V serves as pope; moves his court to Avignon to please the Philip IV of France.

1307-1327 Reign of Edward II of England.

13 October 1307 King Philip IV of France makes an attack on the medieval military order the Knights Templar.

1308 The Teutonic Order acquires Danzig (now Gdańsk) and eastern Pomerania.

1309 The headquarters of the Teutonic Order is moved to a fortified convent at Marienburg in Prussia.

1309 The Knights Hospitaller establish a new headquarters on Rhodes.

1310 Accused of heresy, a trial against the Knights Templar in Paris results in 54 members of the order being burned at the stake.

1312-1337 Mansa Musa I rules the Mali Empire.

1312 Pope Clement V officially abolishes the medieval military order the Knights Templar.

1313-1341 Uzbeg (Özbek) Khan rules the Golden Horde and makes Islam the state religion.

1315-1390 Life of the Persian poet Hafiz Shiraz, considered the greatest Persian poet and among the greatest in the world.

1315 The Mamluks of Egypt install a Muslim puppet ruler in the Nubian kingdom of Dongola.

1316-1335 Abu Sa'id rules the Ilkhanate.

1318-1327 Kebek Khan rules the Chagatai Khanate.

1318-1339 Go-Daigo reigns as emperor of Japan.

Circa 1319 The Italian poet Dante Alighieri completes his epic *The Divine Comedy*.

1320-1325 Reign of Ghiyasuddin Tughluq (aka Ghiyath al-Din Tughluq), founder of the Tughlaq dynasty.

1321-1325 Ghiyasuddin Tughluq built the fortress city of Tughlaqabad in Delhi.

1322 The Ilkhanate and Mamluk Sultanate sign a peace treaty.

1323 The Telangana Kingdom in South India was annexed to the Delhi Sultanate.

1324 Mansa Musa I, the ruler of the Mali Empire, famously visits Cairo and spends an enormous quantity of gold.

Circa 1325 Taríakuri establishes the first Purépecha (Tarascan) capital at Pátzcuaro.

1325-1351 Reign of Muhammad bin Tughluq (born Ulugh Khan) of the Delhi Sultanate.

1325 to circa 1352 Travels of Ibn Battuta.

1326 Prusa (Bursa) falls to Ottoman control shortly after Osman's death; it becomes the capital of the Ottoman Empire.

1327-1377 Reign of Edward III of England.

1327-1333 Hōjō Moritoki reigns as shogun in Japan, the last of the Kamakura Shogunate.

1327 Uzbeg Khan shifts Golden Horde support from the Russian city of Tver to the rising power of Moscow.

1331-1334 Tarmashirin Khan rules the Chagatai Khanate.

1333 The hill upon which Himeji Castle stands was first fortified.

Circa 1333 Nitta Yoshisada attacks and destroys Kamakura, capital of Japan's Kamakura Shogunate.

1333-1336 The Kenmu Restoration, when the Japanese emperor, Go-Daigo, uses rebel warlords to oust the Kamakura Shogunate.

1333-1368 Toghon Temür, the last Yuan emperor, rules China.

1333 The position of deputy shogun (*kanrei*) is created in Japan.

1335 The Ilkhanate disintegrates into smaller states following dynastic disputes.

1336 Timur is born near Samarkand.

1336 The Indian Vijayanagara Empire is founded by Harihara I.

1336 The Italian poet and scholar Petrarch compiles an edition of works by Virgil.

1336 Ashikaga Takauji captures Heiankyo (Kyoto).

July 1336 Ashikaga Takauji defeats Emperor Go-Daigo's chief ally Yoshisada at the Battle of Minatogawa, near Kobe.

1337-1392 Japan has two competing emperors: the Northern and Southern Courts.

1337-1341 Mansa Maghan rules the Mali Empire.

1338 Ashikaga Takauji becomes the new shogun in Japan; it is the beginning of the Ashikaga (Muromachi) Shogunate.

1338-1358 Ashikaga Takauji rules as shogun in Japan.

June 1340 An English fleet of Edward III of England destroys or captures a French fleet at Sluys.

1341-1360 Mansa Sulayman rules the Mali Empire.

1342-1357 Janibeg (Djanibek) rules the Golden Horde.

1345 Traditional date for the founding of the Aztec capital of Tenochtitlán on Lake Texcoco.

1347-1363 Tughlugh Timur rules as the last khan of the Chagatai Khanate. Upon his death, the state disintegrates.

1347-1352 The Black Death plague sweeps across Europe.

July 1347 Edward III of England and his son Edward the Black Prince capture the French city of Calais after a long siege.

1347 Zafar Khan takes the title Abu'l Muzaffar Ala-ud-Din Bahman Shah, founding the Bahmani Sultanate.

Circa 1350 Noh theater becomes popular in Japan.

1350 Traditional date of the arrival of the Great Fleet in New Zealand (Aotearoa).

1350-1352 Japan's shogun, Ashikaga Takauji, battles his brother Tadayoshi.

January 1350 Edward the Black Prince leads a successful defense of Calais against a French attack.

1351-1388 Reign of Firuz (or Feroz) Shah Tughluq of the Delhi Sultanate.

1351 Aztecs celebrate the New Fire Ceremony.

Circa 1352 The Muslim traveler Ibn Battuta visits the Mali Empire, including Timbuktu.

Circa 1352 to circa 1355 Ibn Juzay writes *The Rihla of Ibn Battuta*.

Circa 1353 Giovanni Boccaccio completes his masterpiece, *The Decameron*.

1355 Zhu Yuanzhang, the future Ming Hongwu Emperor, takes over the leadership of the rebel Red Turbans Movement.

1356 Zhu Yuanzhang, leader of the rebel Red Turbans Movement, takes control of Nanjing.

1356 The Hanseatic League is formally founded.

19 September 1356 Edward the Black Prince wins a great victory at the Battle of Poitiers against the French. John II of France is captured.

Circa 1356-1377 Bukka Raya I rules the Vijayanagara Empire.

1358-1375 Muhammad Shah I rules the Bahmani Sultanate.

1359 Edward III of England and Edward the Black Prince march on Rheims but the French city holds out.

1359-1368 Ashikaga Yoshiakira rules as shogun in Japan.

1360 Zhu Yuanzhang, future Ming Hongwu Emperor, defeats the rival rebel leader Chen Youliang at the Battle of Poyang Lake.

May 1360 The Treaty of Brétigny between England and France recognizes Edward III of England's claims to French lands as he renounces his claim to the French throne.

1362-1389 Murad I rules as the sovereign of the Ottoman Empire and brands himself as a sultan.

1362 Lithuanian forces defeat the Golden Horde at the Battle of Blue Waters.

1366 Timur and Amir Husayn take over Transoxania.

1367 Zhu Yuanzhang, future Ming Hongwu Emperor, defeats the rival rebel leader Zhang Shicheng.

1367 Korea sends an embassy to Japan requesting action be taken against the *wakō* (pirates).

1367 The Kremlin's wooden walls and towers are rebuilt with white stone.

1368-1398 Reign of the Hongwu Emperor, founder of the Ming dynasty in China.

1368 The Kremlin is invaded by a Lithuanian army, but the army quickly retreats.

1368 to circa 1394 Ashikaga Yoshimitsu rules as shogun in Japan.

23 January 1368 Zhu Yuanzhang, founder of the Ming dynasty, declares himself emperor of China, taking the reign name Hongwu.

1370 Civil service entrance examinations are reintroduced in China.

Circa 1370 Timur takes sole control of Transoxania.

1370 Edward the Black Prince retakes Limoges from the French and executes 3,000 innocents.

1370 The last Yuan dynasty emperor, Toghon Temür dies at Karakorum.

1370 The Lithuanian army returns to take the Kremlin but retreats once again.

1372-1375 Charles V of France recaptures most of the territory previously gained by Edward III of England, leaving the English only Gascony and Calais.

1373 Julian of Norwich has a near-death experience and receives her famous visions from God.

1374-1387 Mansa Musa II rules the Mali Empire.

1374 John Wycliffe serves on a delegation to resolve disputes between the Church and civil authorities; he sides with the authorities.

Circa 1375 Under the rulership of Nancinpinco, the Chimú conquer the Lambayeque civilization.

1375-1378 Mujahid Shah Bahmani rules the Bahmani Sultanate.

1375-1395 Acamapichtli reigns as leader of the Aztecs.

1377-1399 Reign of Richard II of England.

1377 John Wycliffe is censured by the pope for unorthodox views, appears in London for examination, and is later released.

1378-1417 Western Schism.

1378-1397 Muhammad Shah II rules in the Bahmani Sultanate.

Circa 1380 John Wycliffe and his followers begin translating the Bible from Latin to English.

1380 Russian army defeats the Golden Horde at the Battle of Kulikovo, seen as the turning point in Mongol domination of Russia.

1380 Ch'oe Musŏn leads a successful Korean attack against a large *wakō* pirate fleet at the mouth of the Kum River.

1380-1395 Tokhtamysh rules the Golden Horde during a brief revival.

June 1381 The Peasants' Revolt in England.

1382 The Kremlin is destroyed by Khan Tokhtamysh and his Golden Horde.

1382 Tokhtamysh and the Golden Horde sack Moscow.

1387 Timur sacks Van in Armenia.

Circa 1388-1400 Geoffrey Chaucer composes *The Canterbury Tales*.

1389 The Korean navy attacks the *wakō* pirate bases on Tsushima Island in Japan.

1390 One of the three possible traditional foundation dates of the Haudenosaunee ('People of the Longhouse') Confederacy.

1394-1413 Nasiruddin Muhammad Shah (aka Sultan Mahmud Shah II) rules the Deli Sultanate.

14 April 1395 Timur wins the Battle of the Terek River in southern Russia against the Golden Horde.

12 March 1396 Richard II of England marries Isabella of France, the daughter of Charles VI of France, sealing a three-decade peace between the two countries.

25 September 1396 The Battle of Nicopolis (aka the Nicopolis Crusade), where a Western Christian army is defeated by the Ottoman Turks.

1397 The Kinkaku-ji or 'Golden Pavilion' is built in Heiankyo (Kyoto) by the shogun Ashikaga Yoshimitsu.

1397 The Knights Hospitaller buy Corinth from the Byzantine Empire.

1397-1422 Firuz Shah Bahmani (Taj ud-Din Firuz Shah) rules in the Bahmani Sultanate.

1398-1399 Timur invades the Delhi Sultanate and sacks Delhi.

1398-1402 Reign of the Jianwen Emperor of the Chinese Ming dynasty.

1399 Timur invades Syria and sacks Aleppo.

Circa 1400 The pueblos of Homolovi are abandoned.

Circa 1400 Under the rulership of Minchançaman, the Chimú Empire reaches its greatest extent.

Preface

by Ibolya Horváth

Violence, uprisings, power struggles, wars, climate change, an epidemic, extensive trade networks, and a new world order emerging. Which century does this make you think of? Your first instinct may be to say the 21st. The world may seem like a scary place, with wars going on or looming wherever you look. Discontent over unresolved social issues often erupts into spontaneous or sometimes institutionalized violence, trade wars threaten our globalized way of life, climate change forces farmers to abandon their lands, and despite our advanced medical knowledge, epidemics can still claim millions of lives. It may seem that we are on the verge of a system collapse as the world is changing at a breakneck pace, but almost any century in human history can be described with these words. Of course, the list was intended to describe the 14th century, a time when the world must have seemed even scarier. Almost everywhere in the world, it was a time of monumental change.

In Asia, the four khanates of the Mongol Empire were crumbling. Each of the khanates had forsaken essential parts of their Mongol identity by adopting an urbanized lifestyle, converting to Islam, or encouraging multiculturalism. Nevertheless, the Mongol elite, preoccupied with infighting, largely ignored the needs of their subjects. As so often happens when ordinary people feel forsaken by the elite, discontent grew into unrest, which eventually erupted into rebellions. By the middle of the century, the Yuan were replaced by the Ming in China, and the other three khanates, disintegrating from within, ultimately succumbed to the brutal conquest of Timur. The world, as the people of Asia had known it, was being reshaped. However, despite this upheaval in Asia, Europe may have been an even worse place to live in the 14th century.

Killing 30-50% of the population, the Black Death ravaged Europe, and the destruction it caused was so great that any attempt at returning to what had been 'normal' before was doomed to failure. Not that life had been easy before the plague, as most of the population was trapped within the confines of the feudal system, but with the plague indiscriminately killing the rich and poor, the old and young, and nobody being able to offer any meaningful explanation as to why, let alone provide an effective cure, people must have felt forsaken by God. This feeling found expression in art, fueled societal changes, and made many question the authority of the Church.

Today, we know how viruses spread and what preventive measures are effective, and yet, we have all seen the disruptive power of a pandemic firsthand. We, in the 21st century, also know what causes climate change and how to fight against it, but in the 14th century, such disasters were understood as the will of the gods or God. Nothing reflects this sentiment more clearly than the belief system of the North American Southwest and the Mesoamerican cultures, where various rituals focused on ensuring a good harvest, and even human sacrifices were offered to the rain and sun gods. Yet, a great number of abandoned settlements show that people were, in the end, powerless against nature.

Other parts of the world, such as Oceania and Africa, experienced less upheaval. The Mali Empire thrived under Mansa Musa, trade was booming on the Swahili Coast, and although Islam had taken hold in many parts of Africa, traditional beliefs had not been completely forsaken. Around the same time, several Indigenous cultures were thriving in Oceania, exploring the Pacific, and settling in new territories, such as New Zealand. However, these parts of the world are often neglected by historians.

Regions where written historical records are abundant are, of course, easier to research than trying to make sense of the archaeological record of long-abandoned places, such as the mounds of the Mississippian culture, or reconstructing history based on oral tradition and similarities in artistic styles, as in the case of Benin and Ife in Southwest Africa. Nevertheless, this is no excuse for omitting certain regions from school curricula and educational books on world history.

In this volume, the authors aim to provide a truly global overview of the 14th century, with each region given approximately the same space. It is obviously impossible to cover every event in every country of the world in a single volume, just as you would not be able to visit every city in every country if you traveled around the world for a year. However, you could visit the best-known and a fair number of lesser-known places, try the local cuisine, talk to many different people, and see the differences in culture.

At the end of such a trip, you would most likely conclude that, despite differences in language, religion, traditions, and lifestyle, people all around the world share the same feelings. As humans, we fear illness, the loss of loved ones, natural disasters, and wars. We want our basic needs met, we want the freedom to choose our own path, and we want our voices to be heard by the ruling elite. People in the 14th century felt exactly the same, and when their needs were ignored, they must have felt forsaken by the elite, and in the face of climate change and plague, they must have felt forsaken by their God or gods as well.

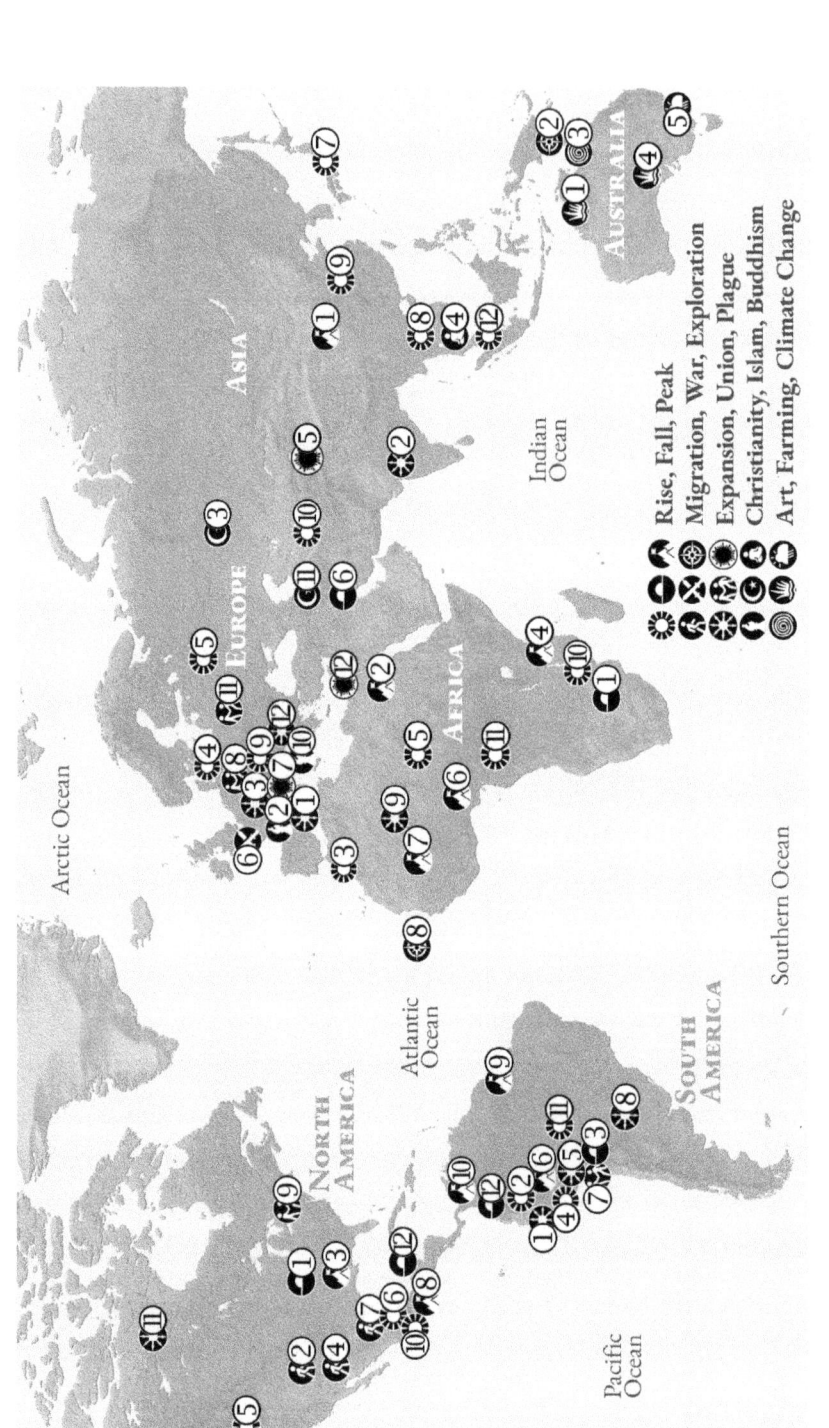

NORTH AMERICA

1. Collapse of Cahokia, last major Mississippian city
2. Ancestral Puebloan migrations
3. Etowah & Moundville mound-building peak
4. Athabaskan expansion into Southwest
5. Growth of Coast Salish & Haida societies
6. Founding of México (Aztec) capital Tenochtitlán
7. Chichimec migrations into Central Mexico
8. Peak of Mixtec city-states
9. Formation of Iroquois Five Nations Confederacy
10. Rise of Tarascan (Purépecha) Empire
11. Consolidation of proto-Inuit Thule culture
12. Collapse of Mayapán, last major Mayan city

SOUTH AMERICA

1. Expansion of Chimú Empire
2. Rise of Chachapoya fortified settlements
3. Fragmentation of Tiwanaku culture
4. Rise of coastal Chancay culture
5. Expansion of Chanka warrior confederation
6. Peak of Andean defensive fortifications
7. Consolidation of Aymara kingdoms
8. Expansion of Guaraní river networks
9. Peak of Marajoara mound-building
10. Urbanization of Muisca chiefdoms
11. Rise of Inca Cusco state
12. Collapse of San Agustín ceremonial centers

EUROPE

1. Crown of Aragon expands into Mediterranean
2. Avignon Papacy sparks Italian political crisis
3. Swiss Confederation grows after Morgarten victory
4. Rise of Hanseatic League trade power
5. Muscovy consolidates under Ivan I & II
6. Hundred Years' War begins, England vs. France
7. Black Death sweeps Europe
8. Golden Bull reshapes Holy Roman Empire
9. Venice rises as maritime superpower
10. Western Schism divides Papacy
11. Union of Krewo unites Poland & Lithuania
12. Ottoman expansion into Balkans, Battle of Kosovo

AFRICA

1. Collapse of Great Zimbabwe's first expansion
2. Mamluk renaissance under al-Nasir Muhammad
3. Rise of Wattasids amid Marinid decline
4. Swahili Coast city-states flourish
5. Rise of Bornu as Kanem collapses
6. Peak of Ife's artistic and spiritual influence
7. Mali Empire at its height under Mansa Musa
8. Portuguese maritime expeditions reach Africa
9. Tuareg seize & rule Timbuktu
10. Rise of Mutapa Kingdom as Zimbabwe declines
11. Rise of Kingdom of Kongo
12. Black Death strikes Egypt & North Africa

ASIA

1. Yuan dynasty consolidates under Temür Khan
2. Delhi Sultanate expands & fragments
3. Golden Horde adopts Islam under Uzbeg Khan
4. Spread of Theravada Buddhism in Southeast Asia
5. Black Death spreads along the Silk Road
6. End of the Ilkhanate & Mongol fragmentation
7. Rise of Japanese Ashikaga Shogunate
8. Rise of the Ayutthaya Kingdom, Southeast Asia
9. Ming rebellion ends Yuan rule
10. Timur rises in Central Asia
11. Emergence of Safavid Sufi Order in Ardabil
12. Emergence of Malacca Sultanate

AUSTRALIA

1. Fire-stick farming and ecological engineering
2. Torres Strait maritime societies & trade networks
3. Rock art & cultural expression in the North
4. Budj Bim aquaculture system in Victoria
5. Climate variability & adaptive resilience

JAPAN

By Mark Cartwright

IN JAPAN, THE MEDIEVAL period was characterized by feudalism, the relationship between lords and vassals, where land ownership and its use were exchanged for military service and loyalty. The aristocracy was replaced by the samurai class as the most powerful social group, shoguns and their regents established themselves as military rulers, while the power of the emperors and Buddhist monasteries declined. The country also witnessed civil wars as warlords and large estate owners, called daimyo (*daimyō*), fought for prominence, and the central government struggled to unify Japan.

The history of medieval Japan is traditionally divided into the following periods.

Kamakura period: 1185-1333

Muromachi period: 1333-1573, including the Sengoku period, 1467-1568

Azuchi-Momoyama period: 1573-1600

Alternatively, the period may be divided into the following two shogunates.

Kamakura Shogunate: 1192-1333

Ashikaga Shogunate: 1338-1573

Kamakura Period

Feudal Relationships

The Kamakura period, or Kamakura *jidai*, began when Minamoto no Yoritomo (1147-1199) defeated the Taira clan at the Battle of Dannoura in 1185. The period is named after Kamakura, a coastal town in Sagami Bay, 48 kilometers (30 miles) southwest of what would become Tokyo (Edo). Kamakura was the base of the Minamoto clan, and it became the capital after Minamoto no Yoritomo sought to distance himself from the former capital at Heiankyo (now Kyoto) and any civil servants and officials who might continue to entertain loyalties to the previous regime. The imperial court remained at Heiankyo, where titles were dispensed, certain taxes collected, and civilian judicial disputes were settled.

Kamakura, protected on three sides by mountains and the sea on the fourth side, was a perfect choice for a military-minded leader. Extra protection was provided by earth fortification walls and two wooden castles: Sugimoto and Sumiyoshi.

Yoritomo established himself here as shogun (*shōgun*), or military dictator of Japan, thus offering the first alternative to the power of the emperor and the imperial court. The shoguns would go on to rule for seven centuries until the Meiji Restoration of 1868. The title had been used before (*seii taishōgun*) but had only been temporary for military commanders on campaign against the Ezo/Emishi (Ainu) in the still-disputed territory in the north of Japan during the 8th century. Yoritomo was able to hold the title of shogun with a new, wider meaning, thanks to his agreement with the young

Emperor Go-Toba (reign 1183-1198), who bestowed it in return for Yoritomo's military protection. The emperor was largely powerless and restricted to ceremonial duties in the entire medieval period, but still able to give legitimacy to shoguns by formally bestowing them their coveted title.

The lack of any written description concerning the precise role of the shogun and the absence of any legal definition meant that the role was easily manipulated by a long line of regents to fit their own purposes. Between 1203 and 1333, 16 regents ruled on behalf of shoguns who were still minors or who acted merely as puppet figureheads. It was not the shogun who ruled Japan, but the shogunate government. This situation would not change until the establishment of the Ashikaga Shogunate in 1338, when regents became a thing of the past, and the shogun once more was the real leader of the country. Even then, though, a government apparatus was in place, which shared out power to prominent members of Japan's military class.

The shogunate government, also known as *bakufu*, which means 'tent government' in reference to its origins as a title held by a commander in the field, was based on the feudal relationship between lord and vassal. Yoritomo enticed members of the rival Taira clan to his, the Minamoto cause, by offering them land and positions if they agreed to be his vassals in the new order. Replacing the dominance of the Japanese emperor and the imperial court, the system Yoritomo introduced saw the shogun distribute land (which was often confiscated from defeated rivals) to his loyal followers and allies in return for their continued support (both personal support and military service through individual private armies of samurai).

Quite early on, it became obvious that the shogun or regent shogun had rather too much on his plate to govern the whole country without any well-defined state apparatus. The system that was in place by the 14th century had developed over the decades, from as early as 1184, when the Kumonjo or Public Documents Office was established. This was then renamed and widened in function as the Mandokoro (Administrative Board) in 1191, as it became the main administration center, and later, it would be given charge of the state treasury. In 1184, the Monchujo was set up, which looked after all legal matters. A new position, a vice-regent to the shogun (*rensho*), was created in 1225. In the same year, the Council of State was formed, the Hyojoshu, which had as its members the top officials, warriors, and scholars of the moment. In 1232, a new law code was established, the Joei Code (*Jōei Shikimoku*), which had 51 articles and established who owned what land, defined the relationship between lords, vassals, and samurai, limited the role of the emperor, and established the taking of legal decisions based on precedence. Finally, in 1249, a High Court, the Hikitsukeshu, was formed, which was especially concerned with any disputes related to land and taxes.

Unlike in Europe, the feudal system of Japan was less contractually based and was a much more personal affair between lords and vassals, with a strong paternalistic influence coming from the former, who were often referred to as *oya* or 'parent.' This 'family' feel was further strengthened by the fact that many lord-vassal relationships were inherited. Some of the loyal followers of the shogun received many estates (*shōen*), which were often geographically disparate or distant from their traditional family homes, and so, rather than manage them directly themselves, they employed the services of an appointed steward (*jitō*) for that purpose, a position that had been used on a smaller scale since the Heian period (794-1185). *Jitō* literally means 'head of the land,' and the position was open to men and women in the early medieval period. Their principal responsibility was to manage the peasants who worked their employer's land and collect the relevant local taxes. Appointed by the shogunate government, stewards never (officially) owned land themselves, that is, until the wheels started to come off the feudal system, but they were entitled to fees (about 10% of the land's produce) and tenure. They were often bound by local customs and also held accountable to national law codes.

The position could be inherited, but there was often not enough money to make a living if the rights to income had to be distributed among several siblings. This situation led to many *jitō* getting into debt as they mortgaged their right to income from a given estate. However, many other *jitō* became powerful in their own right, and their descendants became daimyo, influential feudal landowners. These daimyo ruled with a large degree of autonomy, even if they did have to follow certain rules laid down by the government, such as where to build a castle.

Another layer of estate managers was the *shugo*, or military governor or constable, who had policing and administrative responsibilities in their particular province. In the 14th century, there were 57 such provinces, and so a *shugo* was involved in several estates at once, unlike the *jitō*, who had to worry about only one. A *shugo*, literally meaning 'protector,' made decisions according to local customs and military laws, and, like the *jitō*, they collected regular taxes in kind for the shogunate government, a portion of which they were entitled to keep for themselves. They were also charged with collecting special taxes (*tansen*) for one-off events like coronations and temple-building projects, and organizing labor for state projects like building roads and guesthouses along the routes. Over time, the position of *shugo* became, in effect, one of a regional governor. The *shugo* became ever more powerful, with taxes being directed into their own pockets and such rights as collecting the *tansen* often being given to subordinates as a way to create an alternative lord-vassal relationship without any land exchange being involved. Giving titles and organizing private arrangements with samurai also allowed the *shugo* to build up their own personal armies. Following the failed Mongol invasions of Japan in 1274 and 1281, *shugo* were legally obliged to reside in the province they administered for greater state security, but whether this was always carried out in practice is unclear. By the 14th century, the *shugo* had also assumed the responsibilities of those *jitō* who had not become daimyo, and by the 15th century, most *shugo* inherited the position.

Jitō and *shugo* depended entirely on local sources for their income, not the central government, and this meant that they often made entirely self-interested arrangements. Thus, the shogunate itself became a largely irrelevant and invisible institution at a local level. Farmers often made private deals with officials, giving, for example, a small parcel of land in exchange for a delay in payment of taxes or a negotiated percentage in order to pay their expected fees annually. As a consequence, the whole setup of land ownership in Japan became very complex, with multiple possible landowners for any stretch of land: private individuals (vassal and non-vassals), government officials, religious institutions, the shogunate, and the crown.

Economy

The Kamakura period was generally a good one for the Japanese economy, with trade continuing with China, where gold, mercury, fans, swords, timber, and lacquerware were exchanged for Chinese silk, brocades, perfumes, porcelain, tea, and copper coinage. Coinage was used more frequently, as were bills of credit, sometimes with the unfortunate consequence that people, especially samurai, got into bad debts as they spent beyond their means.

JAPAN 7

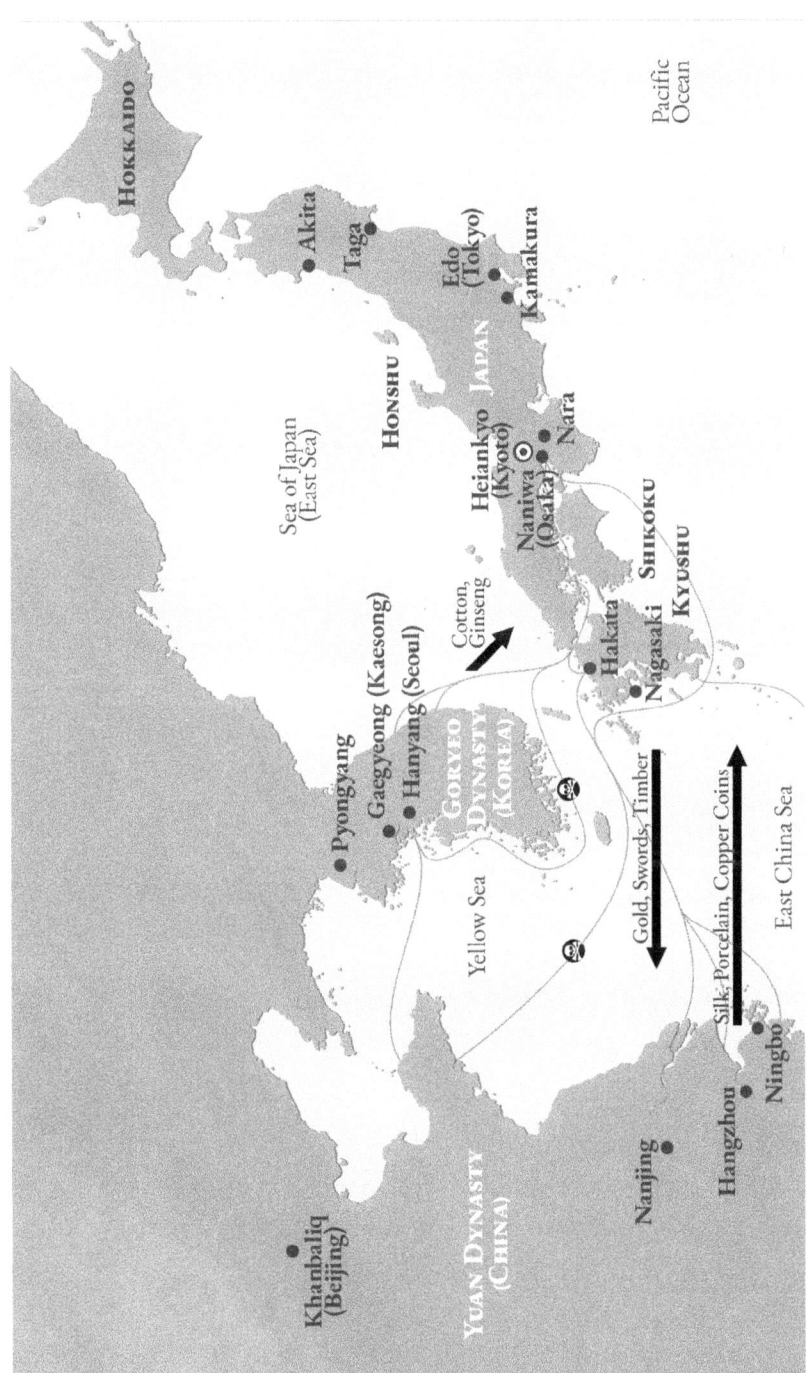

1.1 Medieval Japan and its trade relations with its neighbors

The Kamakura shoguns implemented several land reforms, notably making better use of previously neglected agricultural lands. Technological developments also helped, such as the introduction of a hardier strain of rice from China at the end of the 12th century, the widespread use of double-cropping and fertilizers (compost, manure, and ash), and better tools made of better iron than previously. Less land was left fallow because of inheritance disputes when a male relative was lacking. Villages began to grow in size as the road networks improved, a development helped by the fact that there were, in effect, two capitals (Kamakura and Heiankyo).

Meanwhile, in urban settings, trade guilds (*za*) were established, initially for craftspeople and traders to secure the patronage of a monastery or local lord. Formed by anywhere from 10 to 100 workers or companies, the guilds had the effect of increasing specialization and improving standards. Markets developed in Japan from the 14th century; most towns had a weekly or thrice-monthly market when merchants traveled around their particular regions and farmers sold their surplus goods. Foodstuffs were more available than ever before, thanks to the developments in agricultural techniques and tools. Goods were bartered for other goods, and coins were being used more and more (although they were actually imported from China). Markets were also promoted by local authorities who saw their value as a tax revenue source by standardizing currencies, weights, and measures. Non-food items available at local markets included pottery, tools, cooking utensils, and household furniture. Markets in the capital and other larger cities might have more exotic goods on sale.

Society

The result of the peace and prosperity the country enjoyed was a boom in Japan's population from around 7 million at the start of the Kamakura period to 8.2 million at the end. The essential family unit in Japan was the *ie* (house), which included parents and their children, grandparents, other blood relations, and the household servants and their children. Eldest sons usually inherited the property of the *ie*, but the absence of male offspring could entail bringing in an outsider to act as head of the family (*koshu*)—male children were often adopted for this very purpose, although a female member might also take on the role, too. The wife of the *koshu* was the senior female in the family and was responsible for managing the household duties. The good of the *ie* was meant to take precedence over any individual's, and the three principles to be followed by all were: obligation, obedience, and loyalty.

The society was divided into classes based on their economic function. At the top was the warrior class of samurai, or *bushi* (which had its own internal distinctions based on the feudal relationship between lord and vassal), then the land-owning aristocrats, priests, farmers, and peasants (who paid a land tax to the landowners or the state), artisans, and merchants. Interestingly, the merchants were considered socially inferior to farmers. There were, too, a number of social outcasts, which included those who worked in messy or 'undesirable' professions like butchers and tanners, actors, undertakers, and criminals.

There was some movement between the classes, such as peasants becoming warriors, and women were often used as a tool for social progress via the practice of marrying daughters into families of superior status. This occurred not just among elites but also in rural communities. Women were largely made responsible for the household and its servants, if there were any, but there were also some women warriors and small business proprietors. Women were able to own estates as they were allowed to head families if there was no suitable male relative for the position; they could inherit and keep their own property no matter what happened to their male relatives or husband.

Marriage was a more formal affair among the upper classes, while in rural communities, things were more relaxed; even pre-marital sex was permitted thanks to the established tradition of *yobai* or 'night visit' between lovers. In ancient Japan, a married man often went to live in the family home of his wife, but in the medieval period, this was reversed. In the case of the wives of samurai, they were expected to defend the home in their husband's absence on campaign, and they were given the gift of a knife at their wedding as a symbol of this duty. Many such women learned martial skills.

Divorce was always in favor of the male, who could decide to terminate his marriage simply by writing a letter to his wife. If the couple remained on amicable terms, then a mutual settlement could be made, but the male ultimately had the power to decide such matters. If there were evidence of adultery, then the wife could even be executed. As a wife had no recourse to any legal protection, the only option for many women to escape adulterous or violent husbands was to join a convent. Detailed information regarding women's rights is often lacking in the male-dominated historical record, and practical daily life was, in any case, very likely different from official and legal pronouncements on what women could and could not do.

Religion

Just as Japanese people today enjoy one of the longest life expectancy rates in the world, so too in the medieval period, the Japanese were ahead of almost everyone else. When a person died, most Japanese people thought that the spirit of the deceased then went to the 'Land of Darkness' or *shigo no sekai*. The spirits then might occasionally revisit the world of the living. Those who followed Buddhism believed that people either went to a form of hell, were reincarnated, or went to the Buddhist paradise, the Pure Land. Ancestors were not forgotten and were honored each year in the Obon festival held in July/August, when it was thought they returned to their families for a three-day visit.

Although Shinto continued to be as important as it was in previous periods, during the Kamakura period, two significant new sects of Zen Buddhism were developed: the Jodo Sect (aka Pure Land) and the Jodo Shin Sect (aka True Pure Land). Both sects simplified the religion and stressed that simply chanting the Buddha's name (*nembutsu*) would permit a person of any social class to be reborn in the Amida Buddha's Pure Land paradise. Naturally, Kamakura, therefore, required its own Zen temple. The most important Zen monastery was the Kenchō-ji in Kamakura, built by the regent Hōjō Tokiyori (1227-1263) in 1253. The Kōtoku-in Temple was built in 1252. Unfortunately, a great earthquake circa 1495 caused a tsunami that completely washed away all the temple structures. What remained, largely thanks to its weight of over 93 tons, was the Daibutsu, a giant statue of Amida, or Great Buddha. Another important Zen temple, indeed, today the most important in Japan, was the Engaku-ji monastery, established circa 1283 by Hōjō Tokimune, the regent shogun (reign 1268-1284), and the

Chinese monk Mugaku. The two-story Shari-den building, the only original structure at the site, is thought to enshrine a tooth of the Buddha brought to Kamakura from China. The temple's fine bronze bell is listed as an official National Treasure of Japan. The bell was donated to the temple in 1301 by Hōjō Sadatoki, the regent shogun (reign 1284-1311).

1.2 The Great Buddha of Kamakura

Zen principles of austerity and restraint became very popular with samurai, and its attention to *wabi*—the aesthetic principle of beauty, simplicity, and withdrawal from the bustle of life—made the Japanese tea ceremony a common aristocratic pastime. The austerity of Zen would also influence Japanese ink painting and calligraphy in the Kamakura period, while painting, especially portraiture, became more realistic.

Decline & Kenmu Restoration

At the end of the 13th century, the Kamakura period saw one of the greatest threats to Japan's existence, the two Mongol invasions of Kublai Khan in 1274 and 1281. Kublai Khan had sent a letter to the Japanese government warning of this consequence if they did not pay tribute, but both the shogun and emperor ignored the demand. Fortunately for Japan, the two invasion fleets each met a typhoon and disaster (but not before the second had landed on the beaches of Kyushu), and the winds that either sank or blew the Mongol ships safely away from Japanese shores were given the name *kamikaze*, or 'divine winds.' It seems that the Mongol ships were not particularly well-built either, and so they proved much less seaworthy than they should have been. However, the conflict and the standing in readiness between the invasions (including awaiting an anticipated third attack that never came) nearly brought the state to bankruptcy. The agricultural sector was also severely disrupted by the defense preparations. Rivals to the Hōjō clan now had their best opportunity to challenge the political status quo. Unrest from unpaid samurai and a general lack of control in the provinces, which led to widespread banditry, meant that the Kamakura shoguns were at their most vulnerable.

The disaffection caused by the necessity to keep Japan on a war footing was exploited by Emperor Go-Daigo (reign 1318-1339), who sought to return to the good old days of the emperors before Minamoto no Yoritomo had started the shogunate. The emperor rallied unpaid samurai and ambitious warlords, and made two attempts to grab power, one in 1324 and another in 1331. Neither was successful, and he was exiled for his troubles.

There then followed the incident known as the Kenmu Restoration (1333-1336). Ashikaga Takauji had been sent by the Kamakura Shogunate to deal with Go-Daigo, but, tempted by the power his army offered him, he joined forces with the exiled emperor. Takauji attacked Heiankyo while another rebel warlord, Nitta Yoshisada, attacked Kamakura. The fortifications of Kamakura did their job, but the army of Nitta Yoshisada circumvented them by going around a cape at low tide and attacking the city from the beach. Rather than risk capture, the last leaders of the Hōjō clan committed ritual suicide, ironically near a Buddhist temple called the 'Temple of Victory.' Kamakura was sacked, and the capital was moved back to Heiankyo. The city went into decline after the fall of the Kamakura Shogunate.

Victorious, Takauji wanted to be nothing less than the new shogun, but Go-Daigo refused to give him this title because he did not want to return to a position of subservience. Takauji then defeated Go-Daigo's chief ally Yoshisada at the Battle of Minatogawa near Kobe in July 1336 and then captured Heiankyo. The chaos and fighting of the 1330s were wryly noted by an anonymous sign painter in Heiankyo: "Assaults in the night, armed robberies, falsified documents, easy women ... chopped off heads, monks who defrock themselves and laymen who shave their heads" (Huffman, 43).

Go-Daigo was exiled for a second time, but he established his own court anyway at Yoshino, 95 kilometers (60 miles) south of Heiankyo. Ashikaga Takauji found himself a more compliant puppet emperor, Kōmyō, to act as the state's figurehead, who formally bestowed on his master the coveted title of shogun in 1338, thus inaugurating the Ashikaga Shogunate. With the government established in the Muromachi district of Heiankyo, the decision gave its name to the next period of Japanese history: the Muromachi period, or *Muromachi Jidai* (1333-1573). One loose end was Go-Daigo as there were now two emperors in Japan, a system known as the 'Dual Courts' or 'Northern and Southern Courts,' divided by the major and minor imperial lines rather than mere geography, which would not be resolved until 1392 when the Southern Court ceased to exist after a promise was made and then broken to alternate emperors between the two lines.

The Ashikaga Shogunate

Government

Unlike the relative stability of the preceding period, Japan was now beset with a seemingly endless cycle of civil wars and competition for power between rival warlords, beginning with Ashikaga Takauji fighting his own brother between 1350 and 1352. Takauji was victorious, and Tadayoshi was poisoned, a fate most likely arranged by his brother.

The system of government of the Ashikaga Shogunate followed much the same lines as the Kamakura Shogunate, with a few additions. Foremost among these was the deputy shogun (*kanrei*), usually a position held on a rotation basis by a member of one of three families: the Shiba, Hosokawa, and Hatakeyama. The role was created in 1333, and its key function was to act as a liaison between the shogun and regional military governors and their deputies. Specific oversight of Kamakura was deemed advisable to make sure the Hōjō family did not make a comeback, and this task was put into the hands of the Kantō deputy. Other regions were also considered a risk to the central government, and so there was a similar deputy to supervise Kyushu and northwest Honshu.

The shogunate held control of the central part of Japan, but the outer provinces were left semi-independent. Perhaps ironically for a period known for its general lawlessness, the Ashikaga shoguns did add a few extras to Japan's established law codes. Ashikaga Takauji added 17 articles, which mostly dealt with the expected behavior of samurai. The articles were largely based on the principles famously expressed by Prince Shōtoku (regent of Japan from 594 to 622) in his own 17-article constitution. Another new development was the idea that not only should convicted criminals be punished, but also their families and even the communities in which they lived. This idea of collective responsibility was called *renza* (or *enza*) and sometimes resulted in people connected to the criminal receiving the same punishment. Whether the system reduced crime is a moot point, but it did result in communities trying to resolve criminal cases before they came to the attention of the central authorities.

Economy

The bureaucracy at the capital was relatively efficient, but in the outer provinces, local daimyo ruled their own lands as they saw fit. Local officials and estate managers, such as the *jitō*, found it much more difficult to secure the taxes the state was due from landlords who had no fear of any government reprisals. The state was obliged to find other means to fill its coffers, and these strategies often did much to boost the economy. As landowners and temples tried their hand at money-lending, the number of small businesses grew (especially brewers and distillers), and the government raked off its share through taxes. Another money-spinning scheme was to introduce tolls on roads and impose fees on temples. International trade also did well, and by the beginning of the 15th century, Japan joined the Chinese Ming dynasty's tribute system in 1401. The Ming emperor even recognized the shogun as the 'King of Japan' in return, and goods were exchanged between the two states. Ming porcelain, silk, and bronze coins were popular, while finely worked swords, copper ore, and timber were traded in the other direction.

Agriculture, despite the upheaval of the wars and occasional famines caused by the vagaries of weather that plagued the period, continued to thrive in the longer term, thanks to innovations like double-cropping and the use of fertilizers, which had begun in the Kamakura period. Villages grew in number and size as farmers sought security in numbers and worked together to produce more and benefit from communal projects such as digging irrigation channels and building waterwheels. In the absence of any authority from the central government, villages governed themselves. Small councils were formed, which made decisions regarding laws and punishments, organized community festivals, and decided on regulations within the community. Some villages got together to form leagues or *ikki* for their mutual benefit.

Farmers generally did well in the period, and slavery all but disappeared, but women enjoyed fewer rights than under the Kamakura, with, for example, a convention being established that brides join the household of their husbands, whom, along with their mother-in-law, they were obliged to obey. Although women could still inherit property, there was a return to the convention that the oldest male inherited the family estate in order to reduce the fragmentation of land into parcels too small to be useful for different siblings.

The children of farmers and artisans were taught by their fathers and mothers the practical skills they had acquired through a lifetime of work. Regarding more formal education, this had previously been the exclusive privilege of aristocratic families or those who joined Buddhist monasteries, but in the medieval period, the rising samurai class began to educate their children, too, largely at the schools offered by Buddhist temples. Many prosperous samurai also established libraries of classic Chinese and Japanese literature, which were made accessible to priests and scholars. Nevertheless, the number of people who were literate, even in the upper classes, was only a tiny proportion of the population as a whole, and monks were often called on to assist with paperwork in the secular world.

Culture

The move of the seat of the shogunate from Kamakura brought cultural as well as political consequences because the Ashikaga shoguns wished to beautify their new capital. Consequently, fine palaces, temples, and new art schools sprang up.

The famous Kinkaku-ji or 'Golden Pavilion' was built by shogun Ashikaga Yoshimitsu (reign 1368-1394/5). The shogun acquired the land from the statesman Saionji Kintsune, who had built his own villa on this site of outstanding natural beauty. The new palace complex, which boasted 13 buildings, was completed in 1397, and the shogun took early retirement in 1394/5 in order to pursue the arts in his vast new home. Ashikaga Yoshimitsu may have retired, but he continued to pull the strings of the Japanese government, and he attracted many illustrious visitors to his retreat, notably Emperor Go-Komatsu (reign 1392-1412). The former shogun had made it known that he wished, upon his death, for the site to be converted into a Rinzai Zen Buddhist temple, which it was in 1408. The temple was then renamed Rokuon-ji after Rokuon-in-den, the former shogun's posthumous religious title. The Golden Pavilion is so called because it is lavishly covered in gold foil. There is an association between gold and Pure Land Buddhism, where the former is considered to represent spiritual purity. Further, the Buddhist paradise is thought to abound with gilded pavilions. Unkind commentators suggest the ostentatious covering might also have something to do with Ashikaga Yoshimitsu's high opinion of himself and a wish to demonstrate his great wealth; he did, after all, receive letters from the Ming emperor addressing him as the 'King of Japan,' even after he had retired as shogun. The Golden Pavilion is the only surviving building from the original 14th-century estate.

1.3 Kinkaku-ji Temple or the 'Golden Pavilion,' Kyoto

Ashikaga Yoshimitsu's Kinkaku-ji also saw a flourishing of such crafts as sword-making and ceramics, and many shoguns, especially when they retired from public office, became great patrons of the arts, commissioning painters and sculptors. Collectively, these artistic endeavors became known as Kitayama culture. Performance art was one of the lasting products of this period. Noh (*Nō*) theater developed from the 14th century and derived from older dance and music rituals performed at temples and shrines. In Noh, mask-wearing male actors made highly stylized movements accompanied by music with some brief spoken words to explain the general story, which told of gods, demons, and heroes, and their various moral predicaments. The extravagant and richly embroidered costumes of the actors would greatly influence late medieval and early modern fashion in Japan.

In the medieval period, upper-class women wore perhaps the most famous wardrobe item from Japanese culture, the kimono. Meaning literally 'thing to wear,' the kimono is a woven silk robe tied at the waist by a broad band (obi). Other clothes for both men and women of means tended to be silk, long, and loose-fitting, and both sexes might wear baggy trousers, and women skirt-trousers, too. Women might wear a long robe with a train, the *uchiki*, while men wore short jackets called *haori* or a long jacket (*uchikake* or *kaidori*), fashionable from the Muromachi period. Lower classes typically wore similar clothes, but of more sober coloring and made of woven flax or hemp, and, if working in the fields in summer, both men and women often only wore a loincloth-type garment.

From the late 14th century, cotton clothing became much more common for all classes. The preferred footwear for everyone was sandals (*zōri*), made from either wood, rope, or leather. Country folk might wear straw boots (*zunbe*) in colder weather. The most common headgear was the *kasa*, a straw hat that took many forms, some of which indicated the wearer's social status. A popular accessory for men and women was a hand fan (*uchiwa*), and specifically the folding fan (*ōgi*), which became a status symbol. Women might wear an ornate comb or pin in their hair made from bamboo, wood, ivory, or tortoiseshell, and perhaps decorated with a few embellishments in gold or pearl. A pale complexion was admired on both men and women, and so white powder (*oshiroi*) was worn. Fashionable women wore a red dot on their lower lip made using a flower-based paste or a red lipstick (*beni*). Women also shaved and redrew their eyebrows. Women and samurai were inclined to blacken their teeth in the medieval period, in the process known as *ohaguro*.

The influence of Buddhism on the aristocracy was strong and meant that meat was (at least publicly) frowned upon by many. The samurai and lower classes had no such qualms and consumed meat whenever they could afford to. In the medieval period, most upper-class Japanese laypeople and monks would have eaten two meals a day—one around noon and another in the early evening.

Lower classes might have eaten four meals a day. Men generally ate separately from women, and there were certain rules of etiquette, such as a wife should serve a husband and the eldest daughter-in-law should serve the female head of the household. Food was served on a tray placed in front of the diner, who was seated on the floor. The food was then eaten with chopsticks made of lacquered wood, precious metal, or ivory.

The staple foods for everyone were rice (and lots of it—three portions per person per meal was not uncommon), vegetables, seaweed, seafood, and fruit. Soya bean sauce and paste were popular to give extra taste, as were wasabi (a plant in the same family as horseradish), *sanshō* (ground seedpods of the prickly ash tree), and ginger. Green tea was drunk, usually served after the food, but this was brewed from rough leaves and so different from the fine powder used in the Japanese tea ceremony. Sake or rice wine was drunk by everyone but was reserved for special occasions in the medieval period.

Travel & Piracy

Travel was restricted in the medieval period because of Japan's mountainous terrain and the lack of a well-kept road network. One group that did move around was pilgrims, though limited to those with either the time to do so or the means to pay for expensive travel arrangements. Up to the Edo period, getting around was mostly done on foot, with goods carried by teams of horses or oxen pulling carts, while faster horses were ridden by messengers. Waterways were an important means of transport for both people and goods, especially timber, cotton cloth, rice, and fish. The wealthy were carried about on a palanquin (*kago*)—a bamboo or wooden chair between long poles for the two carriers, one at either end. For the more adventurous, there was maritime trade with both China and Korea, and monks in particular traveled back and forth to study and bring ideas back to their monasteries. Both land and sea travel remained dangerous in medieval Japan, the former thanks to bandits and the latter due to the *wakō* pirates that plagued the high seas.

Wakō translates as 'dwarf pirates,' and although many were from Japan, the term was also indiscriminately applied to any mariners up to no good on the high seas, and so it could include pirates based on the coasts of Korea, Taiwan, and China, to name but a few. There is even evidence that some pirates disguised themselves as Japanese to avoid detection as to where they sailed from. The Chinese called these pirates *wōkòu*, and the Koreans *waegu*. The most notorious pirate base was Japan's Tsushima Island (which also had legitimate ports), where there were plenty of easily defended inlets. The island is rocky and mountainous, so residents struggled to provide enough food for themselves while the local feudal lords, the So, gained handsomely from sponsoring the marauders who seized goods on the high seas. Other important pirate bases in Japan were at Iki Island and Matsuura, near Nagasaki.

At their peak in the 14th century, hundreds of pirate ships plagued the straits between Korea and southern Japan and made four or five major raids on the southern Korean peninsula each year. Many pirates even made it their business to plunder ships and coastal ports on the western side of the Korean peninsula, right up to the northern island of Kanghwa (or Ganghwa). In response, Korea assembled a fleet of ships armed with cannons to face the pirate scourge, with a notable victory credited to Ch'oe Musŏn against a large pirate fleet at the mouth of the Kum River in 1380. In the battle, Ch'oe Musŏn was able to employ cannons thanks to his tireless efforts to develop gunpowder. However, despite several more victories over the years by the Korean navy, including direct attacks on Tsushima Island in 1389 and again in 1419, when 700 suspected pirates were executed, the marauders could not be completely eradicated. The Korean government imposed harsh penalties, including execution, for those caught collaborating with pirates, but they needed the Japanese government to do more, and they sent multiple embassies to the Japanese court for that specific purpose.

The pirates caused enough problems for the Chinese to warrant three separate diplomatic missions to the Japanese court to see what could be done. As with the Korean missions, though, the real problem was that the Japanese had little control over the pirate bases, even if the Chinese began to insist that trade agreements between themselves and Japan would depend on the latter government's efforts to keep the pirates in check. Then, as noted, Chinese pirates grew in number, only adding to the problem of securing the seas for legitimate trading vessels. Several groups of pirates even won battles against Ming armies sent to disband them. Besides the disruption to trade, the devastation which befell coastal communities, and the many thousands of innocents who found themselves sold as slaves, the pirates caused significant tensions in diplomatic relations between China, Korea, and Japan throughout this period. Indeed, the pirates seriously damaged the reputation of Japan in the eyes of their East Asian neighbors in the medieval period.

Bibliography

Beasley, W.G. *The Japanese Experience.* University of California Press, 2000.

Bryant, A.J. *The Samurai.* Osprey Publishing, 1989.

Deal, W.E. *Handbook to Life in Medieval and Early Modern Japan.* Oxford University Press, 2007.

Dougill, J. *Japan's World Heritage Sites.* Tuttle Publishing, 2014.

Ebrey, P.B. *Pre-Modern East Asia.* Cengage Learning, 2013.

Henshall, K. *Historical Dictionary of Japan to 1945.* Scarecrow Press, 2013.

Huffman, J.L. *Japan in World History.* Oxford University Press, 2010.

Lee, K. *A New History of Korea.* Harvard University Asia Center, 1984.

Mason, R.H.P. *A History of Japan.* Tuttle Publishing, 1997.

Peers, C.J. *Soldiers of the Dragon.* Osprey Publishing, 2006.

Pratt, K. *Korea: A Cultural & Historical Dictionary.* Routledge, 1999.

Sansom, G. *A History of Japan to 1334.* Stanford University Press, 1958.

Seth, M.J. *A History of Korea.* Rowman & Littlefield Publishers, 2010.

Tsuda, N. *A History of Japanese Art.* Tuttle Publishing, 2009.

Turnbull, S. *Japanese Castles AD 250-1540.* Osprey Publishing, 2008.

Turnbull, S. *The Mongol Invasions of Japan, 1274 and 1281.* Osprey Publishing, 2010.

Yamamura, K. (ed). *The Cambridge History of Japan, Vol. 3.* Cambridge University Press, 2001.

Image Credits

1.1 Medieval Japan and Its Trade Relations with Its Neighbors © Simeon Netchev
1.2 The Great Buddha of Kamakura. Photo © James Blake Wiener
1.3 Kinkaku-ji Temple or the 'Golden Pavilion.' Photo © James Blake Wiener

The Mongol Empire

By Mark Cartwright

Expert horse riders and archers, the Mongols proved unstoppable in Central Asia and beyond, defeating armies in Iran, Russia, Eastern Europe, China, and many other places. Genghis Khan (reign 1206-1227), first Great Khan or 'universal ruler' of the Mongol peoples, forged the empire by uniting nomadic tribes of the Asian steppe and creating a devastatingly effective army with fast, light, and highly coordinated cavalry. By the 14th century, the Mongols dominated Asia from the Black Sea to the Korean peninsula. The descendants of Genghis each ruled a part of the empire—the four khanates.

Nomads of the Steppe

The Mongols were pastoral nomads of the Asian steppe who herded sheep, goats, horses, camels, and yaks. These tribes moved according to the seasons and lived in temporary camps of circular felt tents or yurts (*gers*). Everyone—men, women, and young children—had to be able to ride well and use a bow for hunting. In the same vein, men and women were usually capable of doing each other's tasks since if one died, the survivor in the partnership had to carry on and look after the family and its herds. Traditionally, Mongol marriages had the aim of cementing clan relationships and strengthening alliances. Indeed, it was the custom to marry outside one's clan group (exogamy), and there was a custom of abducting women from rival tribes as a means to strengthen one clan group and weaken the other. Most marriages, though, would have been designed to reinforce existing bonds between family groups.

Men paid a bride price to their future father-in-law or offered labor as an alternative. As many nomadic men were relatively poor, it was a common custom merely to steal a wife during a raid, never mind any political benefits. In more genteel pre-arranged marriages, the future bride typically brought with her a dowry consisting of such valuables as livestock, jewelry, cloth, servants, and possibly slaves. The dowry might be 'paid' over several years and was usually lower in value than the bride price paid by the groom and his family. The dowry remained the property of the wife and was divided, on her death, among her children. In the ever-practical life of the nomads, sometimes a double marriage might be arranged between two family groups, each one providing a groom and bride, and so the necessity of a bride price from each was avoided. Wives received a small portion of their husband's property, which they managed but then handed on to the youngest son after his father's death.

Mongol society was patrilineal, and polygamy was common among those men who could afford multiple wives and concubines. However, one wife was always selected as senior, and it was her children who would inherit their father's property or position, or both, within the tribe. Women looked after the children and seem to have played an active role in family decision-making, with such sources as the 13th-century *The Secret History of the Mongols* mentioning the wives of rulers making speeches to enthuse warriors and promote loyalty to their husbands. If a husband predeceased his wife, she might be 'adopted' by a junior male relative of his. According to Mongol laws, women could divorce and own their own property, but just how often this was the case in practice is not known. In cases of adultery, both the man and woman were executed.

There was a dedicated space within the yurt for men and women, the former having the west side and the latter the east side where the cooking was done (easily defined since the doorway was traditionally made to face the south). The positioning of the yurts themselves in a camp (*ordu*) was important in imperial and larger camps, with the senior wife having the tent nearest to the west, the most junior wife to the east, and the concubines, children, and servants some way behind. Women were responsible for both setting up and packing up camps, putting the yurts and the family's belongings onto the carts, which they usually drove, and packing any pack animals like horses and camels.

The climate of Mongolia is often harsh; the typical weather of the Asian steppe is cold, dry, and windy. Winters can be long—from September to May—and bitterly cold (down to -34 degrees Celsius or -30 degrees Fahrenheit). Summers are short but can be hot, reaching a temperature over 30 degrees Celsius (86 degrees Fahrenheit). Reflecting this, clothing was warm, durable, and practical. Sheep provided fleeces and wool to make felt, and goats were herded in large numbers and were the principal source of leather. Felt was not only used for blankets and the yurts (tents); felt from sheep's wool and animal furs were the most common materials to make clothing, which was remarkably similar for both men and women: silk or cotton undergarments, baggy trousers, thick felt or leather boots, and a conical hat made from felt and fur.

The most recognizable piece of outer clothing, still widely worn today, was the *deel*. This long one-piece robe-jacket was folded over and closed on the left side of the chest (left breast doubled over the right) with a button or tie positioned just below the right armpit. Some *deel* had pockets, and the sleeves typically went only down to the elbow. The outer lining of the robe was of cotton or silk, and heavier versions had an additional fur or felt lining or a quilt padding. The inner lining was typically turned over a little to the outside of the garment at the sleeves and hem. For those who could afford it, the robe might have some exotic fur trim at the collar and edges. Through hunting, trade, or tribute from conquered peoples, the Mongols acquired furs such as sable, squirrel, rabbit, fox, monkey, dog, goat, and wolf. Exotic or difficult to obtain furs like snow leopard and lynx were especially prized and reserved for the elite members of society. In the coldest periods, fur garments were worn in a double layer with the inner layer having the hair on the inside and the outer layer the opposite way around.

A wide leather belt was worn, which had useful hanging pouches and might be decorated with ornate metal pieces (metal of any kind being a rarity for nomadic peoples). The belts of women were even more decorative than those of the men. In winter, a heavy coat of fur or felt was worn over the *deel* robe. Under the robe, another thin robe might be worn, or a simple cotton or silk undershirt. Trousers were worn under the ever-present robe. Winter trousers could be made entirely from fur or have cotton, wool, or silk padding, the latter being an excellent light insulator.

Boots were made from felt or leather, with the sole usually being a thickened layer of felt, and the boots high enough to tuck in the trousers. Boots had no heels and were fastened tight using laces. The feet were kept warm with thick felt stockings. The classic Mongol hat was conical and made from felt and fur with flaps for the ears and an upturned brim at the front. Sometimes the brim was divided into two. In summer a light headcloth might be worn to keep off the sun. Elite men and women distinguished themselves by sporting a few peacock feathers in their hats. One of the few areas where women differentiated themselves from men, and then only elite women, was the elaborate *boqta* headdress, which had pearls and feathers for decoration. One can still see these headdresses today when, for example, Kazakh women attend traditional festivities. While both men and women wore earrings, women also added metal, pearl, and feather decorations to their hair. Men, on the other hand, did not have much opportunity to do the same, as they seem to have shaved the crown of their head, sometimes leaving only a thin strip of hair at the front of the head with locks dangling down to the eyebrows. The hair left on the back of the head was commonly grown long and tied into two braids. In medieval illustrations, Mongol men often have a wispy goatee beard and drooping mustache.

Making felt, leather, and clothes, and then repairing them, were all tasks expected of Mongol women. Washing was one chore that did not happen very often due to the lack of water in the usually arid steppe environment. Foreign travelers of the period frequently comment on the dirtiness of the Mongols and their clothing and such habits as wiping their hands on their trousers after eating. In any case, regular washing was not desirable for nomadic outer clothing because it was often greased with animal fat to make it wind- and waterproof.

Another consequence of nomadic life was the absence of a large number of material possessions; thus, cloth and clothing were one of the important assets of a family and were given as gifts and as part of a bride's dowry. Male friends and blood brothers often exchanged a leather belt, while rulers gave sumptuous clothing to fellow rulers as diplomatic gifts and to senior officials on special occasions such as royal births and weddings, or to reward loyal service. Even the absence of clothing had a significance such as when belts and hats were removed before making prayers (including by the khans), belts of onlookers had to be removed and slung over the shoulder during succession ceremonies to demonstrate obedience, and sometimes the accused in a law court was stripped before sentence.

As nomadic herders of (in order of importance) sheep, goats, horses, Bactrian camels, and, at higher elevations, yaks, the Mongol people were much keener to keep their animals alive rather than eat them. Besides the much-needed wool, the animals provided a steady supply of milk (to make butter, cheese, yogurt, and drinks) and dung (to be burned as fuel). Oxen, although not herded in great numbers, were also useful as a means to pull carts.

The Mongol diet was mostly dairy based. Butter was made and stored in leather pouches but was, instead of salting, given a longer shelf life by the boiling process of its manufacture. A common food was fresh yogurt, cream was added to dishes, and another staple was *qurut* or dried milk curds. Cheese was often dried and cured by placing it on top of a yurt and exposing it to the wind and sun. *Qurut* was typically fermented or boiled in milk and was handy for travelers and warriors.

A welcome addition to the everyday diet would have been any herd animal that had died of natural causes or was too old to keep up with the herd. Meat was typically boiled and more rarely roasted because this process takes longer and so needed more precious fuel. Dried meat (*si'usun*) was an especially useful staple for travelers and roaming Mongol warriors. According to the chronicler Jean de Joinville (1224-1317), Mongol riders also placed a portion of raw meat under their saddles, and the movement of the animal and rider would eventually pound all the blood out of it and make a flattened steak. This is the origin story of 'steak tartare,' a menu item found around the world and associated with the Mongolian people, known (incorrectly) by many other nations in the Middle Ages as 'Tartars.'

In the harsh steppe environment, nothing was wasted and even the marrow of animal bones was eaten with the leftovers, then boiled in a broth to which curd or millet was added. Being frugal, the Mongols often killed an animal by cutting open its chest and squeezing the heart or cutting an artery. In this way, no blood was lost and could be used to make sausages. Another dietary supplement was any animals caught as a result of hunting, such as deer, antelopes, wild boars, marmots, wolves, foxes, and many wild birds (using snares and falconry). Freshwater fish were also sometimes eaten when possible but seem not to have appealed to most nomads.

Nomads are also gatherers, and the Mongols collected useful dietary supplements such as wild vegetables, roots, tubers, mushrooms, grains, berries, and other fruit they came across in nature or via trade. The Mongol mutton and vegetable dish known as *sulen* (or *shulen*)—which is a broth, soup or stew depending how many extras are added—spread in popularity across the Mongol Empire and is still today eaten in many parts of Asia.

As the empire spread, so the Mongol people added bread, noodles, and grain-based foods to their diet, as well as exotic spices. Ever-willing to adopt elements of the cultures they conquered, they experimented with new dishes—for example, the dessert baklava, the honey, nuts, and layers of wafer-thin pastry dessert now found everywhere but especially popular in Turkey, Greece, the Middle East, and North Africa. The Mongolian term *bakla* means 'pile up in layers' and one of the earliest known recipes for the dessert derives from a Chinese encyclopedia written at the time of the Mongol domination of that country.

Many herbs were collected and used as medicine for diseases, illnesses, and injuries. Eating certain parts of wild animals considered to have potent spirits, such as wolves and even marmots, was thought to help with certain ailments, too. Donkey meat was considered a good remedy for wind and depression, while bear paws helped increase one's resistance to cold temperatures. Such concoctions as powdered tiger bone dissolved in liquor, which is attributed all sorts of benefits for the body, is still a popular medicinal drink today in parts of East Asia. Curiously, the Mongols rarely drank fresh milk as they were lactose deficient. Horse blood was drunk when water was in short supply, draining it from the animal's neck without killing it. Tea—in the form of concentrated black tea bricks boiled in milk—was widely adopted from the 14th century.

Drinking large quantities of alcohol was a very important part of Mongol culture, and any important festival or gathering included rituals where all guests, both men and women, were expected to drink along to the beat of a drum or handclaps. *Kumis* was one of the most popular Mongol drinks and was typically made from fermented mare's milk (although the milk of sheep, oxen, camels, and yaks could be used, too). The drink was made by churning the milk in large leather bags using a wooden paddle, a process that took several hours. Known to the Mongols as *airagh*, it was an alcoholic summer drink and, because a season's supply required up to 60 horses, being able to drink it regularly was also a status symbol. The slightly fizzy drink was only 1-3% alcoholic, but this could be increased by various levels of distillation, the most laborious of which removed all solids and left a clear drink known as *qara kumis* or 'black kumis.' Naturally, the Great Khan had his own unique and plentiful supply of *airagh*, provided by herds kept in the hunting park at the capital Xanadu for his exclusive pleasure. A small quantity of *airagh* was often flicked into the air to appease any evil spirits or consecrate a herd and, similarly, a small offering of the drink and a small piece of meat was often dedicated to deceased relatives.

Still drunk today, it is often described as having a sour taste with an aftertaste of almonds.

Other alcoholic drinks included honey wine, known as *boal*, and as the empire expanded, so the Mongols were exposed to more and stronger alternatives than their mare's milk brew. Millet beer (*buza*), wine from grapes or rice, and many types of distilled liquors were drunk. The latter type, generally called *arqi* by the Mongols, were typically made from many varieties of fruit and grains and could be wickedly strong, up to 60 proof in some cases. Drinking to excess by both men and women seems to have been a social norm without any stigma attached to it (even having a certain honor), although cases of obesity and gout were common, and many early deaths of Mongol leaders are attributed to alcoholism.

Feasts were held on the rare occasions that Mongol nomads got together in one place, such as a meeting of tribal chiefs to elect a new leader or to celebrate important birthdays, weddings, and so on. Special occasions and feasts warranted meat dishes to be served; traditional dishes and how to cook them were recorded in the *Yinshan Zhengyao*, a sort of entertaining manual for the Mongol imperial court. Written by Hu Sihui in 1330, the title may be translated as 'Proper and Essential Things for the Emperor's Food and Drink,' and the recipes included roast wolf soup and *jasa'a* (mountain oysters), and for the morning after, a detoxifying dried orange peel puree. These events were attended by both men and women, and there was often a prescribed order of seating, eating, and drinking, all depending on the seniority of the participants. Not receiving one's bowl before a less senior member of the clan could lead to fights.

To stock up for special feasts and wintertime, special hunts were organized. Mongols were proficient hunters; they trained from a very young age, their horses were small but sturdy beasts with excellent stamina, and they had a great weapon, the Mongol composite bow. Made of multiple layers of wood, bamboo, or horn, the bow was strong, flexible and, because it was strung against its natural curve, it could shoot arrows with a high degree of accuracy and penetration. Arrowheads tended to be made from bone and, much more rarely, metal, while shafts were made from wood, reed, or a combination of both, and fletching from bird feathers. Hunters could shoot with accuracy while riding their horses at speed, thanks to stirrups and wooden saddles with a high back and front, which gave better stability.

To make a hunt a success, the Mongols participated in great numbers in a coordinated annual attack on a designated area of steppe. This strategy was called the *nerge* (aka *jerge* or *jarga*) and was traditionally held early each winter over at least a month-long period. During the *nerge* a long line of riders covering up to 130 kilometers (80 miles) marked out by flags moved from the outer end inward to eventually enclose a large pre-selected geographical area. The riders, accompanied by hunting dogs, then gradually moved, over a period of several weeks, in toward a smaller pre-designated circular zone, also marked out with flags beforehand, so that the animals driven there could more easily be killed. The riders worked in shifts to ensure no animals escaped the cordon, and anyone who did let an animal through the line was severely punished. Once the animals were penned in, only the khan could open the hunting with the first shot, and anyone starting off before him was executed. After the hunt, some animals were deliberately allowed to escape the entrapment in order to ensure the conservation of the game for future hunts. A nine-day feast traditionally marked the climax and close of the *nerge*.

Although nomadic life generally saw men do the hunting and women do the cooking, the division of labor was not always so clear, and often both sexes could perform the tasks of the other, including using a bow and riding. Women had rather more rights than in most other Asian cultures at the time and were also actively involved in religion.

The Mongols' religion had no sacred texts or particular ceremonies but was, rather, a mix of animism, ancestor worship, and shamanism. Instances of the elements of fire, earth, and water, impressive geographical sites like mountains, and natural phenomena such as storms were considered to possess spirits. Directions, places, and natural features were held important by the Mongols because they were considered as contact points with spirits. Natural phenomena, especially thunder and lightning, which is particularly impressive on the wide plains of the Asian steppe, were held in awe as the work of the gods. Earth and water spirits, in particular, acted as protectors; for example, it was thought that moving water, such as rivers, was capable of blocking and even nullifying evil. To ensure the gods and spirits had a favorable influence on human affairs, certain rituals and taboos were observed. Taboos, designed not to offend any spirits, included not shedding royal blood (considered along with a person's bones to contain the soul), not urinating or washing objects or one's person in rivers, not stepping on the threshold of a yurt, and not putting a knife anywhere near a fire. The conventions were taken seriously, and anyone caught breaking them risked severe punishments, even death in some cases.

Shamans were the nearest thing the Mongols had to a priesthood, and they could be both men (*bo'e*) or, more rarely, women (*iduqan*). It was quite common for shamans to pass on their position and skills to their children, although one might also become a shaman following a near-death experience or by displaying a particular sensitivity to the spirit world. Robes worn by shamans often carried symbols such as a drum and hobbyhorse, representing the guardian and protector spirit of the Mongol people. Shamans were believed capable of reading signs such as the cracks in sheep's shoulder bones, allowing them to divine future events. Those shamans who had success in their various predictions achieved a position of great prestige in the local community, sometimes rivaling the tribal chief, a position they sometimes held themselves. An ability to alter the weather was another shamanic skill, particularly as a bringer of rain to the often arid steppe. Shamans could help with medical problems and return a troubled spirit back to its rightful body.

The Mongols' concern to bury their dead with the deceased's weapons and personal possessions indicates some sort of belief in an afterlife. They seem to have considered the afterlife some sort of continuation of this one, and so one's social status and even profession continued as before. At the same time, Mongols believed that ancestors (*ongghot*) were not unreachable in a remote afterlife but were capable of overseeing the well-being of their descendants. In gratitude for protection, ancestors were regularly offered small food and drink offerings at mealtimes. In addition, the interior of yurts often displayed pictures or finely dressed effigies representing the family's ancestors. When moving camp, all the group's effigies were placed in the same wagon and then supervised by a shaman.

Other religions were present among the Mongols, notably Nestorian Christianity and, from the 14th century, Tibetan Buddhism (Lamaism) became popular, perhaps thanks to its shamanistic elements. Islam was also widely adopted in the western khanates. Above all, though, there was a widespread belief in the principal two deities: the Earth or Mother Goddess, known as Etugen (aka Itugen), who represented fertility, and Tengri (*Gok Monggke Tenggeri*), the 'Blue Sky' or 'Eternal Heaven.' This latter deity was seen as a protector god, and, crucially, he was thought by the tribal elites to have given the Mongol people a divine right to rule the entire world. Genghis Khan and his successors would put this idea into devastating practice by conquering almost the entire continent of Asia and creating the largest empire ever seen up to that time in history.

The Four Khanates

The Mongol nomadic tribes were used to a tough life, were highly mobile by nature, and were trained from childhood to ride horses and shoot bows. These qualities would make them into excellent warriors able to endure long and complex campaigns, cover vast amounts of territory in a short space of time, and survive on only the absolute minimum of supplies. Even the role of women and their chores of camp-making and transportation helped the Mongol army as they provided the vital logistic support for their husband warriors. Genghis Khan was perhaps the first Mongol leader to realize that if only the various tribes and clans could be united, the Mongols could master the world.

Genghis, born Temüjin circa 1162, overcame a harsh childhood, became a great leader through a ruthless mixture of diplomacy, warfare, and terror, and in 1206, in a grand meeting of all tribal leaders (a *kurultai*), he was formally recognized as the Great Khan or 'universal ruler' of the Mongols. Genghis Khan attempted to further unify his realm by insisting that the hitherto only spoken Mongol language was made into a written one using the script of the Uighur Turks and by introducing a lasting law code, the *Yasa*. Communication was greatly helped by the establishment of the *Yam*, a network of staging posts that messengers could use for resupply as they rode across the state. The empire had already begun in earnest, but it was about to get a whole lot bigger.

Mongol tribal leaders had traditionally achieved and then maintained their position of power by distributing war booty among their loyal followers, and Genghis was no different. The Mongol people were thus reorganized to specifically gear the state for perpetual warfare. Ninety-eight units known as *minghan* or 'thousands' were created (and then later expanded), which were tribal units expected to provide the army with a levy of 1,000 men. The khan also had his own personal bodyguard of 10,000 men, the *kesikten*, which was the elite standing army of the Mongols and which trained commanders for the other divisions. A third source of troops was the armies raised from allies and conquered states. Later, when Kublai Khan (reign 1260-1294) established the Yuan dynasty in China (1271-1368), Mongol armies there were composed entirely of professional soldiers.

Mongol leaders ensured loyalty and increased their chances of success by promoting commanders based on merit rather than the use of clan seniority as had been the case before Genghis. Motivation was high because booty was shared equally, and there was even a dedicated body, the *jarqu*, which ensured booty was distributed correctly (for example, horses, slaves, precious metals, textiles, high-quality manufactured goods, and even food). Commanders could expect to receive both booty and land or tribute from conquered peoples. Ordinary soldiers could expect rewards, too. At the same time, any soldier or commander who disobeyed orders was severely punished, lashings being the most common method.

Warriors were prepared from childhood thanks to the Mongol tradition of having both young boys and girls participate in competitions of athletics, horse racing, wrestling, hunting, and archery.

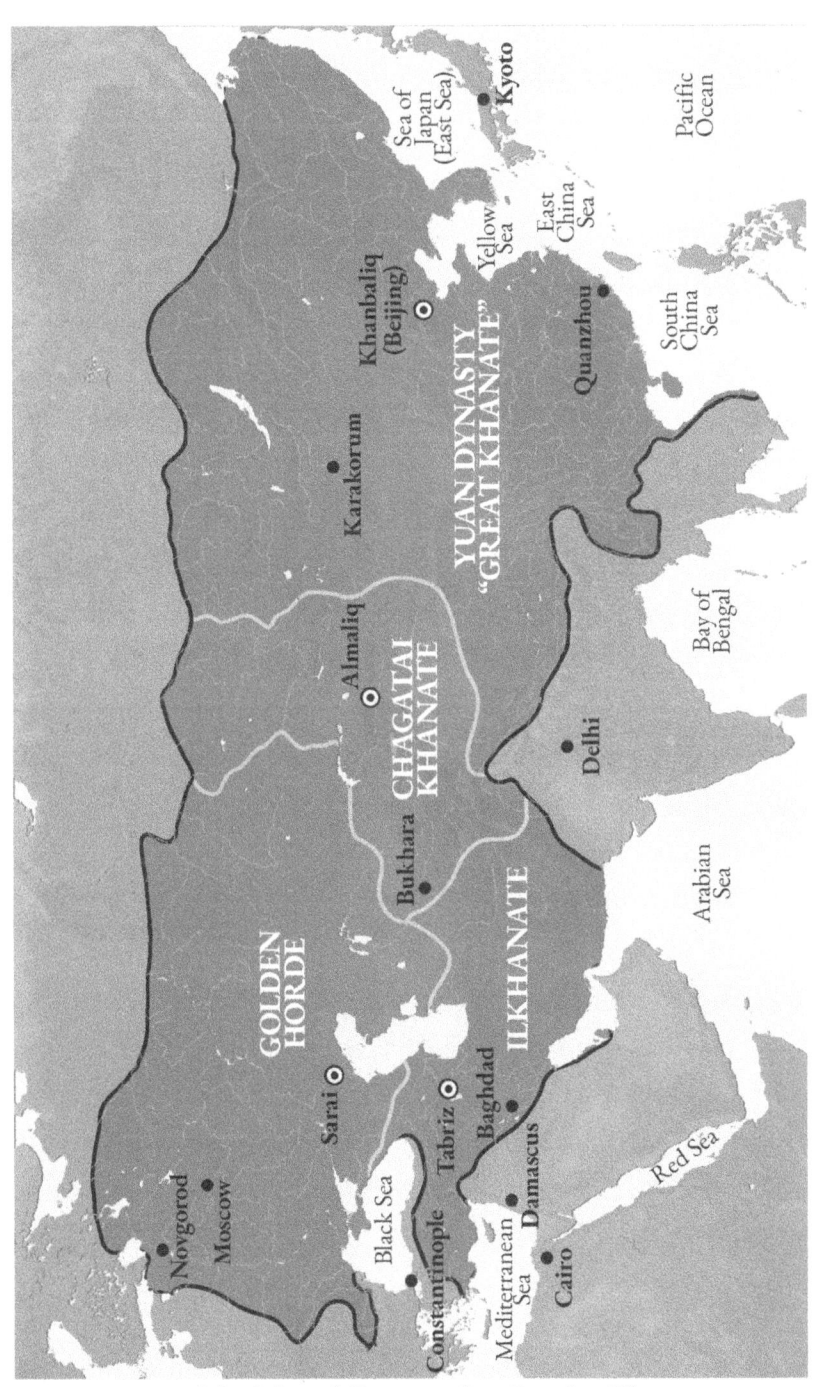

2.1 The Mongol Empire after Genghis Khan

The Mongol warriors—mostly men but sometimes women, too—were, then, already proficient at using battle-axes, lances (often hooked to pull enemy riders from their mounts), spears, daggers, long knives, and sometimes swords, which were typically short, light, and with a single cutting edge. The Mongol weapon of choice was the composite bow; a typical mounted archer carried two or three bows and around 30 light and 30 heavier arrows in a quiver. Additional standard equipment included a horsehair lasso, a coil of rope, an axe, a file for making arrowheads, a sewing repair kit, a leather bag for food and to use as a float when crossing rivers, two leather bottles for liquids, and a cooking pot. Men slept in light versions of the classic yurt, one carried for every ten riders. The Mongols had both light and heavy cavalry, and each rider typically had up to 16 spare horses, giving them a very long range of maneuver. On the battlefield, cavalry units responded to orders conveyed by gongs and drums (although, interestingly, the very first attack was always conducted in silence). Mongol armor was light so as not to impede the speed of cavalry riders, but if worn, it was typically made of thick quilted felt or leather. Learning from the Chinese, a silk undershirt might be worn as this had the handy consequence of wrapping around the arrowhead if one was struck, protecting the wound and making the arrow easier to withdraw. The head was protected by either an iron or hardened leather helmet, sometimes with a neck guard and a central top spike, or ball and plume. An alternative was the traditional Mongol hat. Horses were sometimes given armor; plate armor was restricted to the horse's head, but, otherwise, some mounts were completely covered with padded armor.

2.2 Recreation of a mounted warrior of the Mongol Empire

Mongol armies moved extremely quickly and attempted to outmaneuver their opponents using speed and coordination. The aim was to only engage the enemy when absolutely necessary and to commit large numbers only when a specific weak spot had been identified. This strategy was designed to give maximum results for minimal losses. Cavalry units of around 1,000 men (a *minghan*) were subdivided into units of 100 (a *jagun*), which was in turn divided into units of 10 (an *arban*). The Mongols were usually outnumbered by their enemies in field battles but overcame this disadvantage by superior speed and tactics. A classic Mongol strategy was to attack with a small force and then feign a retreat, which led the enemy back to a larger Mongol force. Another favored maneuver was the *tulughma*, that is to attack with a central body of cavalry—heavy cavalry in the front lines and lighter units behind, who then moved through gaps in the front lines, and while these moved forward as one, cavalry units moved on the wings to envelop the enemy forces. The tactic was a smaller-scale version of the *nerge*. Ambush was another common tactic, as was using smoke from burning grass or dust clouds to mask troop movements, or attacking at the least expected time, such as during a blizzard.

One of the most successful strategies employed in Mongol warfare was terror. When a city was captured, for example, the entire civilian population could be executed—men, women, children, priests, even the cats and dogs—with a handful of survivors allowed to escape and tell of the atrocity in the neighboring towns. Consequently, when towns heard of the Mongols' approach, many surrendered without a fight in the hope of clemency, which was often given.

Genghis's first target was the Jin state in northern China, but he soon turned the whole Asian world upside down in less than two decades. Genghis had decreed that after his death, his empire was to be divided among his four sons, Jochi, Chagatai, Tolui, and Ögedei, although Jochi would predecease his father in 1227. Genghis died later the same year, but the unified empire would endure until 1260. The descendants of Genghis each ruled a part of the empire—the four khanates—the most powerful of which was the Mongol Yuan dynasty in China (1271-1368), established by Kublai Khan (reign 1260-1294). The Golden Horde, centered on the western Eurasian steppe, was founded by Batu Khan (died 1255) around 1227. The Chagatai Khanate covered what is today mostly Uzbekistan, southern Kazakhstan, and western Tajikistan. The Ilkhanate (1260-1335) was established by Hulegu (died 1265) and encompassed what is today Iran and parts of Turkmenistan, Turkey, Iraq, Armenia, Afghanistan, and Pakistan.

Kublai was succeeded by his grandson Temür Öljeyitü as khan and emperor of China (reign 1295-1307), who, continuing with the same institutions and many of the same officials appointed by his predecessor, enjoyed a peaceful and successful reign. There then followed a long line of short-reigning rulers who struggled to balance the competing pro-Chinese and pro-Mongol traditionalists that divided the government at all levels. This rivalry sometimes broke out into violence, with one emperor being assassinated and another thrown out following a coup. By the mid-14th century, the Yuan rulers had been beset by a devastating combination of unusually cold winters, famines, plagues, and flooding of the Yellow River, which all combined to bring hyperinflation when the government tried to solve the problems of a damaged infrastructure by printing too much paper money. There followed widespread banditry and uprisings by an overtaxed peasantry. Worse, some of the local elites and provincial administrators in southern China were colluding with the bandits, smugglers, and even religious leaders to take over entire towns. Yuan China was disintegrating from within.

The Yuan rulers had not helped themselves by squabbling over power, creating an overblown bureaucracy, and wasting revenue and land resources on a few favored princes and generals. Most importantly of all, they failed to quash numerous rebellions, including that perpetrated by a group known as the Red Turban Movement, an offshoot of the Buddhist White Lotus Movement, led by a peasant called Zhu Yuanzhang (1328-1398). Zhu Yuanzhang's first major coup had been the capture of Nanjing in 1356, and, after he had taken Beijing, the last Yuan emperor of a unified China, Toghon Temür (reign 1333-1368), fled to Mongolia and the old, now largely abandoned capital, Karakorum. The Yuan would, thus, continue to rule in Mongolia under the new name of the Northern Yuan dynasty (1368-1635).

In the 13th century, all three western khanates constantly fought each other in border disputes, but by 1304, there was finally a relative peace across Asia, a period known as the Pax Mongolica. By the 14th century, the Mongols became part of the sedentary societies they had so easily overwhelmed, and many converted from traditional

Shamanism to Tibetan Buddhism or Islam. This was a general symptom of the Mongols not only losing part of their cultural identity but also their famed military prowess. Border conflicts continued on all sides despite the general 'peace,' but the reign of Kebek (reign 1318-1327) brought some economic prosperity in the Chagatai Khanate, largely thanks to his promotion of currency use. The small silver coins now used widely across the khanate were known as *kebeks* after the khan himself, and their name would survive in Russia, as their term *kopeika* became kopecks. Kebek also centralized the state and formed a new and more secure capital at Qarshi (in southern Uzbekistan).

The next significant Chagataid ruler was Tarmashirin (reign 1331-1334), who converted to Islam and promoted that religion in his realm. This conversion did not, however, put off the khan from launching raids into the Muslim sultanate of Delhi. There were, too, problems now at home as traditional Mongols, most of whom practiced Shamanism, Tibetan Buddhism (Lamaism), or Nestorian Christianity, saw the move toward Islam as a betrayal of their Mongol roots. This ill feeling culminated in a rebellion, which overthrew Tarmashirin in 1334; although, as it turned out, most of the subsequent khans would also be Muslim, and the western part of the state, in particular, became dominated by that religion. The state effectively split into eastern (Mawarannahr or Transoxania) and western (Moghulistan) halves, with many local tribal chiefs then ignoring the governments of both. In addition, local Turkic emirs took control of the southern part of the state. Further disruption was caused by the arrival of the Black Death in the region during the 1340s. By the mid-14th century, the Mongol elite had largely become part of the sedentary societies they had once sought to conquer, and the last khan, Tughlugh Timur (reign 1347-1363), could not prevent the disintegration of the khanate as a definable political entity.

The Ilkhanate, centered on Persia, regularly had to defend its territories against neighboring states. There were unsuccessful diplomatic relations with the West to form an alliance against the Mamluks of Egypt, although trade agreements were established with Italian city-states. The last decade of the 13th century saw dynastic wrangles between the Ilkhans Baidu and Gaikhatu, vast overspending by the state caused by ill-advised handouts to favored aristocrats, and the disastrous introduction of paper money, which nobody could quite get used to. The persistent wars with neighbors did not help either and greatly disrupted the lucrative camel caravans that crisscrossed Asia. Even agriculture was suffering, a situation first brought about by the Mongols' destruction of the ancient qanat irrigation system when they had first invaded the region from the 1220s. These underground canals had ensured desert areas were made suitable for farming, but their repairs needed intense labor, which the Mongols struggled to provide in areas where wars had led the peasantry to permanently seek safer areas to live.

Ghazan (reign 1295-1304), who took power thanks to a wave of unpopularity regarding Baidu, sorted out the economy by issuing a new and centrally controlled coinage. Significantly, considering the failure of paper money, Ghazan's coins sometimes carried the legend 'real money.' Ghazan converted to Islam in 1295, but this did not stop him from attacking the Mamluk Sultanate, briefly capturing Aleppo and Damascus in November 1299, and then again attacking Syria in 1303. Ghazan's conversion to Islam, however, saw the Ilkhanate officially become a Muslim empire. Ghazan's coins now bore the legend: 'Emperor of Islam.' This shift resulted in many Christian churches, Buddhist temples, and other non-Muslim places of worship being destroyed, but some escaped the purge, especially in areas where the Muslim population was not the majority, such as the northeastern part of the state (today's Georgia and Armenia).

From 1304, the Pax Mongolica allowed the new ruler, Ilkhan Öljaitü (reign 1304-1316), the brother of Ghazan, to complete construction of a new capital at Sultaniyya, located just south of its predecessor, Tabriz. The capital was adorned with beautiful domed mosques and fortified walls with octagonal towers, but little remains today, except the ruined tomb of the man who oversaw its growth. Öljaitü converted to Shiite (Shia) Islam in 1310, and the religion would be widely adopted as well as influential in terms of general culture, art, and architecture. The cultural achievements are perhaps best seen in the figure of Rashid al-Din Hamadani (1247-1318), grand vizier of the Ilkhanate, who famously wrote a history of the known world, the *Compendium of Chronicles*, an invaluable source of Mongol history for modern scholars.

In 1322, a peace treaty was finally drawn up with the Mamluks, and the state seemed as healthy as it had ever been. However, in 1335, the death of Ghazan's son and successor, Abu Sa'id (reign 1316-1335), brought another series of dynastic squabbles—not helped by the young *ilkhan* requiring a regent in the early part of his reign, the overly ambitious General Choban. The political instability was then made much worse by the lack of an heir when Abu Sa'id died, perhaps from poisoning in 1335. The struggle for power centered on different Muslim factions, and many of the protagonists did not even make the history books, never mind win overall domination over their rivals. This time, the lack of unity was fatal to the Ilkhanate, which broke up into competing micro-khanates, making them vulnerable to the Golden Horde, which was still thriving.

The longest-lasting of the great Mongol khanates, the Golden Horde, stretched from the Black Sea to Siberia at its peak in the first half of the 14th century. Its name, *Zolotaya Orda*, is Russian and derives from the informal name for the golden-colored palace tent (*hordo* in Middle Mongolian) its rulers used. The horde was further subdivided into the Blue Horde (descendants of Batu) and the subordinate White Horde (descendants of Batu's brother Orda). The first capital was Sarai Batu, but this was later replaced by Sarai Berke or New Sarai (often simply called Sarai), which was strategically located on the lower Volga River and became a great trade and cultural center. The Golden Horde, whose population and culture was a mix of Mongol and Turkic tribal peoples, had long battled its neighbors, including the Ilkhanate and the Byzantine Empire, with varying degrees of success, and it faced several serious challenges from both Russia and Lithuania. On the other hand, the Golden Horde maintained lucrative trade relations across the continent, in particular, with the Italian trading states of Genoa and Venice, and with the Mamluks of Egypt, to whom the Golden Horde sent military aid and slaves. Relations between the Golden Horde and the Byzantine Empire were improved when Khan Toqta (reign 1291-1312) married the daughter of the emperor, Andronikos II Palaiologos (reign 1282-1328). Tribute was extracted from conquered peoples, often collected by intermediaries such as the Russian princes.

The Golden Horde, as with the other khanates, gradually changed from within, as the small Mongol minority (the smallest of all the khans) assimilated and adopted elements of the Turkic culture of the Mamluks. In the 1280s, for example, Turkic replaced Mongolian script on Golden Horde coins. Then, under the rule of Uzbeg (aka Öz Beg or Özbek, reign 1313-1341), Islam was made the state religion. Uzbeg's reign was also characterized by an increase in challenges from neighbors, notably the Lithuanians, Poles, and various Russian principalities, whom he tried to constantly play off against each other to avoid a united anti-Golden Horde front. The task was far from easy. It seemed that whenever the Golden Horde fought the Russians, the Lithuanians nibbled off a bit more of the khanate in Eastern Europe. The Osmanli (Ottoman) Sultanate in Anatolia was another threat, particularly to the well-established trade connections with the Mamluks.

In the mid-14th century, fortunes declined when the Black Death struck (indeed, this plague may well have originated in Golden Horde territory), killing millions and disrupting the camel caravan routes upon which the economic wealth of the Golden Horde depended. Squabbles between Uzbeg's successors created a series of damaging rivalries and factions that divided the Golden Horde elite. From 1360, there was rarely a single recognized ruler of the Golden Horde, and civil wars were frequent. The long decline really set in following a brutal attack by Timur (aka Tamerlane, reign 1380-1395) in 1395. The Golden Horde ruler Tokhtamysh (circa 1376-1395) had been installed as a puppet ruler by Timur, and he oversaw something of a resurgence in the khanate's fortunes. The strongest principality of the Rus to the north was Muscovy, and the Grand Prince of Moscow, Dmitrii Donskoi, defeated a Golden Horde army in 1380 at the Battle of Kulikovo. Tokhtamysh then got his revenge and even sacked Moscow in 1382. Tokhtamysh then unwisely sought greater independence from his former mentor Timur, who was by then intent on conquering all of Central Asia and all four of the original Mongol khanates.

Timur, a Muslim Turkic chieftain who claimed Mongol descent, grew up in the Chagatai Khanate, and he participated in the successful campaigns of that state. He briefly served as a minister under Ilyas Khoja (died 1368), the governor of Transoxania and son of Tughlugh Timur, the last khan of the Chagatai Khanate.

THE MONGOL EMPIRE   51

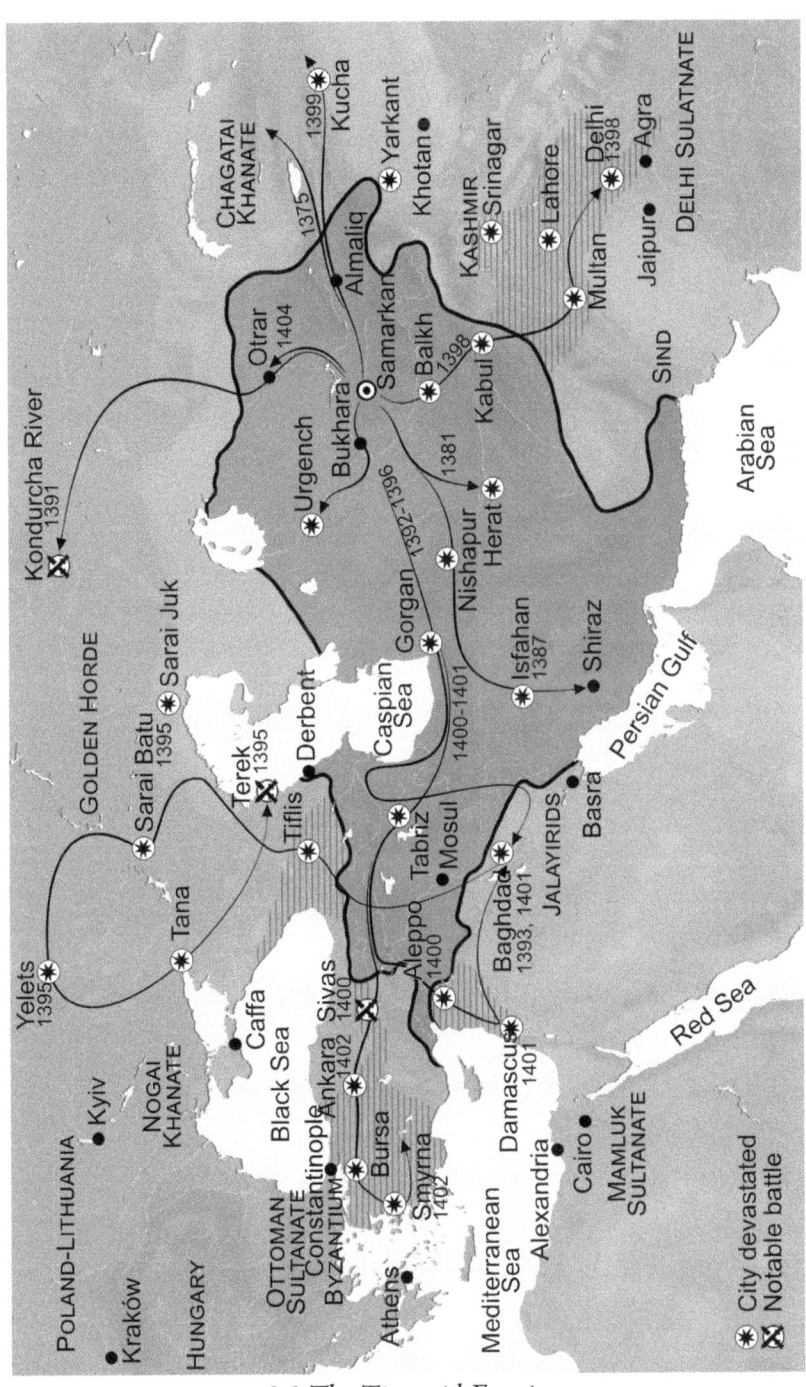

2.3 The Timurid Empire

Timur then allied himself with Amir Husayn, his brother-in-law, and they managed to take over Transoxania by 1366. Following the death of Husayn, Timur took sole control of Transoxania around 1370, and he used the connections of one of his many wives to the Mongol khans to legitimize his claim as its new ruler.

From the 1370s, Timur had his eye on more of the former territories of the Chagatai Khanate and the Ilkhanate. Like the Mongols before him, Timur attacked with speed and where it was least expected. Troops of various origins were loyal to Timur since his success rate at providing promised booty was extremely high. Timur, who almost always led his troops personally, "was undeniably a highly gifted and successful general. But he indulged in destruction and wanton cruelty to an extent that Chingiz [Genghis] would have considered pointless" (Morgan, 176). Stories abounded of the lengths Timur went to terrorize conquered peoples, such as cementing captured victims alive into a tower or erecting a battle memorial made of the bones of the defeated. The idea, not a new one, was to ensure other cities in the region capitulated rather than face such terrible acts of vengeance, but the violence was always excessive, against both non-Muslims and Muslims.

Timur's vast Timurid Empire eventually stretched from the Mediterranean in the west to the frontiers of China in the east and from the Caspian and Aral Seas in the north to the Persian Gulf and Arabian Sea in the south. By the 1390s, Central Asia was under his control, including parts of Persia. Timur then attacked the Golden Horde in 1395. At the Battle of the Terek River in southern Russia on 14 April 1395, Timur obliterated the army of Tokhtamysh and forced him to flee. Victory enabled Timur to occupy Moscow for a year and conquer most of the territory along the lower Volga, and he ruthlessly sacked Sarai, to the permanent detriment of the city's fortunes. In addition, his destruction of Sarai's extensive archives has been a permanent lament of historians of the Golden Horde ever since. Just like Sarai, the Golden Horde never regained the status it had enjoyed prior to Timur's passing through.

Still not satisfied with his gains, Timur's next target was the wealth of India. In the winter of 1398-9, he invaded the subcontinent and defeated an army of Nasiruddin Muhammad Shah Tughluq (aka Sultan Mahmud Shah II, reign 1394-1413) at Panipat. Timur then moved on another 80 kilometers (50 miles) or so to loot and sack the great city of Delhi, capital of the Delhi Sultanate (1206-1526). Timur's insatiable appetite for conquest and plunder continued in his latter years. He invaded Syria and sacked Aleppo in 1399. Baghdad was sacked in 1401. The next year, it was Anatolia's turn to be ravaged. Finally, an audacious expedition to attack Ming China was underway when the conqueror of Central Asia died en route in February 1405.

Although infamous for his barbarous treatment of conquered peoples, Timur's empire did register several cultural achievements. Samarkand was made the capital, and Timur ensured its beautification and cultural enrichment by forcibly relocating certain conquered peoples to it, notably scholars, artists, architects, and artisans. Samarkand had once been a great administrative center of the Mongol Empire and was still a major stopping point on the Silk Road. Timur expanded Samarkand slightly adjacent to the older city, which had been sacked by Genghis Khan. Timur's Samarkand became a great metropolis, and he named various quarters of its suburbs after the cities he had conquered. The city's reputation spread far and wide thanks to its fine buildings and beautiful gardens, becoming a byword in Western Europe for the exotic and little-known gardened cities of Central Asia. Timur invested heavily in buildings with a religious function, particularly Muslim shrines and mosques, many of which were beautifully and painstakingly decorated with gilding and mosaic pieces of precious turquoise and azure. Unfortunately, not a great deal survives today, but there is the Great Mosque, the Timurid tomb-complex of Shāh-i Zinda, and the Gūr-i Amīr, the massive domed tomb that contains Timur's embalmed remains.

No Timurid ruler ever gained the successes its founder had enjoyed, and the empire suffered for Timur's lack of skill or ambition as a statesman since the nomadic warrior failed to create any lasting administrative institutions in his conquered lands. While Timur's empire rapidly shrank, the Timurid dynasty did, at least, continue to dominate in Turkestan and neighboring regions well into the 16th century, and Samarkand, in particular, continued to thrive as a cultural center.

Bibliography

Broadbridge, A.F. *Women and the Making of the Mongol Empire.* Cambridge University Press, 2018.

Buell, P.D. *Historical Dictionary of the Mongol World Empire.* Rowman & Littlefield Publishers, 2018.

Ebrey, P.B. *Pre-Modern East Asia.* Cengage Learning, 2013.

Lane, G. *Daily Life in the Mongol Empire.* Hackett Publishing Company, Inc., 2009.

May, T. *The Mongol Empire.* Edinburgh University Press, 2018.

Mansingh, Surjit. *Historical Dictionary of India.* Orient Paperbacks, India, 2007.

Morgan, D. *The Mongols.* Wiley-Blackwell, 2019.

Rossabi, M. *A History of China.* Wiley-Blackwell, 2013.

Saunders, J.J. *The History of the Mongol Conquests.* University of Pennsylvania Press, 2001.

Turnbull, S. *Genghis Khan & the Mongol Conquests 1190-1400.* Osprey Publishing, 2003.

Turnbull, S. *Mongol Warrior 1200-1350.* Osprey Publishing, 2003.

Turnbull, S. *The Mongols.* Osprey Publishing, 1980.

Image Credits

2.1 The Mongol Empire After Genghis Khan. Map © Simeon Netchev

2.2 Genghis Khan: The Exhibition. Photo by William Cho, ArtScience Museum, Singapore, CC BY-SA 2.0, https://www.flickr.com/photos/adforce1/5465078899/

2.3 The Timurid Empire. Map © Simeon Netchev

CHINA

By Mark Cartwright

CHINA WAS RULED BY the Mongol Yuan dynasty from 1271 to 1368 after Kublai Khan (reign 1260-1294) defeated the Song dynasty, which had reigned since 960, and established himself, as all nomadic leaders before him had dreamed of, as the emperor of China. The Mongols were helped by many Song generals defecting or surrendering their armies, and the fact that the imperial court was beset by infighting between the child emperor's advisors. Ultimately, the empress dowager and her young son, Emperor Gongzong (reign 1274-75), surrendered along with their capital, Lin'an, on 28 March 1276. The Song royals were taken prisoner to Kublai's new capital at Beijing (Daidu). Groups of loyalists fought on for three more years, installing two more young emperors in the process (Duanzong and Dibing), but the Mongols swept all before them. Finally, on 19 March 1279, a great naval battle was won at Yaishan (aka Yamen), near modern-day Macao; the Mongol conquest of China was complete. It was the first time that the country had been unified since the 9th century, not that this was much consolation to the countless dead, robbed, and displaced across China.

Yuan Dynasty

Making himself emperor of China, Kublai gave himself the reign name Shizu and, in 1271, his new dynasty the name 'Yuan,' meaning either 'origin' or 'center, main pivot.' Beginning with Kublai, Mongol rulers made some superficial attempts to appeal to their new Chinese subjects by adopting such traditions as emperor's robes, traveling in a sedan chair, and surrounding themselves with Confucian advisors. The real power, though, remained in Mongol hands as key administrative positions in the newly created twelve semi-autonomous provinces that China and northern Korea (annexed in 1270) were now divided into largely went to Mongols, especially to members of the very large Mongol imperial bodyguard. The traditional six Chinese ministries, in place since the Tang dynasty (618-907), continued as before, but there were Mongol institutions, too, like the Shumi Yuan or 'Ministry of War.'

From the Han dynasty onwards (206 BCE to 220 CE), the civil service examinations allowed the state to find the best candidates to staff the vast bureaucracy that governed China. These exams were a means for a young male of any class to enter the bureaucracy and so become a part of the gentry class of scholar-officials. The exams had multiple levels and were extremely difficult to pass, requiring extensive knowledge of Confucian classics, law, government, and oratory, among other subjects. For the state, the system supplied not only able candidates who were selected on merit but also ensured an entire class developed that had sympathy with the ruling status quo. Kublai abolished the civil service examinations, which would have favored Chinese officials with their Confucian education—they were reinstated in 1313, but Mongols still received advantages.

Although many Chinese officials continued to work as before, they were subject to random and secret inspections by Mongol-trusted censors. The Mongol regional official known as the *jarquchi* was appointed to Chinese territories, and these officials, along with representatives of the various Mongol clans, made up a local government for each province. The Mongol police force, the *tutqaul*, was given the task of ensuring roads were kept free from bandits, and Western Asians, particularly Muslims, were often given roles in the financial side of government, such as finance ministers and tax inspectors.

Kublai ensured that Mongols always gained an advantage in China by officially classing them as superior in rank to the Chinese. There were four official Yuan ranks, based on perceived loyalty to the Yuan rulers.

Mongols
Semu: people from Central Asia and speakers of Turkic languages
Hanren: Northern Chinese, Tibetans, Khitans, Jurchen, and others
Nanren: Southern Chinese formally ruled by the Song

Being a member of one of the above four classes had repercussions for an individual's tax status, their treatment by the judicial system, and their eligibility for positions in the state administration (there was a 25% capped quota for Southern Chinese people, for example). Differences in treatment included the Northern Chinese being taxed by household, while the Southern Chinese had to pay according to the area of land they owned. Punishments were a particularly striking area of difference with, for example, a Mongol found guilty of murder only having to pay a fine, while a Southern Chinese person convicted of mere theft was fined and then tattooed as a criminal. The new law code introduced in 1270, however, had only 135 capital crimes, half the number found in the code used by the Song.

There were other measures of segregation, too, such as forbidding Chinese to take Mongol names, wear Mongol clothes, or learn the Mongol language. Intermarriage was discouraged. Rather than being a solely racially motivated policy, though, Kublai and his successors were most concerned with controlling their subjects, making it easier to identify who was who and ensuring there were no rebellions; Chinese people were forbidden to carry weapons or congregate in public, for example.

At least traditional religions were permitted to continue as long as they did not threaten the state, although Buddhism was generally favored over traditional Chinese Confucianism. The Mongols' own preference for Shamanism showed no signs of change, although Kublai himself converted to Tibetan (Lamaist) Buddhism. Further, despite the obvious discrimination, Southerners kept their classical Chinese culture very much alive through private meetings and the arts, often producing paintings, poetry, and plays, which conveyed within them subtle protests against the Yuan regime. The latter art form, which included puppet theater as well as live actors, boomed under the Yuan because of its visual appeal and striking stories; the Mongols, unable to speak Chinese, had little time for prose and poetry.

Kublai Khan was particularly interested in re-establishing the Chinese tribute system, which had been neglected during the latter part of the Song's reign. The system had states pay symbolic and material tribute to China's dominant position as the center of the known world, the 'Middle Kingdom.' Not only was it a means to further legitimize his position as Chinese emperor, but it could also bring in useful material goods and help expand international trade. There was also the matter that Mongol rulers legitimized their position through conquest and the distribution of booty to their followers to ensure loyalty and continued service. Kublai, then, embarked on a series of campaigns to bring China's neighbors back to their former position of subservience to the emperor. Japan was twice invaded (1274 and 1281), but each time staunch resistance and fortuitous storms, the kamikaze or 'divine winds,' forced a retreat. Like Japan, Southeast Asia was attacked in various land and naval campaigns, but it also proved an elusive prize with invasions of Vietnam (1281 and 1286), Burma (1277 and 1287, now Myanmar), and Java (1292), achieving only limited success but at least gaining regular tribute from the Pagan Kingdom in Burma and the Champa and Dai Viet kingdoms of Vietnam. It seemed that conducting naval warfare overseas and the unfamiliar climate of Southeast Asia were insurmountable obstacles to Yuan expansion. Kublai never gave up on Japan, though, and continued to send unsuccessful diplomatic missions to persuade the country to join the Chinese tribute system.

In other parts of Asia, to the west, there was relative peace, although there was a major rebellion in Tibet in the early 1290s, and the other descendants of Genghis Khan continued to nibble at China's western borders. Nevertheless, the Mongols managed to expose China to a wider world. This was especially true in regard to the West with contacts through Persia and, thanks to missionaries, ambassadors, and travelers like Marco Polo (1254-1324), Europe. Of more concrete benefit to the Mongols and Chinese than world fame, the Yuan also promoted international trade. Artisans and craftworkers were given a more elevated status than previously and granted tax exemptions. Merchants, not being producers but 'exchangers,' had been discriminated against under the Song, and these, too, now benefited from more favorable tax measures, low-cost loans, and the end of sumptuary regulations.

3.1 Figure of a Mongol, earthenware sculpture, 14th century, China

Merchants were encouraged to use paper money, currency exchanges were better regulated, and more roads, canals (including the Grand Canal connecting southern and northern China), and the use of ocean-going ships aided the transport of goods. The effect of these policies was to create a boom in crafts and trade, especially of silk and fine porcelain, the latter product now being supervised by a specific government agency, paving the way for the later Ming potters to gain worldwide fame of their own. Trade also brought a greater exchange of ideas and technologies, such as Persian expertise in astronomical observations, maps, luxury textile weaving, and irrigation coming to China, and gunpowder weapons, printing, the mariner's compass, and paper money reaching the West.

Kublai's successor, Temür Öljeyitü (reign 1295-1307), continuing with the same institutions and officials, enjoyed a peaceful and successful reign, but was followed by a long decline in the 14th century, beset by famines, plagues, floods, widespread banditry, and peasant uprisings. The Mongol rulers also squabbled among themselves for power and failed to quash numerous rebellions, including that perpetrated by a group known as the Red Turban Movement led by a peasant called Zhu Yuanzhang (1328-1398).

Born in Anhui Province, eastern China, Zhu Yuanzhang's peasant family suffered extreme poverty, and his parents often found themselves having to move home just to avoid rent collectors. An even greater disaster struck with the plague that hit China in the 1340s. Both his father and eldest brother succumbed to the disease, and the family was left penniless. By now 16 years of age, Zhu was obliged to join a Buddhist monastery, where at least he could find food and shelter. Unfortunately, the monastery was not doing too well either, and Zhu sometimes had to beg in the street for his daily bread. The young man roamed around central China for several years, but he did eventually return to the monastery in Anhui.

The Red Turbans, so called because their members wore that color headgear, were actually an offshoot of the radical Buddhist White Lotus Movement. The Reds had sprung up as part of the wider peasant reaction to the Yuan policy of using forced labor on government construction projects, particularly on the Grand Canal and Yellow River. Most active in northern China, the rebels frequently clashed with Mongol forces, and in one such episode, the monastery where Zhu was staying was burned down. Zhu, now 24 and with few other options, decided to join the Red Turbans. Slowly, he made himself more and more vital to the cause. He married the daughter of one of the movement's leaders and then took over their leadership himself in 1355.

Establishing his power base in the Yangzi valley, Zhu eventually had 20,000-30,000 men under his command. Zhu replaced the Red Turbans' traditional policy aim of reinstating the old Song dynasty (960-1279) with his own personal ambitions to rule, and he gained wider support by ditching the anti-Confucian policies that had alienated the educated classes. Alone among the many rebel leaders of the period, Zhu understood that to establish a stable government, he needed administrators, not just warriors out for loot.

Zhu Yuanzhang's first major step to dominance in China was the capture of Nanjing in 1356. The Mongol rulers had not helped their cause by dismissing their most able general, Chancellor Toghto, the year before, on the grounds that he was too pro-Chinese. Zhu's successes continued, and he defeated his two main rival rebel leaders and their personal armies. First to go was Chen Youliang, who had declared himself Han emperor in 1360. Chen was killed and his army defeated at the Battle of Poyang Lake in 1363. Next came Zhang Shicheng, a salt smuggler and pirate with a large naval force, who was defeated in 1367. When Han Lin'er then died—he who had claimed to be the rightful heir to the line of Song emperors—Zhu was left the most powerful leader in China, and, after chasing the remnants of the Mongol army back to Mongolia, he declared himself emperor on 23 January 1368, the day of the New Lunar Year.

Ming Dynasty

Zhu would take the reign name Hongwu (meaning 'abundantly martial'), and the dynasty he founded would be known as Ming (meaning 'bright' or 'light'). The new emperor sought to establish his legitimacy by reinstating the traditional sacrifices Chinese rulers made to Heaven and Earth. For the same reason, other Confucian and Buddhist rituals saw a return, too. Whatever his legitimacy, Hongwu would stamp out any lingering rebel movements in the next two decades and reign until 1398. His successors continued his efforts to unify China through a strong centralized government and so consolidated the Ming dynasty's grip on power. It was the beginning of another golden era of Chinese history.

Hongwu was wary of losing his throne in the same violent way he had gained it, and so he was determined to impose a strong centralized government on China, with him personally exercising control over all matters. The institution of the Chinese emperor would return to that of old—the absolute monarch and possessor of a divine mandate to rule, the so-called Mandate of Heaven. To strengthen his position, even the secretariat, a position which had previously acted as a bureaucratic limit on an emperor's power, was abolished (although not until 1380, and it would return under later emperors). Any dissenting officials were ruthlessly punished or executed, and to ensure Hongwu's control spread far beyond the capital in Nanjing, the provincial governments were reorganized with imperial family members placed at their heads. At the same time, local authorities were given just enough autonomy that they could create a balance of power with these regional heads and so ensure no one—family, friend, or foe—ever rose to challenge the emperor.

The emperor, himself a beneficiary of free Buddhist education, was an advocate of learning for all, and he promoted local schools to that end. In 1370, Hongwu reintroduced the civil service examination system, which would continue right into the 20th century. Regarding the arts, a flourishing would only really occur under Hongwu's successors, but he did found a painting academy in Nanjing. Other policies carried out by Hongwu included the compilation of a draconian law code (the *Da Ming lü* or 'Grand Pronouncements'); land and tax obligations were meticulously registered, hereditary military service continued to be imposed on the peasantry in threatened regions (as it had been under the Mongols), international trade was curbed as all things foreign were considered a threat to the regime, and the old tribute system required of neighboring states was revived. The reduction in commerce compared to the more internationally minded Mongols meant that agriculture was once more the focus of government economic policy. Following the devastation of large swathes of China after the Mongol invasion and the rebellions during the Yuan dynasty's death throes, land for cultivation was meticulously registered and redistributed back to the peasantry, areas were drained, irrigation systems were improved, and some areas were reforested. The region of the southwest was conquered, and a new province was created: Guizhou.

3.2 The Ming dynasty of China

Perhaps initially more a hyper-paranoid ruler with some good intentions than an evil despot per se, Hongwu had no qualms about punishing his officials, as this quote attributed to him illustrates: "In the morning I punish a few; by evening others commit the same crime. I punish these in the evening and by the morning again there are violations. Although the corpses of the first have not been removed, already others follow in their path ... Day and night I cannot rest" (Brinkley, 168).

As time wore on, though, Hongwu became more erratic and paranoid. Regular punishments and purges of the state bureaucracy were carried out, most infamously in 1376 when several thousand officials were executed following accusations of mismanaging the grain tax. Anyone who took exception to the emperor's bias toward Buddhism was similarly dealt with. From 1380, there was an even bigger purge, which saw 15,000 officials and their relatives executed when Hongwu thought he had discovered an assassination plot by his chancellor, Hu Weiyong. The purge, beginning with the chancellor's execution, went on for over a decade and rooted out any person with even the slightest connection—real or imagined—to Weiyong. Such was the effect of this reign of terror and the lack of enthusiasm among the educated scholar class to participate in the government; Hongwu was obliged to compel bureaucrats to accept official appointments and ban resignations. Even the military did not escape, and the three top Ming generals were executed between 1393 and 1395. By now in his mid-60s, it seems that the tighter Hongwu held on to power, the less grip he felt he had.

Hongwu had 26 sons, but his carefully groomed heir was to be his first son, Zhu Biao, whom he had with Empress Ma. However, Biao's early death in 1392 would cause a reshuffling of the court hierarchy, which had dire consequences.

3.3 Burial site of Ming Hongwu, the first Ming emperor, and Sun Zhongshan (Sun Yat-sen), Nanjing

When Hongwu died in 1398, he was succeeded by his second choice as heir, Biao's eldest son, Zhu Yunwen (aka Huidi), who took the reign name of Jianwen Emperor (reign 1398-1402). This became the established method of the Ming dynasty to choose heirs to the throne; the eldest son of the empress was first in line and, if he died before taking office, his eldest son would inherit.

Unfortunately for the new emperor, his grandfather's policy of jumping a generation was not welcomed by all, especially not Hongwu's second son, known as the Prince of Yan (and as Zhu Di, born 1360). The prince was ambitious; he had already shown himself an able military commander in campaigns against the Mongols and wanted the throne for himself. Significantly, the prince's claim was backed by his large army stationed in the northeastern provinces of China and meant to protect the area around Beijing. The final straw was Jianwen's decision to remove the title of prince from the first and other sons of an emperor, the Prince of Yan included. The ex-prince began to incite rebellion, questioning Jianwen's legitimacy to rule and spreading rumors that the young emperor was unduly influenced by corrupt and self-serving officials.

A bitter civil war followed, and it would last, on and off, for three years. The Prince of Yan, with a better-organized army and more able commanders at his disposal, was the final victor, and he became Emperor Chengzu, taking the reign name Yongle Emperor, meaning 'Eternal Contentment' or 'Eternal Joy.' The Jianwen Emperor simply disappeared. There were some accounts that he had been killed during the civil war when a fire broke out in the imperial palace at Nanjing. Another, more intriguing rumor spread that the former emperor had managed to escape the city disguised as a monk. Some scholars have suggested that one of the reasons the Yongle Emperor sponsored the famous seven voyages of the explorer Zheng He (starting from 1403) was to find out if the Jianwen Emperor really had escaped alive and was in hiding somewhere in Southeast Asia, plotting a comeback. Whatever his fate, nothing more was ever heard of the Ming dynasty's second emperor.

Having taken the throne by force, and given the importance in Chinese culture that the emperor was supposed to be the Son of Heaven and specially chosen by God to rule, the Yongle Emperor spent much of his long reign trying to legitimize his position. A purge was carried out in the civil service, sparked by the refusal of the noted Confucian scholar-official Fang Xiaoru to draft the proclamation of Yongle's enthronement. Xiaoru was executed by dismemberment, any of his known associates in the government were executed, and so were all his relatives to the tenth degree. The emperor ordered the scholar-officials at the state archives to destroy documents and falsify the historical records so that Jianwen was 'airbrushed' out of Chinese imperial history. The whole civil war was noted as a mere 'quelling of disturbances' in the official records. Discussion of the discredited Jianwen officials was taboo, and possessing any of their writings was forbidden; anyone caught doing so received the death penalty.

Nevertheless, some historical records remain from Jianwen's reign, and they indicate the young emperor had reversed some of the policies of his grandfather. Hongwu had centralized the government and removed many of the political limits on the emperor's power. For example, he eliminated the secretariat of ministers, a position that had advised emperors. Jianwen restored some of the powers to the most senior ministers in his government, and he also revised a number of the harsher laws in his grandfather's law code. We know that Hongwu had favored the Buddhist and Taoist monasteries, but Jianwen removed some of these privileges. Hongwu oversaw a resurgence in Han Chinese power and established a dynasty that saw unprecedented economic growth and a flourishing of the arts. A harsh ruler probably not much loved by anyone, the first Ming emperor set the foundations for his successors to build upon and transform China into a world powerhouse. The emperor's posthumous name, to which sacrifices were made in his honor, is Ming Taizu.

Despite some external pressures in the first half of the 15th century, Ming China was flourishing. The economic prosperity also created a boom in the arts as a richer class of gentry developed, with money to spend and a great desire to show off their appreciation of fine art to any visitors to their homes. Aesthetic tastes were not limited to the classical arts either; gardens became a popular way for the well-off to entertain guests and display one's culture. The walled gardens of Suzhou became particularly famous, where specially chosen rocks, tended pine trees and bamboo, pavilions, and walkways were all arranged to create a harmonious imitation of the scenes seen in landscape paintings.

Thanks to better printing presses, more books were printed than ever before, volumes were illustrated using woodblock prints to make them more attractive, and literature was itself made more accessible by being written in the vernacular language. There were books on how to live a good life, handbooks of etiquette, commentaries on classic texts, military treatises, notes for exam preparation, collections of woodblock prints, anthologies of poems, erotic works, and, of course, fiction. *Shuihuzhuan* (about a group of well-meaning bandits), *Xiyouji* (about a priest who journeys to India to collect Buddhist scriptures), and *Jin Ping Mei* (a risqué satire of the Ming government, examining the life of a wealthy merchant) were all famous novels written in the vernacular during the Ming dynasty. The *Romance of the Three Kingdoms* (*Sanguo yanyi*), written in the 14th or 15th century and often attributed to Luo Guanzhong, remains to this day one of the most popular of all Chinese novels with its fantastic tales interwoven with historical figures during the fall of the Han dynasty and the beginning of the Three Kingdoms period.

The *Yongle Dadian* was created during the reign of Emperor Yongle, a massive encyclopedia of all important Chinese literary works that had survived up to that point. The work, taking up over 22,000 chapters, was too large to be printed, and, unfortunately, most of the original was lost; however, around 800 chapters still exist in various libraries outside of China.

Finally, space must be allowed for the blue-and-white porcelain wares that have come to symbolize the Ming dynasty for many people today. Although artists of the Ming dynasty produced a wide range of pottery, it is this fine 'china' that was exported with unprecedented success. Actually made in earlier dynasties but perfected to new levels of craftsmanship under the Ming, porcelain—a hard, pure white, and translucent ceramic—was made at such noted centers as Jingdezhen and sold across China and to an appreciative world market that had not yet learnt the secret of making it. In the first period of Ming rule, blue-and-white porcelain was the most highly prized, as it had been under the Mongol rulers of the Yuan dynasty. The blue (cobalt oxide sourced from Central Asia, particularly Iran) was painted onto the porcelain body and then covered with a glaze called *yingqing*. An alternative but less common color was red and orange, achieved by using copper instead of cobalt. Early designs were often influenced by the high demand from Arab clients, who wanted the decoration on the porcelain to mimic the intricate abstract floral designs of their own textiles and carpets.

In the centuries that followed, the Ming dynasty oversaw an unprecedented growth in China's population and general economic prosperity. Notable achievements of Ming China included the construction of the Forbidden City—the imperial residence in Beijing—a blossoming of literature and the arts, the far-flung explorations of Zheng He, and porcelain production.

Eventually, though, the same old problems that had beset previous regimes bedeviled the Ming emperors: court factions, infighting, and corruption, along with government overspending and a disenchanted peasantry, which fueled rebellions. As a consequence, the economically, politically (and some would say morally) impoverished Ming could not resist the invasion of the Manchus, who established the Qing dynasty from 1644.

3.4 Bottle with peony scroll, porcelain painted with cobalt blue under a transparent glaze (Jingdezhen ware), mid-14th century, China

Bibliography

Buell, P.D. *Historical Dictionary of the Mongol World Empire.* Rowman & Littlefield Publishers, 2018.

Clunas, C. *Art in China.* Oxford University Press, 2009.

Dawson, R.S. *The Chinese Experience.* Orion Books: Phoenix Press, 2019.

Dillon, M. *China: A Cultural & Historical Dictionary.* Routledge, 1998.

Ebrey, P.B. *Pre-Modern East Asia.* Cengage Learning, 2013.

May, T. *The Mongol Empire.* Edinburgh University Press, 2018.

Morgan, D. *The Mongols.* Wiley-Blackwell, 2019.

Polo, M. *The Travels of Marco Polo.* Penguin Classics, 1958.

Rossabi, M. *A History of China.* Wiley-Blackwell, 2013.

Saunders, J.J. *The History of the Mongol Conquests.* University of Pennsylvania Press, 2001.

Turnbull, S. *Genghis Khan & the Mongol Conquests 1190-1400.* Osprey Publishing, 2003.

Image Credits

3.1 Figure of a Mongol, the Metropolitan Museum of Art, public domain, https://www.metmuseum.org/art/collection/search/74174

3.2 The Ming Dynasty of China. Map © Simeon Netchev

3.3 Ming Xiaoling (Emperor Hongwu Tomb). Photo by Gary Todd, public domain, https://www.flickr.com/photos/101561334@N08/10150994034

3.4 Bottle with Peony Scroll, the Metropolitan Museum of Art, public domain, https://www.metmuseum.org/art/collection/search/49216

India

By Patit Paban Mishra

Delhi Sultanate

IN 1192, THE VICTORY of Muhammad of Ghor over the Rajput king, Prithviraj Chauhan III (reign circa 1177-1192), led to foreign rule being established in the Indian subcontinent. The Mamluks styled themselves as sultans from 1206, and the Delhi Sultanate, with its rulers following Islam, continued until 1526. The Khalji period (1290-1320) marked the beginning of the ascendancy of Indian Muslims, and their empire even extended to southern India. They were followed by the Tughlaqs (1320-1413), whose rule initially saw economic life accelerate but also brought the gradual decline of the Delhi Sultanate.

Ghiyasuddin (aka Ghiyath al-Din Tughluq, reign 1320-1325) was the founder of the Tughlaq dynasty. He was governor of the northwest provinces at the time of Nasiruddin Khusrau Shah (reign 1320), a Hindu convert. The Turk tribes did not reconcile to the rule of a converted Muslim, as they believed in Turkish superiority.

Ghiyasuddin gathered around him the nobility and became the sultan after deposing Khusrau. He suppressed the recalcitrant Hindu rajas and undertook a policy of territorial aggrandizement. In 1323, the Telangana Kingdom in South India was annexed. The Tughlaq army plundered Jajnagar in Odisha. East and South Bengal were incorporated into the Delhi Sultanate, while North Bengal remained a vassal state.

As a capable military commander, the sultan revamped the army organization, making it battle-ready. Agriculture was also improved, and revenue officers were explicitly ordered not to be harsh with cultivators. Bridges, roads, and canals were constructed. The postal system became more efficient. The sultan had a fair sense of justice, and he prohibited inhumane punishment, but thieves and corrupt revenue officials were not spared. On a personal level, the sultan was a strict disciplinarian and a strict follower of Islamic laws, eschewing alcohol as well as worldly pleasures.

Between 1321 and 1325, Ghiyasuddin Tughluq built the fortress city of Tughlaqabad in Delhi. It was the capital, and a strong fortress designed for defense. The palace-fortress enclave was constructed by checking the Jamuna River's flow, resulting in the creation of an artificial lake, which surrounded the city in the eastern direction of the fort. Tughlaqabad occupied a massive area of rectangular shape, encompassed by walls ranging from 15 to 30 meters (49 to 98 feet), with a thickness of about 10 meters (33 feet). The bastions, having two stories and gargantuan towers, surrounded the palace, audience halls, tombs, and mosque. The sloping walls, called batter, were a novelty of Tughlaqabad.

The mausoleum of Ghiyasuddin Tughluq was located on the southern side of the fortress. Built by the sultan, the tomb is in the shape of a pentagon surrounded by fortified walls with an angle of 75 degrees. Built of red sandstone with a dome of white marble, the archways present a perfect combination of arch and beam, blending the trabeate and arcuate architectural methods. The interior, containing the sarcophagus, has a single chamber surmounted by a dome. A legend mentions the discord between the sultan and the Sufi saint, Khawaja Nizamuddin Auliya (1236-1325); after the sultan did not permit the workers to be employed by the saint, he uttered the famous prophecy, "*Hunuz Dilli dur ast*" (Delhi is yet far away).

Ghiyasuddin could not reach the capital from Bengal and was killed when the wooden pavilion built in his honor collapsed.

Muhammad bin Tughluq (born Ulugh Khan, reign 1325-1351) became the sultan of Delhi after his father's death, even though he has been blamed for the event by some historians. He believed in the divine right of kingship and undertook a policy of conquest, sending expeditionary forces to Khurasan, Nagarkot, Qarajal, Mewar, Telangana, and Malabar. Diplomatic relations were established with many Asian countries. His empire was the most extensive among the medieval sultans and, following a liberal policy, he appointed officials irrespective of caste, creed, or religion. He constructed the royal residence of Jahanpanah along with the Begumpuri Mosque.

The projects of the sultan often failed due to improper execution and the unpopularity of the schemes. The creation of another capital in Daulatabad, taxation in the doab region, and the introduction of token currency created great hardship for his subjects and invited opposition. The sultan's experiments were grand failures, and his reign period witnessed dissent and rebellions. The governors of the northwestern province and Bengal were given harsh punishments. Independent kingdoms came into existence, such as Malabar, Vijayanagara, and Bahmani. The most controversial figure of medieval India, he was averse to any advice and, unable to hold his vast empire together, he failed as a ruler. At the time of his death in 1351, the disintegration of the Delhi Sultanate had already begun.

The cousin of Muhammad bin Tughluq, Firuz (or Feroz) Shah Tughluq, ascended the throne in 1351 and ruled until 1388. Although not a capable military leader like his predecessors, the sultan was a great builder of cities, monuments, and public buildings. He imposed the four taxes sanctioned by the Islamic laws, including a tax on non-Muslims. Depending on the priestly classes, or the *ulemas*, the state was intolerant toward the *dhimmis* (non-Muslims) and the Shias. His campaign to Jajnagar (Odisha) in 1361 destroyed the famous Puri Jagannatha Temple. Firuz did not attempt to retrieve the territories lost by his predecessor, and his military organization was fragile. His fondness for keeping a large retinue of slaves resulted in the depletion of the state coffers.

Firuz, a patron of learning, established 30 madrasas (Islamic schools) and three colleges. Although intolerant of Hindus, he ordered the translation of religious scriptures into Persian. His humanitarian measures included the building of orphanages and charitable hospitals. His construction activities included establishing scores of towns, undertaking irrigation works, and digging public wells. Firuz took special care in maintaining and repairing famous monuments, like the Qutub Minar, the Jama Masjid (public mosque), and the mausoleums of some of the earlier sultans. Jaunpur, Hissar, Fatehabad, and Firozpur were just some of the urban centers that thrived during his reign.

Firuz resided in the newly built city of Firuzabad in Delhi; its ruins, Feroz Shah Kotla, are still extant. The old fort-city of Tughlaqabad was abandoned, and the new capital was constructed with a rectangular plan of about 800 by 400 meters (2,625 by 1,312 feet). A fortified stone wall surrounded the town, with the main entrance on the western side.

4.1 Qutub Minar, Delhi

It encompassed the quarters of the guards and soldiers, a rectangular-shaped Mahall-i Bari Amm (Palace of the Public Court), and a square pillared hall for transacting the private business of the sultan. On rectangular and square-shaped courts stood residential quarters of the royalty, Hawa Mahal (Palace of the Winds), Kushk-i-Shikar (Hunting Palace), mosque pigeon-tower, *baoli* (stepped well), and exquisite gardens with running water and fountains. The sultan's abode was Kushk-i-Feroze. Friday prayers were offered in the public mosque, the Jama Masjid, with its spacious courtyard and series of cells. One of the city's unique features is the pillar of Mauryan Emperor Ashoka (reign circa 268 to circa 232 BCE), raised on a three-tiered pyramid-like structure. It was removed from its original location in Topra (now Topra Kalan) in the district of Ambala, Haryana. The pillar, encased in reed and raw animal skins, was moved with the help of a 42-wheel carriage drawn by about 200 people. On the banks of the River Jamuna, it was ferried and carried to the present location. In 1356, stone friezes were placed around it.

After the death of his eldest son, Fateh Khan, in 1374, Firuz's health started to decline, which led to civil wars and infighting over the future of the throne. His grandson Tughluq Shah (aka Tughlaq Shah, reign 1388-1389) became the next sultan after his death. The experiments of Muhammad bin Tughluq, the weakness of Firuz, the incompetent successors that followed, the depletion of state resources, and the wars in South India were all responsible for the ultimate downfall of the Tughlaq dynasty. Tughluq Shah was assassinated by nobles proclaiming loyalty to his cousin, Abu Bakr Shah (reign 1389-1390). Muhammad Shah (reign 1390-1393), in turn, deposed Abu Bakr. By 1394, the Tughlaq Empire covered an area of just eleven kilometers (seven miles) from Delhi to Palam. Alauddin Sikandar, son of Muhammad Shah, then ruled for some months in 1394. His younger brother Nasiruddin Muhammad Shah (aka Sultan Mahmud Shah II, reign 1394-1413) was the last member of the Tughlaq dynasty. The sack and plunder of Delhi by Timur (1336-1405) in 1398 was the last blow from which the dynasty did not recover.

Bahmani Sultanate

Out of the turbulent conditions that prevailed during the later years of Muhammad bin Tughluq's reign, a number of independent dynasties emerged, casting off the yoke of central authority. Among them, the Bahmani Sultanate, encompassing much of present-day Karnataka, Maharashtra, and Andhra Pradesh, with its capital at Gulbarga (modern-day Kalaburagi), rose as a formidable power.

Muhammad bin Tughluq's misguided experiments and the tyranny of cruel governors estranged the nobility. Among the most disquieted were the Amiran-i-Sadah, guardians of civil order and military command. Sensing their disaffection, the sultan sent Aziz Khammar, governor of Malwa, against the defiant noble Ismail Mukh Afghan, who, rallying the discontented, seized Devagiri (Daulatabad). Mukh soon yielded the mantle to a young and valiant soldier, Zafar Khan, who, in 1347, took the title Abu'l Muzaffar Ala-ud-Din Bahman Shah, claiming descent from the royal house of Persia. From his capital at Gulbarga, the new sultan set about forging a realm worthy of his name. Dabhol, Goa, Kolhapur, and Telangana bowed to his authority. By 1358, his dominion stretched from Daulatabad to Bhongir (aka Bhuvanagiri), from the Wainganga River to the Krishna River. Victorious over the Hindu chieftains of Karnataka, he amassed immense treasure, securing the wealth and power upon which the Bahmani Sultanate would stand for generations.

During the reign of Bahman Shah's successor, Muhammad Shah I (reign 1358-1375), hostilities broke out with Bukka Raya I of Vijayanagara and Kapaya Nayaka of Warangal. At the heart of the conflict lay the Raichur doab and the fortress of Kauthal, coveted prizes and constant bones of contention. This rivalry was but a revival of an age-old contest for economic ascendancy. The doab's strategic location, coupled with the richness of its fertile lands, rendered it a prize no ruler could ignore. The struggle was no single war, but an incessant series of encounters, sieges, and punitive raids fought relentlessly over the course of many years. In the Tamil South, the Nayakas, once governors under Vijayanagara, commanded rich lands, swift cavalry, and strong infantry. They were very much loyal to Vijayanagara. In the middle of the 1360s, Muhammad Shah marched deep into the Raichur doab, seizing forts along the Tungabhadra River. Bukka Raya sought help from the Nayakas from Tanjore (now Thanjavur) and Gingee. From the protracted war that followed, nobody emerged victorious. Kapaya Nayaka acknowledged the suzerainty of the Bahmani Sultanate and ceded Golconda after being defeated in the Battle of Kauthal in 1366. It was alleged that 400,000 Hindus were massacred in the territory of Bukka Raya. Nevertheless, a considerable part of the Raichur doab was retained by him.

Muhammad Shah I was a capable ruler consolidating his sultanate. The army was thoroughly revamped. His domain was divided into four *tarafs* (provinces): Daulatabad, Berar, Bidar, and Gulbarga. Sultan Mujahid Shah Bahmani (reign 1375-1378), son of Sultan Muhammad Shah I, was nurtured in the royal household of Gulbarga amid the refinements of courtly culture, the discipline of martial arts, the study of Islamic scholarship, and the elegance of Persianate tradition. From his father, he inherited not only a throne but also a fierce rivalry with the Vijayanagara Empire for mastery over the Raichur doab. Relations between the two powers were marked by relentless military raids, frequent saber-rattling, and, on occasion, the formal exchange of envoys. Mujahid assembled a formidable army of seasoned cavalry, companies of archers, and ranks of war elephants, and, in 1376, he set forth from his capital at Gulbarga toward the Raichur doab. Advancing steadily, his forces captured several forts along the way and pressed onward toward Vijayanagara, the imperial capital itself. After fierce and unyielding battles, Mujahid was compelled to sue for peace, and a fragile truce was struck. Yet his brief reign was troubled from both within and without. Though his court glittered with poets, scholars, and architects, it seethed with intrigue among the Bahmani nobility, foreign-born Afaqis, and native Deccanis, who vied for honor and favor.

In 1378, during a hunting expedition near Gulbarga, his cousin, Daud Shah, driven by rank jealousy, struck Mujahid down. In his short life, Mujahid had sought to bend the Deccan to Bahmani will, to guard its borders, and to display the splendor of its court. His life is a testament to the violent world of 14th-century Deccan. The claim of Daud to the throne was weak, and he ruled for barely a year. The Bahmani nobility at that time was fractured into powerful, competing factions, and many were against him. Soon after, he faced opposition from another claimant, Muhammad Shah II (grandson of Bahman Shah), who had stronger legitimacy and wider backing among the *amirs* (nobles). He defeated Daud Shah, deposed him, and became the sultan in 1378. The rule of Daud was thus more of an interregnum between stronger sultans and devoid of any noteworthy features.

Muhammad Shah II's (reign 1378-1397) proclivity was toward consolidation and diplomacy. Muhammad looked toward the prosperity of the sultanate through commercial relations. The state revenue considerably increased due to improvements in agriculture. He was a patron of the arts and literature. He was followed by Firuz Shah Bahmani (aka Taj ud-Din Firuz Shah, reign 1397-1422), who adorned the Bahmani court with intellectuals from Persia, Central Asia, and Arabia. Firuz Shah's administrative reforms strengthened the sultanate's governance. He improved revenue assessment, encouraged agricultural productivity, and invested in public works. His religious policy was noted for its comparative tolerance, as he welcomed Hindu nobles into positions of influence and respected the customs of his non-Muslim subjects. His military ambition resulted in successful military campaigns. Firuz Shah turned his attention toward the archenemy Vijayanagara, but his three expeditions did not produce any decisive result.

Vijayanagara Empire

The Vijayanagara Empire was probably founded in 1336 by Harihara I (reign 1336 to circa 1356), the first ruler of the Sangama dynasty, along with his brother Bukka Raya I (reign circa 1356-1377). With its capital at Vijayanagara (City of Victory), the empire rose to prominence as a formidable South Indian power. Harihara and Bukka were serving under the Kakatiyas and Kampili rulers, but they were captured by the Delhi sultans and converted to Islam.

INDIA 87

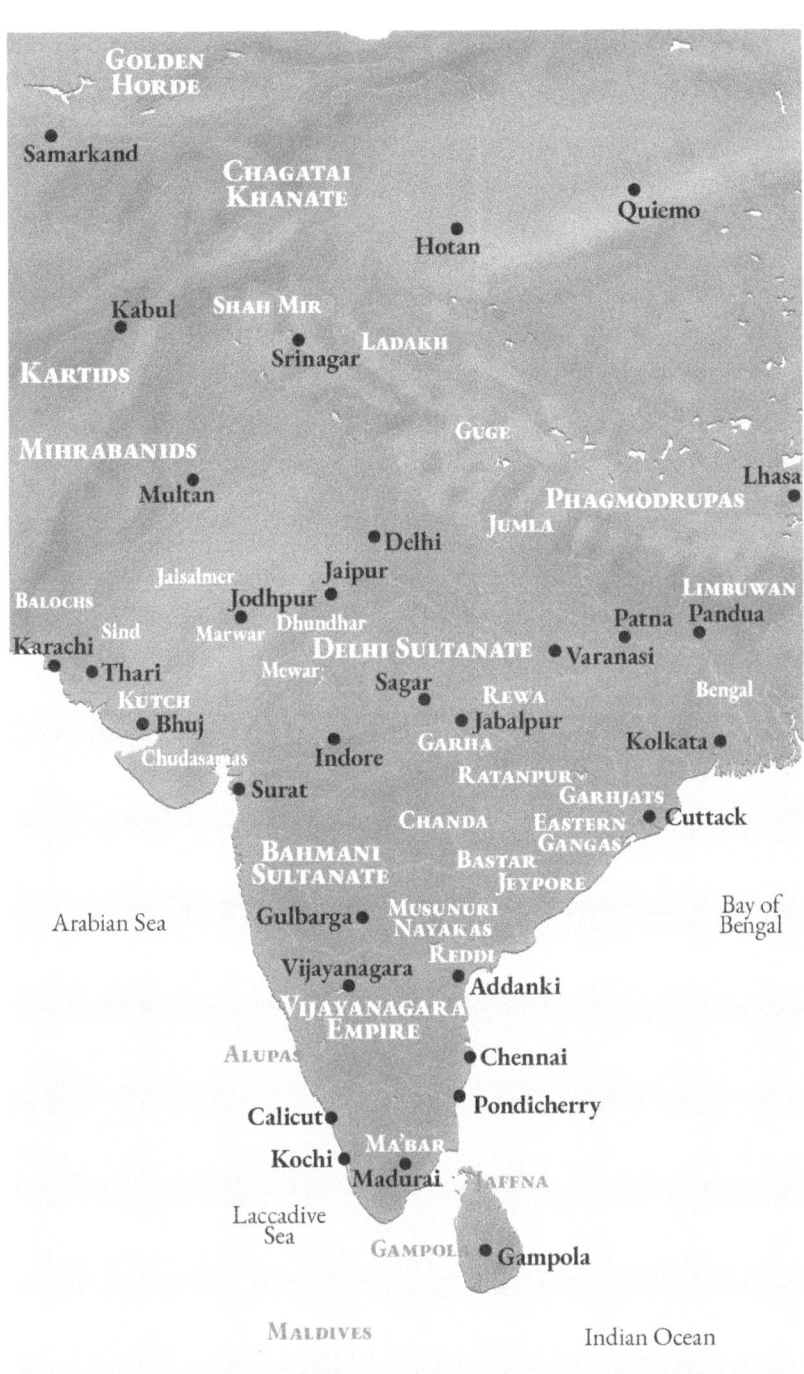

4.2 Medieval India circa 1360

Tradition, woven with fact and fiction, holds that they were reconverted to Hinduism under the guidance of a sage named Vidyaranya (aka Madhavacharya), a respected saint of the Sringeri Sharada Peetham, and founded the new dynasty on the banks of the River Tungabhadra. Harihara chose Hampi as the capital and styled himself as Purvapaschima Samudradhishvara (Lord of the Eastern and Western Sea). Another title bestowed on him was Karnataka Vidya Vilasa, signifying his scholarship. The architect of the nascent kingdom, he consolidated his territory, and most of modern Tamil Nadu, Karnataka, and Andhra Pradesh came under his sway. His tenure was distinguished by a period of stability, the effective mobilization of state revenues, and the restoration of local governance institutions that had languished amid years of disorder.

Following the death of Harihara I in circa 1356, his brother Bukka Raya I ascended the throne of the Vijayanagara Empire. With a dynamic vision and strong leadership, Bukka ushered in a new era of expansion and consolidation. Often hailed as the true architect of Vijayanagara's imperial power, Bukka's reign—which spanned over two decades—saw the empire grow in territorial might and cultural prestige. He not only extended its political boundaries but also laid the foundation for a rich religious and cultural synthesis that would define Vijayanagara for generations to come. As the empire's second ruler, he pursued aggressive military campaigns, vanquishing the Madurai Sultanate and controlling territories and fortresses in the Krishna-Tungabhadra doab. One of Bukka's most notable achievements was the conquest of the Rameswaram region, a symbolic act of asserting Hindu dominance and spiritual sovereignty. By restoring temples desecrated during earlier invasions and supporting Brahmanical institutions, Bukka not only gained political legitimacy but also won the allegiance of local elites and the populace.

Administratively, Bukka continued and refined the system instituted by his brother. He fostered an efficient revenue collection apparatus, ensured stability through local chieftains and governors, and strengthened ties with prominent religious and intellectual centers. His support for temple construction and restoration played a vital role in reviving Hindu cultural identity in the south of the Indian subcontinent. One of the most famous examples of his patronage is the Vijayanagara-style temple architecture, which would reach its zenith in later centuries but found its roots during Bukka's reign. Bukka Raya I's court was endowed with scholars, dramatists, and poets. He maintained correspondence with foreign rulers and emissaries, including those from China and Persia. Such interactions not only enhanced Vijayanagara's prestige but also facilitated trade and cultural exchange.

Bukka died in 1377 and was succeeded by his son Harihara II, with the title of Maharajadhiraja (King of Kings). The third monarch of the Sangama line, he presided over the Vijayanagara Empire from 1377 to 1404 and is chiefly remembered for his consolidation of imperial gains, astute military leadership, cultural patronage, and a concerted effort to fortify the administrative framework of the state. A defining aspect of his kingship was the extension of imperial control along the western littoral. This coastal region, with its lucrative ports and vital trade arteries, had long attracted the interest of both indigenous powers and foreign traders. Harihara II launched a series of successful campaigns across the Konkan region and the modern-day coastal stretches of Karnataka, ultimately pushing the frontiers of Vijayanagara to the shores of the Arabian Sea. This expansion invigorated maritime commerce, forging trade links with distant lands such as Persia and Arabia.

Harihara II's reign was also marked by continued rivalry with the Bahmani Sultanate to the north. The Deccan plateau, by this period, had evolved into a contested heartland, a perennial battleground between the Hindu Vijayanagara Empire and the Islamic Bahmani realm. While a decisive victory remained elusive, Harihara II managed to uphold the empire's defensive lines and maintained a significant presence in critical regions like the Tungabhadra doab—an area prized for both its strategic position and fertile plains.

A devout adherent of Shaivism, Harihara II nevertheless practiced an inclusive form of rule, embracing the religious diversity of his subjects. His era saw considerable support extended to temples and institutions of learning, particularly those associated with the worship of Lord Shiva. Architectural activity flourished, with enhancements to sacred edifices and the establishment of new shrines. Moreover, he actively nurtured the literary traditions of both Sanskrit and Kannada, fostering a vibrant intellectual culture at court and beyond. On the administrative front, Harihara II strengthened the inherited system of governance, striking a careful balance between central oversight and regional autonomy. Local governors retained a measure of independence under the suzerainty of the imperial court, while reforms to the taxation system aimed to streamline revenue collection and reduce inefficiencies.

Harihara II's death in 1404 closed a chapter of relative stability and consolidation. He left behind an empire broader in reach and more firmly grounded than the one he had inherited. His reign signified a shift from expansionist fervor to measured statecraft, laying the groundwork for the future evolution of the Vijayanagara polity. Though less renowned than some of his successors, his steady hand and enduring reforms secured his place among the empire's pivotal rulers.

The Eastern Gangas

The Eastern Ganga dynasty, often referred to as the Imperial Gangas (1038-1434), flourished in the historical region of Kalinga, encompassing present-day Odisha and parts of northern Andhra Pradesh. It emerged as one of the most refined, resilient, and culturally vibrant dynasties in Indian history. Renowned for its steadfast patronage of art, literature, and monumental architecture, the dynasty profoundly shaped the cultural landscape of eastern India. Its maritime engagements facilitated the dissemination of Indian cultural ideals across Southeast Asia, enriching transoceanic exchanges. Although its political authority waned by the 14th century, the dynasty's artistic and architectural legacies endured through the ages. The revered Jagannatha Temple continues to draw thousands of pilgrims from across India and abroad, while the awe-inspiring Sun Temple at Konark stands as a timeless testament to their aesthetic sophistication and engineering mastery.

The lineage commenced with Vajrahasta V (reign 1038-1079), and by the 14th century, the dynasty's authority faced political challenges and foreign incursions. Narasimha Deva II's reign (1278-1306) was marked by strategic military campaigns aimed at countering external threats and consolidating the kingdom's frontiers. Territories earlier seized by the Bengal nawabs were recovered, and his forces advanced as far as the banks of the Ganges, issuing land grants to affirm authority. Recalcitrant feudatories were subdued, further strengthening central control.

Bhanu Deva II (reign 1306-1328), son of Narasimha Deva II, witnessed an incursion by the Delhi Sultanate under Ulugh Khan (later reigned as Muhammad bin Tughlugh), son of Ghiyasuddin

Tughluq, who advanced against Jajnagar. The invasion was repelled by Sriram Senapati, commander-in-chief of Bhanu Deva II's forces. Hampered by the challenging terrain of Odisha, which proved unsuitable for sustaining a prolonged campaign, Ulugh Khan withdrew toward Delhi. The engagement was indecisive, if, indeed, a full-scale battle took place at all. Narasimha Deva III (reign 1328-1352) enjoyed comparative calm and prosperity. He strengthened the defense of the kingdom by undertaking large-scale fortification to check invasions from Delhi. He ordered additions to the Puri Jagannath Temple and provided grants to temples.

The next ruler, Bhanu Deva III (reign 1352-1378), faced several invasions. In 1353, the Bengal ruler Shamsuddin Ilyas Shah invaded, then the Vijayanagara ruler Bukka Raya I defeated the Ganga emperor, then came an invading army from the neighboring Reddis of Kondaveedu, and finally Sultan Firuz Shah Tughluq marched up to Jajnagar via Khiching in Mayurbhanj. The Ganga ruler fled to Telangana. There was large-scale destruction of temples by the marauding army of the sultan. Bhanu Deva III sued for peace by paying tribute, but after the sultan's departure, the Ganga emperor asserted his independence and preserved the stability of the kingdom to a large extent.

During the reign of Narasimha Deva IV (reign 1378-1425), the empire endured repeated invasions, which greatly strained its strength. The sultan of Jaunpur launched an incursion into the Ganga dominions, compelling the latter to pay tribute. From the south, the Reddi rulers emerged as a formidable threat. In 1381, the Reddis defeated the Ganga forces and seized Simhachalam. A decade later, they renewed their offensive, forcing the Ganga monarch to sue for peace. These successive military confrontations weakened the empire considerably. However, following the decline of the Reddis brought about by internal civil strife, the Ganga ruler regained much of the lost territory and reasserted his authority. Thereafter, he relied chiefly upon diplomacy and internal consolidation to meet the challenges of the time.

Narasimha Deva IV continued the tradition of royal patronage, bestowing generous endowments upon temples, granting lands to Brahmins, and making substantial donations to religious institutions. Court scholars and poets enjoyed his favor, and copper-plate charters were issued to confirm land grants bestowed upon loyal nobles and sacred establishments. By this period, Ganga political power had been reduced largely to a ceremonial role. The dynasty remained a venerable symbol of Odisha's glorious past, even as real authority passed into the hands of the Gajapatis.

Bibliography

Ahmad, M. *Sultan Firoz Shah Tughlaq, 1351-1388 A.D.* Chugh Publications, 1978.

Aiyangar, S.K. *Vijayanagara: History and Legacy.* Aryan Books International, 2000.

Ashrafi, A. *The Khilji and Tughlaq Dynasties.* Shree Publishers, 2022.

Eaton, R.M. *India in the Persianate Age, 1000-1765.* University of California Press, 2019.

Farooqui, S.A. *A Comprehensive History of Medieval India: Twelfth to the Mid-Eighteenth Century.* Pearson Education India, 2011.

Habib, I. *Economic History of India, AD 1206-1526: the period of the Delhi Sultanate and the Vijayanagara Empire.* Tulika Books, 2017.

Husain, A.M. *Tughlaq Dynasty.* Spink, 1963.

Khan, A.N. *Islamic Architecture in South Asia: Pakistan, India, Bangladesh.* Oxford University Press, 2003.

Kulke, H. *A History of India.* 4th ed. Routledge, 2004.

Majumdar, R.C. (ed). *The Delhi Sultanate (1300-1526 AD), Vol. 6.* Bharatiya Vidya Bhavan, 1989.

Mathur, R. *Medieval Indian History.* Murari Lal & Sons, 1970.

Michell, G. *Vijayanagara: Splendour in Ruins.* Alkazi Collection of Photography; Mapin Publishing, 2008.

Michell, G. and M. Zebrowski. *The New Cambridge History of India: Architecture and Art of the Deccan Sultanates.* Cambridge University Press, 1999.

Mishra, P.P. *An Encyclopaedia in Spatio-Temporal Dimensions: Biography, Culture, and Religion.* Cambridge Scholars Publishing Ltd., 2024.

Mishra, P.P. "Bahmani Sultanate." In *The Encyclopedia of Empire*, edited by J. MacKenzie. Wiley-Blackwell, 2016.

Mishra, P.P. "Delhi Sultanate." In *Berkshire Encyclopedia of World History, Vol. 2.* Edited by W.H. McNeill. Berkshire Publishing Group, 2005.

Mishra, P.P. "Eastern Ganga and Gajapati Empires." In *The Encyclopedia of Empire*, edited by J. MacKenzie. Wiley-Blackwell, 2016.

Mishra, P.P. *Kalinga and Southeast Asia: A Saga of Shared Civilization.* Black Eagle, 2025.

Panda, S.K. *The State and Statecraft in Medieval Orissa under the Later Eastern Gangas (A.D. 1038–1434).* K.P. Bagchi & Co., 1995.

Panigrahi, K.C. *History of Orissa: Hindu Period.* Kitab Mahal, 1981.

Ramanujan, S.R. *Vijayanagara: The Never to Be Forgotten Empire.* Notion Press, 2019.

Rani, A. *Tughlaq Architecture of Delhi.* Bharati Prakashan, 1991.

Rao, G.S.P. *Krishnadeva Raya: The Great Poet-Emperor of Vijayanagara.* Potti Sreeramulu Telugu University, 2004.

Ray, A. *The Sultanate of Delhi.* Routledge, 2019.

Sastri, K.A.N. *A History of South India: From Prehistoric Times to the Fall of Vijayanagar.* Oxford University Press, 1975.

Sherwani, H.K. *The Bahmanis of the Deccan.* Munshiram Manoharlal, 1985.

Stein, B. *Vijayanagara.* Cambridge University Press, 1989.

Syed, M.H. *History of Delhi Sultanate.* Anmol Publications Pvt Ltd, 1970.

Wink, A. *Al-Hind: The Making of the Indo-Islamic World, Vol. III: Indo-Islamic Society, 14th–18th Centuries.* Brill, 2004.

Yazdani, G. *The Early History of the Deccan.* Oxford University Press, 1960.

Image Credits

4.1 Qutub Minar in Delhi. Photo by A. Savin, Wikipedia, Free Art License, https://commons.wikimedia.org/wiki/File:Qutub_Minar_in_Delhi_03-2016.jpg

4.2 Medieval India Circa 1360. Map © Simeon Netchev

Africa

By Mark Cartwright and Joshua J. Mark

The Mali Empire

THE LARGEST EMPIRE OF 14th-century Africa, the Mali Empire (1240-1645), was founded by Sundiata Keita, a Malinke prince (reign 1230-1255), following his victory over the kingdom of Sosso (circa 1180-1235) in a decisive battle at Krina (aka Kirina) in 1235. In 1240, Sundiata captured the old Ghana capital. Forming a centralized government of tribal leaders and a number of influential Arab merchants, this assembly (*gbara*) declared Sundiata the supreme monarch and gave him such honorary titles as *Mari Diata* (Lord Lion). The name Sundiata gave to his empire was Mali, meaning 'the place where the king lives.' It was also decreed that all future kings would be selected from the Keita clan, although the title was not necessarily given to the eldest son of a ruler, which sometimes led to fierce disputes among candidates.

The *mansa*, or king, would be assisted by an assembly of elders and local chiefs throughout the Mali Empire's history, with audiences held in the royal palace or under a large tree. The king was also the supreme source of justice, but he did make use of legal advisors. In addition, the king was helped by a number of key ministers such as the chief of the army and master of the granaries (later treasury), as well as other officials like the master of ceremonies and leader of the royal orchestra. Nevertheless, the *mansa* acted as a supreme monarch and monopolized key trade goods—for example, only he was permitted to possess gold nuggets; traders had to make do with gold dust. The king had certain mystical qualities attributed to him, and all slaves were to be exclusively loyal to him. No person had the right to be in the king's presence when he ate, for example, and all visitors before him had to be barefoot and bow down and pour dust over their heads. Such was this cult of leadership and the extreme centralization of government in a single figure that the fortunes of the empire rose and fell depending on the talents, or lack of them, possessed by a particular king.

These problems of governance were yet to come, though, and Sundiata would continue to expand his territory to include the old kingdoms of Ghana, Walata, Tadmekka, and Songhai. Niani, now no longer in existence but probably located on a plain near the all-year-round navigable Sankarani River, was selected as the empire's capital. It was protected by mountains and was close to the two key sources of trade goods: forests and waterways.

Tribute was acquired from conquered chiefdoms, although many local chiefs were permitted to continue to rule their own people but with a Mali-appointed governor to assist them, often backed by a garrison. Additional guarantees of loyalty included taking royal hostages and keeping them at the capital. This federation prospered, developing over the 14th century into one of Africa's richest ever empires whose wealth would astound both Europe and Arabia.

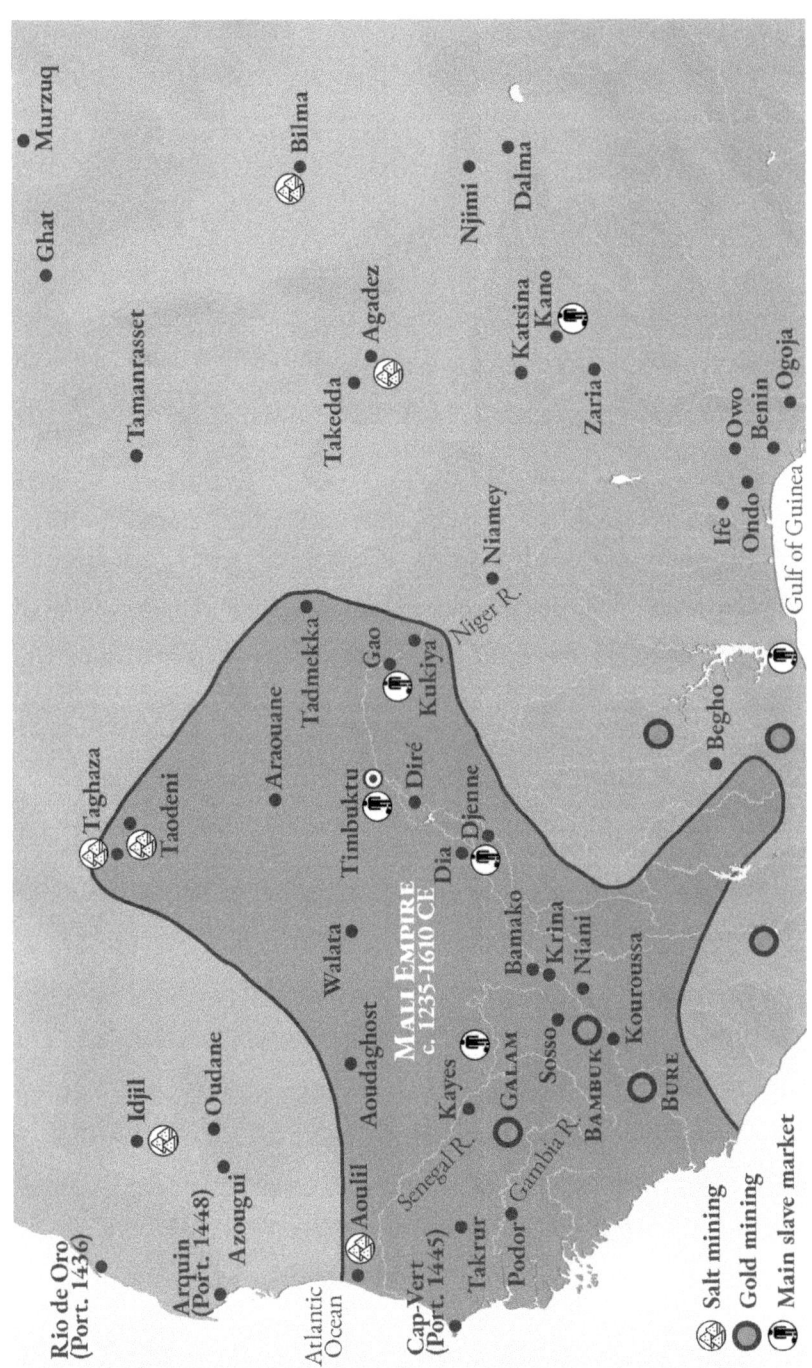

5.1 The Mali Empire

Further, and perhaps more important for the ordinary people of Mali, foreign visitors noted the high degree of justice they saw, the safety with which one could travel from place to place, and the abundance of food in all villages.

The Mali Empire prospered thanks to trade and its prime location, situated between the rainforests of southern West Africa and the powerful Muslim caliphates of North Africa. The Niger River provided ready access to Africa's interior and Atlantic coast, while the Berber-controlled camel caravans that crossed the Sahara Desert ensured valuable commodities came from the north. The Mali rulers had a triple income: they taxed the passage of trade goods, bought goods and sold them on at much higher prices, and had access to their own valuable natural resources. Significantly, the Mali Empire controlled the rich gold-bearing regions of Galam, Bambuk, and Bure. One of the main trade exchanges was gold dust for salt from the Sahara. Gold was in particular demand from European powers like Castile in Spain, and Venice and Genoa in Italy, where coinage was now being minted in the precious metal.

The greatest ever ruler of the Mali Empire, Mansa Musa I, the grand nephew of the founder Sundiata Keita, took power in 1312 and would reign until 1337. Mansa Musa gained the throne after his predecessor, Mansa Abu Bakr II, sailed out into the Atlantic with a large fleet of ships and was never seen again. Exploration's loss was Mali's gain, and Mansa Musa, nominated to rule while Abu Bakr II satisfied his curiosity as to what lay over the horizon, would become one of the greatest rulers in the entire history of Africa.

With an army numbering around 100,000 men, including an armored cavalry corps of 10,000 horses, and with the talented general Saran Mandian, Mansa Musa was able to extend and maintain Mali's vast empire, doubling its territory and making it second in size only to that of the Mongol Empire at the time. Mali controlled lands up to the Gambia and lower Senegal in the west; in the north, tribes were subdued along the whole length of the Western Sahara border region; in the east, control spread up to Gao on the Niger River and, to the south, the Bure region and the forests of what became known as the Gold Coast came under Mali oversight. This latter region was left semi-independent because gold production had always been much higher when more autonomy was granted there.

To better govern this vast expanse of land containing a multitude of tribes and ethnic groups, Mansa Musa divided his empire into provinces with each one ruled by a governor (*farba*) appointed personally by him. The administration was further improved with greater records kept and sent to the centralized government offices at Niani. The wealth of the state increased thanks to taxes on trade, the Mali-controlled copper and gold mines, and the imposition of tribute from conquered tribes. Mansa Musa thus became extremely wealthy, perhaps even the richest person in history.

When he arrived in Cairo in July 1324 en route to Mecca, he caused an absolute sensation. In an extreme gesture of largesse, Mansa Musa would give away so much gold and his entourage spend so much shopping in the markets of the city that the value of gold dinar in Cairo crashed by 20% (in relation to the silver dirham); it would take twelve years for the flooded gold market to recover. The king of Mali had also given 50,000 gold dinars to the sultan of Egypt merely as a first-meeting gesture, and news of his Cairo visit even reached Europe. In Spain, a mapmaker was inspired to create Europe's first detailed map of West Africa. Created circa 1375, the map, part of the *Catalan Atlas*, has Mansa Musa sitting regally on a throne, wearing an impressive gold crown, and holding a golden staff in one hand and, somewhat gleefully, a huge nugget or orb of gold in the other. It was such tales of gold that would inspire later European explorers to brave disease, warlike tribes, and inhospitable terrain to find the fabled riches of Timbuktu, the golden city of the desert that nobody quite knew where to place on the map even in the 18th century.

The area around Timbuktu has been inhabited since the Neolithic period as evidenced by Iron Age tumuli, megaliths, and remains of now abandoned villages. It was, however, around 1100 that Timbuktu was founded by Tuareg herders, the nomads of the southern Sahara, as an advantageous spot where land and river routes coincided. According to one legend, the herders dug a well at the site and asked an old woman called Buktu to look after it whenever they were away. In the Tuareg language Tamashek, the word for 'place' is *tin*, and so Timbuktu derives from the name the Tuareg gave the place, *Tin'Buktu*, meaning 'place of Buktu.' A more modern but less romantic interpretation of the origin of the city's name is that it merely means 'the place between dunes.' From these humble Tuareg beginnings, Timbuktu would develop into an important autonomous desert port, becoming the most important trading city in the Sudan region (the area from the West Coast to Central Africa, stretching along the southern border of the Sahara Desert). The city would be monopolized and then taken over by the Mali kings, who made it into one of the most important and most cosmopolitan trade centers in Africa.

Timbuktu's golden period was in the 14th century. Such lucrative goods as ivory, textiles, horses (important for military use), glassware, weapons, sugar, kola nuts (a mild stimulant), cereals (e.g., sorghum and millet), spices, stone beads, craft products, and enslaved people passed through the city. Goods were bartered or paid for using an agreed-upon commodity such as copper or gold ingots, set quantities of salt or ivory, or even cowry shells (which came from Persia).

Mansa Musa was inspired by the holy sites he saw in Arabia, and on his return to Mali, he built a dazzling audience chamber at Niani and mosques at Gao and Timbuktu. These included the 'great mosque' in Timbuktu, also known as Djinguereber Mosque, or Jingereber. The buildings were designed by the famous architect Ishak al-Tuedjin (died 1346 and also a noted poet) from Andalusian Granada, who had been enticed from Cairo following Mansa Musa's visit there. The mosque was completed by 1330, and al-Tuedjin lived the rest of his life in Mali. A royal palace or *madugu* was built in the capital city and Timbuktu, along with fortification walls to protect the latter city against raids by the Tuareg. Due to the lack of stone in the region, Mali buildings were typically constructed using beaten earth (*banco*) reinforced with wood, which often sticks out in beams from the exterior surfaces. Despite the limited materials, the mosques in particular are imposing structures with huge wooden doors and tiered minarets. Other buildings included large warehouses (*fondacs*) for storing goods before they were transported elsewhere, which had up to 40 apartments for merchants to live in.

Mansa Musa was also inspired by the universities he had seen on his pilgrimage, and he brought back to Mali both books and scholars. The king greatly encouraged Islamic learning, especially at Timbuktu, which, with its mosques, universities, and many Koranic schools, became not only the holiest city in the Sudan region of West Africa but also an internationally famous center of culture and religious study. In addition, Mansa Musa sent native religious scholars to Fez in Morocco to learn what they could and then return to Mali as teachers. Studies were actually much wider than religion and included history, geography, astronomy, and medicine. Great libraries were built up with tens of thousands of books and manuscripts, many of which survive today.

Despite the spread of Islam, ancient indigenous animist beliefs continued to be practiced, especially in rural communities. Islamic studies were conducted in Arabic, not native languages, and this further impeded its popularity outside the educated clerical class of towns and cities. Even the Islam that did take hold in Mali was a particular variation of that practiced in the Arab world, perhaps because Mali rulers could not afford to completely dismiss the indigenous religious practices and beliefs that the majority of their people clung to.

Mansa Musa was succeeded first by his son Mansa Maghan I (reign 1337-1341), who had also ruled as regent while his father had been on his famous pilgrimage, and then by his brother Mansa Sulayman (circa 1341-1360). That Maghan's reign lasted only four years and his place was taken by his uncle would suggest foul play, but concrete evidence is lacking. Mansa Sulayman did continue his brother's promotion of Islam, and the Mali Empire would prosper for another century or so before new trade routes were opened up by the Portuguese. The discovery of new goldfields and access to the southern coast of West Africa meant that by the mid-15th century, Mali no longer monopolized trade in the region. Significantly, the Mali *mansas* were also guilty of fighting among themselves as civil wars wracked the empire. As a consequence, first the Tuareg attacked Mali cities like Timbuktu, and then the burgeoning Songhai Kingdom, ruled by King Sunni Ali (reign 1464-1492), definitively took over most of the Mali territories in the 1460s.

Timbuktu and the Mali Empire in general received international attention in the Middle Ages thanks to descriptions in the works of Muslim travelers. The region was visited and described by the famed explorer from Tangier, Morocco, Ibn Battuta (1304 to circa 1369), who traveled throughout West Africa, among many other places in the world.

Ibn Battuta's Travels

Ibn Battuta's expeditions took him further than any other traveler of his time and resulted in his famous work, *The Rihla of Ibn Battuta*. 'Rihla' is actually not the book's title, but its genre: travel literature. The book's actual title is *A Gift to Those Who Contemplate the Wonders of Cities and the Marvels of Traveling*. Battuta kept no journal on his travels, and his Rihla was composed from memory and embellished upon by the scholar Ibn Juzay al-Kalbi (1321-1357) between circa 1352-1355.

Ibn Battuta traveled the Islamic world and Far East in the 14th century, covering 120,000 kilometers (75,000 miles) between 1325 and circa 1352, visiting 40 countries and crossing three continents. He seems to have gone by the name Shams al-Din in his lifetime and came from an educated background, a family of qadis (judges, from the Arabic *qāḍī*), and was devoted to his religion. When he felt it was time to go on his first pilgrimage to Mecca in 1325, he initially does not seem to have entertained any thoughts of going further than Mecca. He traveled across North Africa to Tunis, then went to Alexandria, Egypt, in the company of a caravan for protection on the road (a strategy he would often employ throughout his travels). In Alexandria, he met a devout mystic named Burhan al-Din who prophesied that he would visit Sind (Pakistan), India, and China and would enjoy the hospitality of al-Din's three brothers who lived in those regions.

Later in Alexandria, while staying with Sheik al-Murshidi, Ibn Battuta had a dream in which he was carried by a great bird to Mecca, but then beyond to lands he had never thought to see. The Sheik interpreted this dream for him as a sign that he would successfully reach Mecca but that his travels would take him much further. These experiences in Alexandria caused Ibn Battuta to re-think his original plan of returning home after the pilgrimage and he began to consider travel simply for its own sake, valuing the journey over the destination. From Alexandria he went to Cairo and from there moved on through Palestine and Syria toward Mecca. Arriving in Mecca in October 1326, Battuta carefully relates the experience of the Kaaba (also spelled Ka'ba) as thousands of pilgrims surged around the center of the world, where the celestial realm intersects with the kingdoms of the earth.

With the pilgrimage concluded, Battuta could return home, but he was now traveling simply for the love of travel. In 1326-1331, he crossed Persia to the Zagros Mountains, visited the city of Shiraz, famous at the time for its beauty and magnificent gardens, rode in the retinue of a Mongol ruler, visited Baghdad, and took ship to Yemen during which he survived a storm at sea.

The year 1331 or 1332 found him exploring Africa and then moving on to Anatolia (Turkey) where he escorted a princess to Constantinople (Istanbul) and visited the Hagia Sophia. At some point between 1332 and 1333, upon finding that a ship to India would take too long to arrive, he set out on foot and crossed Central Asia to finally arrive in India almost a year after the time it would have taken the ship to bring him there. In India, the sultan of Delhi hired him as one of the chief judges of the city. From India he visited China, where he was again appointed as a judge, and moved on to the Maldives, again becoming a judge. From the Maldives he went to Ceylon (Sri Lanka), Malaysia, traveled back through India, and made his way slowly through the Middle East.

AFRICA 107

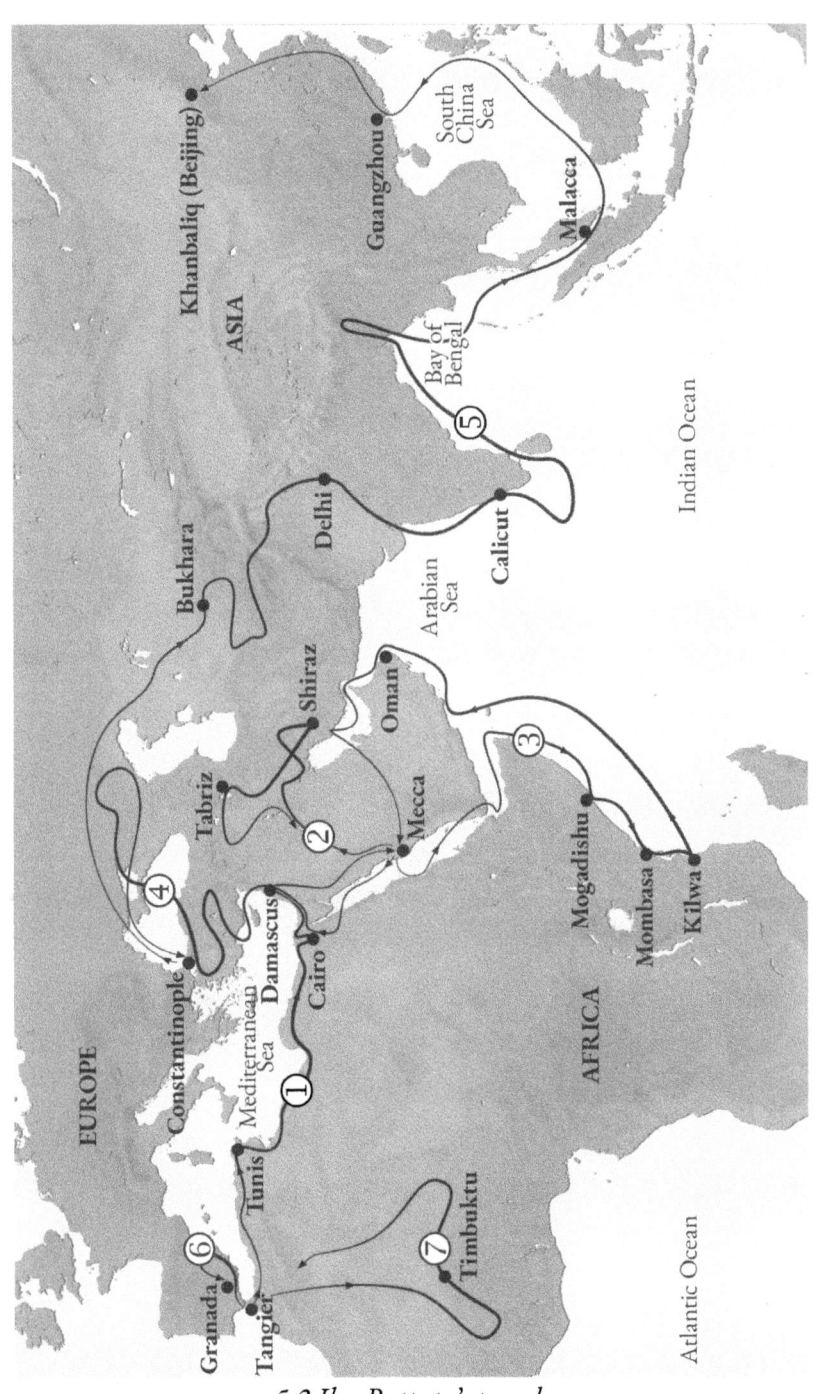

5.2 Ibn Battuta's travels

In the course of his journeys he had married seven times, fathered a number of children, bought and sold slaves, had great riches and fine apartments, counseled kings and rode with princesses but had also traveled with nothing to his name but his trousers and the hope of finding some food, been shipwrecked, robbed, and had his life threatened by a sultan. Finally, his thoughts turned to home and he traveled through Syria at the height of the plague in 1348, noting how death was all around him (he is recognized today as one of the first writers to record the plague in detail). Battuta detoured to Sardinia and traveled through Spain until he met up with a group of Muslims who were heading to Tangier. He arrived back in Morocco sometime in late 1348. Finding that his father and mother had died recently from the plague and that his friends were gone or dead, he set out again, returning to Spain and then taking a trip across to Timbuktu and the trading center of Gao, only returning home again to Morocco circa 1352.

He settled in the city of Fez, where Sultan Abu Inan heard his story and was so impressed that he asked for it to be written down. The sultan either assigned the scribe Ibn Juzay al-Kalbi or Ibn Battuta chose him for the job (having met him earlier on his travels). Following the dictation of his travels to Ibn Juzay, he vanishes from history but was most probably given a government post in the city by the sultan. He died, probably in Fez, in either 1368 or 1369.

Trans-Saharan Travel & Trade

Fez, like the other great North African cities of Marrakesh, Tunis, and Cairo, was an important starting or destination point for the trans-Saharan caravans. Long before the great trans-Saharan caravans of the medieval period, there was a more localized trade between nomadic desert peoples and the tribes of the savanna region south of the Sahara, often called the Sudan region. Rock salt from the Sahara itself, which was badly needed in the salt-impoverished savanna, was exchanged for cereals (e.g., rice, sorghum, and millet), which could not be grown in the desert. The large camel caravans that traveled the minimum 1,000 kilometers (620 miles) to cross the entire Sahara Desert really took off from the 8th century. Routes would shift over the centuries like the sand dunes of the desert as empires rose and fell either side of the Sahara, and as new resources were discovered that could be exploited in the trade that never ceased.

A typical caravan could have 500 camels, but some of the annual ones had up to 12,000 camels in them. These great caravans usually traveled in the best season for travel, winter. To avoid the heat of the midday sun, caravans typically set off at dawn to the call of horns and kettledrums, then rested in the shade of tents during the middle of the day, and moved on again in the late afternoon, continuing until well after dark.

The journey across the Sahara could take at least from 40 to 60 days, and it was only made possible by stopping at oases along the way, but even with these water stops, the journey was brutal and hazardous. That there were established routes, and that Arab medieval writers were so particular in mapping them, is strong evidence that any improvised deviation, the taking of shortcuts or the missing of the next oases through poor navigation or a sandstorm, was very likely to bring disaster. Other dangers included bandits, venomous snakes, scorpions, and the supernatural demons that desert people often believed haunted certain parts of the Sahara.

The chief limit on a caravan was how much water it could carry and how quickly it could get to the next water source along the route. Besides the stars and the smell of the sand and vegetation, a desert Berber, as today, used many other indicators of direction such as the height of the sun and moon, the lay of the land, mountains on the horizon, the shadows of the dunes, wind direction, the spray of sand blown from the peaks of dunes, ancient eroded gullies, the distribution of rocks and pebbles, the presence of mirages, and the position of camel dung, which is pointed in shape with the point always in the direction of the next water source.

What exactly was worth all the bother of transporting over large distances very much depended on the particular wealthy elites in the north and south of the desert, something that changed not only because of tastes and fashion but also the rise and fall of states and their access to goods that could be exchanged.

Salt was the major commodity going south and was exchanged for gold, ivory, hides, and enslaved people (from African tribes conquered by the sub-Saharan empires). Goods were gathered up from across the entire West African region and channeled along the Niger and Senegal Rivers to trading 'ports' like Timbuktu. As the Sudan region saw new and richer empires rise, like the Mali Empire and Songhai Empire, so a wealthy elite sought evermore exotic and expensive goods from North Africa and the wider Mediterranean.

Besides salt, the caravans transported southward glazed pottery (luxury vases, cups, oil lamps, and incense burners), precious and semi-precious stones (especially garnet and amazonite), cowrie shells and copper wire to be used as currencies, copper ingots, horses, manufactured goods, fine cloth, beads, coral, dates, raisins, and glassware (cups, goblets, and perfume bottles). As the Sudanese empires spread their influence, and new powers rose, such as Hausaland, so this brought in new goods to the trans-Saharan trade like kola nuts (a mild stimulant), ostrich feathers, perfumes, and tobacco.

Hausaland

Hausaland was located in the Sahel region between the Niger River and Lake Chad in north Central Africa in what is today northern Nigeria. The Sahel is the semi-arid strip of land running across Africa between the Sahara Desert in the north and the savanna grassland to the south. Hausaland, specifically, stretched from the Aïr Mountains (north) to the Jos plateau (south) and from Borno (east) to the Niger valley (west). This region saw the development of towns by the Hausa-speaking people from 1000 to 1300.

The exact origins of the Hausa cities are not known, but theories include a migration of peoples from the southern Sahara who, abandoning their own lands following the increased desiccation of that area, established new settlements in what would become known as Hausaland. An alternative theory suggests that the Hausa people originally lived on the western shore of Lake Chad and when the lake shrank (as a consequence of the same climatic changes that affected the Sahara) they occupied this new and fertile land and then eventually spread to the immediate north and west. Unfortunately, there is still no archaeological evidence to support either of these two theories. As a consequence, there is a third hypothesis, which is that the Hausa had not migrated from anywhere but were indigenous to the region. Support for this theory lies in the fact that there is no tradition of migration in Hausa oral history.

Traditionally, there were seven city-states (the *Hausa bakwai*)—Biram, Daura, Gobir, Kano, Katsina, Rano, and Zaria (aka Zazzau)—but there were, in fact, many more, including Garun Gobas, Gwari, Jukun (aka Kwararafa), Kebbi, Nupe, Yawuri (or Yauri), Yoruba, and Zamfara.

Each city had its own king or ruler, the *sarkin kasa*, who was advised by a chief councilor or vizier, the *galadima*, and a small council of elders—typically consisting of nine members who also determined the next ruler in line. Various officials were appointed by the king to, for example, collect taxes and customs duties, lead the city's cavalry units or infantry, maintain security on roadways, and look after certain crops. The city ruled over various smaller chiefdoms or villages in its immediate vicinity, each ruled by a chief or *sarkin gari*. The third tier of this political pyramid was the family clan or *gida*, many of which made up an individual village.

Rural Hausa populations were farmers who worked the land, which belonged to the community as a whole. The Hausa states traded gold, ivory, salt, iron, tin, weapons, horses, dyed cotton cloth, kola nuts, glassware, metalware, ostrich feathers, and hides. Cities specialized in the manufacture or trade of certain goods—for example, dyes (especially indigo) at Katsina and Daura, or silver jewelry at Kebbi and Zamfara. Goods were exchanged in kind, although salt, cloth, and enslaved people were often used as standardized forms of commodity currency.

Unlike much of Sub-Saharan Africa, the area occupied by Hausaland was largely untouched by Islam until the 14th century. Finally, though, a form of Islam was adopted and adapted following contact with Muslim merchants, missionaries, and scholars, who came from the east, the Niger River bend area. Islam was typically blended with traditional animist rituals and so took on its own distinct character in the region. Not having any commercial incentive to gain favor with foreign merchants like the Hausa rulers and elite, rural populations proved as difficult as in other parts of Africa to fully convert to the new religion, despite (or perhaps because of) sometimes brutal methods such as the destruction of shrines and the burning of ancient sacred groves. Despite this resistance from some chiefs and much of the rural populace, Islam did eventually take a strong hold in the region. Mosques were built in the cities, and one of the oldest surviving remnants of these early structures is the dried mud Gobarau Minaret of the mosque at Katsina, which dates to the early 15th century.

Spread of Islam in Africa

Islam spread from the Middle East to take hold across North Africa during the second half of the 7th century when the Umayyad Caliphate (661-750) of Damascus conquered that area by military force. From there, it spread via Islamized Berbers (who had been variously coerced or enticed to convert) in the 8th century along the trade routes that crisscrossed West Africa, moving from the east coast into the interior of Central Africa, finally reaching Lake Chad. Meanwhile, the religion also spread down through Egypt and swung westward through the Sudan region below the Sahara Desert. A third wave brought the religion to Africa's eastern shores, the Horn of Africa and the Swahili Coast, directly from Arabia and the Persian Gulf.

Once the religion had reached the savanna region, which spreads across Africa below the Sahara Desert, it was adopted by ruling African elites, although very often indigenous beliefs and rituals continued to be practiced or were even blended with the new religion. As Muslim traders penetrated deeper into Africa, so the religion spread from one empire to another, taking hold first at Gao in 985 and then within the Ghana Empire from the late 10th century. From there, the religion spread eastward to the Mali Empire. With the adoption of Islam by the rulers of the kingdom of Kanem between the 11th and 13th centuries and Hausaland from the late 14th century, the religion's encirclement of Africa south of the Sahara Desert was complete.

Aside from genuine spiritual conviction, African leaders may have recognized that adopting Islam (or seeming to) or, at the least, tolerating it would be beneficial to trade. Islam had profound effects on all aspects of daily life and society, but these did vary over time and place. The coming of Islam saw a general decline in the status of certain groups in ancient African communities. In contrast, an association with Islam sometimes brought a certain prestige. Men and women's roles sometimes changed, some African communities having previously given women a more equal status with men than was the case under Muslim laws. Some African societies were matrilineal, and these changed to a patrilineal system. More superficial changes included the changing of names to those favored by Muslims. Clothing changed, too, with women, in particular, encouraged to dress more modestly and adolescents to cover their nudity.

In East Africa, Islam faced stiff competition from Christianity, which was firmly entrenched in Nubia and states such as the kingdoms of Faras (aka Nobatia), Dongola, and Alodia, and in the kingdom of Axum in what is today Ethiopia. It was not until the 14th century and military intervention from the Mamluk Sultanate of Egypt (1250-1517) that these Christian kingdoms became Muslim, the exception being the kingdom of Abyssinia.

Islam had more immediate success further south on the Swahili Coast. From the mid-8th century, Muslim traders from Arabia and Egypt began to permanently settle in towns and trading centers along the Swahili Coast. The local Bantu peoples and Arabs mixed, as did their languages, with intermarrying being common, and there was a blending of cultural practices that led to the evolution of a unique Swahili culture. However, even on the Swahili Coast, which adopted Islam with perhaps more success than anywhere else, many converts continued the practice of appeasing spirits who were believed to bring illness and other misfortunes. Ancestors continued to be worshipped, in some cities women enjoyed better rights than they did under strictly sharia law, and, in a very un-Islamic practice, cemeteries were filled with tombs where precious goods were buried with the dead.

Islamic architecture also spread with the religion, with mosques being built wherever there were worshippers. However, just like the religion itself, there were minor local differences. Mosques on the Swahili Coast, for example, had neither the minarets nor inner courtyard typical of mosques elsewhere in the Islamic world.

Swahili Coast

The Swahili Coast on the shores of East Africa included a number of important independent trading cities from Mogadishu in Somalia at its northern end to Kilwa in the south, an island located in modern-day southern Tanzania. Major ports and towns in between, over 35 in total, included Brava, Pate, Kismayo, Malindi, Mombasa, Pemba, Zanzibar, and Mafia. In addition to these main sites, there are some 400 other smaller ancient sites dotted along the eastern coastal area. The term Swahili derives from the Arabic word *sāḥil* (coast) and so means 'people of the coast.' It not only refers to the coastal region of East Africa but also to the language spoken there, a form of the indigenous African language Bantu, which emerged in the middle of the first millennium. Later, many Arabic terms were mixed in and Swahili became the lingua franca of East Africa, even if different dialects did develop.

Swahili cities were independent from each other and usually governed by a single ruler, but details of how these were chosen are lacking, aside from some cases of one ruler nominating his successor. The social structure of the city-states generally had three levels. The ruling class—governors, merchants, craftworkers, and holders of religious office—was composed of those with a mixed Arab and African ancestry. The second group was made up of slaves who were Native Africans of unmixed ancestry, and the third group was Arab and Persian traders who had not settled permanently.

These city-states, with the exception of Mogadishu, rarely exerted any form of wider political control beyond their immediate vicinity. Neither was there even very much cultural influence over the mainland interior. As many cities could not produce enough food, though, there must have been some arrangement with local tribes on the mainland who provided sorghum, rice, bananas, yams, coconuts, and more.

Precious metals, ivory, cotton cloth, pottery, tortoise shells, timber, incense, spices, rock crystal, salt, grain, rice, hardwoods, perfumes, rhino horns, animal hides, and enslaved people came to the Swahili city-states from Africa's interior. These goods could be sold in the cities themselves, passed on to other African communities (after payment of duties to the cities' rulers), or exported away from the continent by sea. In the other direction, pottery, precious metal jewelry, glassware, glass beads, faience, silk, and Ming porcelain came from Arabia, Persia, India, China, and Southeast Asia. Again, the foreign products were both consumed in the Swahili city-states and traded on to African settlements throughout East and Southern Africa. Finally, Swahili city-states also manufactured goods for both their own residents and for trade, such as pottery, cloth, and highly decorated *siwa*, the typical brass trumpet of the region.

Merchants exchanged these goods in a system of barter where one commodity was exchanged for another, but some of the larger cities, like Kilwa, were able to mint their own copper coinage from the 11th or 12th century. There were also commonly agreed-upon currency commodities such as copper ingots or cowrie shells.

Domestic housing along the Swahili Coast typically consisted of rectangular wattle-and-daub or mud-brick buildings with palm-leaf gabled roofs. Better housing, such as found at Kilwa, was made from stone and was mostly of one story. Swahili stone houses typically had two very long but narrow rooms (their width was limited by the length of mangrove poles needed to support the coral roofing) with few windows, making their interiors dark but cool. There were smaller private chambers with many wall niches set at the back; there is often an inner courtyard with large windows, and a toilet chamber and washrooms. Decoration was achieved by adding carved wooden window and door frames, window grilles, or even setting rows of porcelain bowls into the ceilings. Larger houses had well-watered gardens and orchards. Buildings were constructed very close together, often sharing a wall, and so cities frequently had very narrow and maze-like streets.

Mosques were smaller than elsewhere in the Muslim world and given very little decoration. One of the best surviving monuments on the Swahili Coast is the Great Mosque, also known as the Friday Mosque, at Kilwa. Constructed from coral rock blocks in the 14th century and added to in the subsequent century, the structure incorporated parts of an earlier mosque of the 10th-11th century. It has impressive monolithic coral columns that support a high vaulted ceiling, octagonal columns creating 30 arched bays, and a four-meter square room (43 square feet) with a domed roof.

5.3 Great Mosque of Kilwa, Tanzania

Kilwa had many other fine and imposing buildings. The Husuni Kubwa Palace ('Large Fort' in Swahili) was located on a sandstone promontory just outside the city and was reached by a monumental staircase cut into the rock. The buildings were mostly of one story and constructed using dressed blocks cut from the natural rock faces of Kilwa. It was a large complex covering almost 10,000 square meters (1 hectare; 2.5 acres) and included a spacious audience hall, courtyard with tiered seating or steps, domed ceilings, storerooms (covering half of the palace's area), and a pool. Although the architecture is similar to buildings seen in Aden with its domes, pavilions, and barrel vaults, the Kilwa architects added their own unique twist by embedding pieces of Chinese porcelain into the white lime plaster of the exterior walls for decorative effect. The roofing was made from flat pieces of coral supported by a dense framework of mangrove poles. The palace and other buildings for the ruling elite and wealthy included such luxuries as indoor plumbing. The palace walls and those of the mosque and one house have another point of interest, several examples of ancient graffiti that show both Arab and local trading ships. A different kind of wall writing, and just as important, is an inscription that reveals the name of the ruler who commissioned it, al-Hasan ibn Suleiman (reign 1320-1333), and thus we have an approximate date of construction.

Another impressive structure is the Husuni Ndogo or 'Small Fort,' which consists of a large rectangular courtyard with a stone well completely encircled by a sandstone circuit wall and only one entrance gate. Its precise purpose is unknown, but it may have functioned as a place for travelers to stay, a barracks, or even a market. The city boasted additional mosques as well as many small, well-watered gardens, some with orchards. Large warehouses were built of coral rock, too. The palace, Great Mosque, and general attention to architecture at Kilwa led Ibn Battuta to famously describe it as "one of the most beautiful towns in the world" (quoted in Spielvogel, 233). Indeed, Kilwa became the most prosperous of all the Swahili Coast cities, overtaking Mogadishu, thanks to gold from Zimbabwe that reached Sofala, Kilwa's trading post further south in modern Mozambique, founded perhaps around 1300. This gold was easily acquired from surface deposits across the Zimbabwean plateau and in the tributaries of the Zambezi River.

Zimbabwe

The kingdom of Zimbabwe, of which Great Zimbabwe was its capital, was formed by the Shona, a Bantu-speaking people who had first migrated to Southern Africa in the 2nd century. The exact confines of the kingdom are not known except that its heartland was in central Mashonaland (northern Zimbabwe). The region of the Zimbabwe plateau, located between the Limpopo River in the south and the Zambezi River in the north, is composed of temperate grasslands that are free of the tsetse fly, although rainfall has always been unpredictable with the threat of drought at least once a decade. Small bands of nomadic hunter-gatherers had inhabited the area long before the Shona pastoralists arrived with their livestock and iron-smelting technology and, indeed, the two groups would continue to compete for territory right into the modern era.

The cumulative archaeological evidence points to a society that, from the 10th century, prospered from farming (especially of sorghum, millet, pumpkins, and watermelons), animal husbandry, hunting, and localized trade (using local iron, copper, and gold deposits). As these communities prospered, and as their trade network expanded to the great trade centers of the Swahili Coast, so they were able to build more impressive stone monuments. Great Zimbabwe, located some 30 kilometers (19 miles) southeast of modern Masvingo, is only the largest of over 300 Iron Age stone sites in the region, which today covers modern Zimbabwe and Mozambique.

Zimbabwean society, as in other parts of Southern Africa, was dominated by male family heads who competed with their peers for power and influence. One of the main methods of acquiring such power was the ownership of cattle. The number of a man's wives was another indicator of success because this corresponded to the labor at his disposal. Women were expected to sow, tend, and harvest crops, prepare food, and fetch water. Unmarried men hunted, herded animals, and made clothing. Men who had no property of their own might become a dependent of a man with property, who allowed them to assist in herding duties in return for food and shelter. Such dependents were another indicator of a male's success in Zimbabwean society.

The chief of a tribe was likely the wealthiest male, although the post was usually hereditary among the Shona. A chief had no army to support his authority, and so it is probable that most chiefs sought to accommodate the views of their community's senior males and subordinate chiefs under their nominal control. Archaeological evidence of fire destruction at some sites suggests there were occasional conflicts between competing groups. The male children of the tribe's herd-owning men were educated with their peers for a number of months in isolation from the community. The boys were taught hunting skills, had to endure physical hardship and endurance tests, and were taught the traditions and customs of the tribe. At the end of the training period, they were circumcised and given a new name, which meant the boys had become men. Girls were also given group education where they were prepared for their future roles as wives and mothers. When a girl did marry, she left her home and lived with the family of her husband, her father presenting a dowry of cattle.

That Great Zimbabwe had trade links with other states further afield is evidenced by finds of even non-African goods that came via merchants of the East African coast, 400 kilometers (250 miles) away. Gold, ivory, and copper (often cast in X-shaped ingots) were exchanged for such exotic luxury goods as Chinese Ming porcelain and carved faience from Persia. There were no markets, and this trade was done by barter for the benefit of the ruling elite. There is, then, ample evidence of the wealth this interregional trade brought to the city, not only in finds of foreign luxury artifacts but also in both its architecture and art. However, by the 15th century, any links with coastal trade had ceased. The precise causes of Great Zimbabwe's decline are not known, but competition from rival states and the working out of gold deposits are the most likely explanations. There may have been problems caused by overpopulation, too, such as overworking of the land and deforestation, a situation perhaps brought to crisis point by a series of droughts.

Unfortunately for posterity, the site of Great Zimbabwe was systematically looted of anything of value during the European colonialists' activities in the area in the 1890s. Those artifacts that have found their way into the public arena are almost always without any information as to the context in which they were found. A number of finely carved soapstone figures have been found that include eight representations of birds perched on monoliths over one meter (three feet) in height. The bird is known as the Zimbabwe Bird and does not resemble any bird in nature; it appears on the flag of the country today. Other sculptures include cattle and highly stylized nude female figures.

Ife

Another region best known for its impressive sculptures was modern Nigeria, in southern West Africa. Ife is particularly famous today for the magnificent metal sculptures its artists produced, which include serene-looking human heads so masterfully crafted that Europeans once wrongly considered them the work of another civilization.

Ife (aka Ile-Ife) flourished between the 11th and 15th centuries as the capital and principal religious center of the Yoruba kingdom of Ife, which prospered thanks to trade connections with other West African kingdoms. Located along the Guinea coast, Ife controlled the rainforest to the west of the Niger River delta. Very little is known about the state apparatus of Ife and how it controlled its territory. Even information on the economy of Ife is sparse. It is likely that Ife, and the whole area of the West African rainforest in general, prospered thanks to iron-smelting technology that could produce iron tools like the hoe and so, in turn, bring forth plentiful harvests of food such as okra, yams, dates, palm oil, and fish.

5.4 Human head, terracotta, 12th-15th century; Ife people, Southwest Nigeria

Goods that could be traded with kingdoms to the north included kola nuts, pepper, gold, and ivory. Enslaved people were also sent northward and so Ife was indirectly connected to the camel caravan trade routes that crossed the Sahara and reached such cities as Tripoli on the Mediterranean coast. Goods exchanged for those provided by Ife would have been principally salt from the Sahara and luxury goods for the Ife elite, who controlled the trade. The luxury items would have included swords, copper, brass, jewelry, perfumes, and horses.

By the beginning of the 11th century, Ife had grown to become a large walled city with several large stone buildings, including a palace, workshops, and shrines. Some of the city's streets were paved with terracotta tiles to make them more resistant to rain. Similarly, many courtyards were paved with small pieces of pottery and quartz pebbles to create geometrical designs. Some courtyards have altars consisting of a low semicircular structure with the neck of a pottery vessel placed within it. The majority of housing was made using clay, and unfortunately these have long since perished, but a clue to their original decorative appearance is finds of many small pottery disks that were stuck into them to create a mosaic effect.

The Yoruba considered the site of Ife the exact place of creation, that is, where the gods descended from heaven and created the world as we know it. There are several versions of the creation myth, and details vary. The creator god Oduduwa separated earth from water. Living creatures were made by Obatala. The first humans were sent forth to rule over twelve cities and so became their first kings and queens. From these figures, all subsequent rulers claimed descendance. Specifically at Ife, the first divine ruler was Oni, whose name means 'king.'

The king was likely also the head of Ife's religion—a blend of animism, ancestor worship, and other traditional practices. Sacrifices and offerings were made to both gods and ancestors. There was (and still is among the Yoruba today) a belief that a person's character (*ìwà*) reflected their inner energy (*àṣẹ*) and that this energy is present in all things natural and divine. The energy was thought to reside primarily within a person's head, which may explain why the art of Ife typically concentrates on this part of the body. Further, because the energy of powerful people like chiefs can be dangerous, it is necessary that their mouths or even the whole face be covered with a veil—another feature commonly represented in Ife art. *Àṣẹ* is often represented as a cone, yet another symbol frequently seen in the headdresses of human representations in Ife sculpture.

The metal sculptures of naturalistic and life-size human heads for which Ife is still famous for today were made from the 11th to 15th centuries according to chemical analysis, and cast using the lost-wax casting process. Twelve heads were found together in a royal compound at Ife in 1938, and several more have been discovered since, including a pure copper mask. The head sculptures were cast in brass and sometimes also made from pottery. The human heads are all unique, but their precise purpose is not known. They may represent rulers, gods, revered ancestors, or have been used for some religious purpose. Many heads have vertical lines down the face and these may represent the ritual scars that marked an individual's passage from childhood to adulthood. The problem with this theory is that scarification was not widely practiced among the Yoruba people. Alternatively, the scars may have differentiated more local groups within the wider Yoruba population, reflected the practice of wearing temporary facial markings for rituals, perhaps represented the shadows created by the veils rulers commonly wore or, most simply, have been a form of aesthetic decoration. The heads have another interesting feature: a series of punched holes around the lips and jawline, possibly for the attachment of beards or veils made of glass beads. These veils are still worn today in the region on special occasions and their ceremonial significance is here summarized by the Zimbabwean archaeologist and art historian Peter Garlake: "The life-size brass heads of Ife are powerful expressions of serenity born of divine authority. This was the most important quality of any ruler ... The veils are intended to make extraordinary potency of a ruler's words less likely to cause fear and hurt. Mystery masks majesty" (117).

One exceptional piece of Ife sculpture that is not a head is a bronze figure of a standing chief who wears a kilt-like garment, many necklaces—including one with a double bow insignia—anklets, and a beaded hat with a high frontal decoration. The figure holds in one hand a forest buffalo horn, likely used as a container of medicine, and in the other hand a short staff. Dating to the 14th century, the figure now resides in the National Museum Lagos, Nigeria.

The sculptures of Ife very likely influenced those produced in the kingdom of Benin, also in modern Nigeria. Certainly, in Benin oral traditions, it was the king of Ife who sent a master craftsman southward to Benin in the late 13th century to spread his sculptural skills, and this may reflect the historical movement of iron-working Yoruba peoples in the territory of the Edo in Benin. The Edo tradition also states that it was they who invited Prince Oranmiyan of Ife to rule them and it is his son, Eweka, who became the first king of Benin. Points of similarity between the art of the two cultures include the use of a leopard in connection with death and snakes, such as those that entwine the gables of the Benin palace and a relief from Ife. Archaeology, however, has yet to establish any firm connection between these states that successively dominated the southern portion of West Africa above the Bight of Benin.

Benin

Formed in the 13th century as a state proper, the kingdom of Benin was populated by the Kwa-speaking Edo people and covered, at its peak, an area of some 400 kilometers (250 miles) in length and 200 kilometers (125 miles) in width. The heartland was a circle around the capital, also called Benin, extending some 60 kilometers (37 miles) in all directions, and it was ruled directly by the king. Next came an outer band of territory governed by royal princes, and finally a third ring of tribes that offered tribute to but were not directly ruled by the king of Benin. The kingdom prospered thanks to regional trade, with Benin seemingly acting as a middle-trader between other kingdoms, passing on goods that it did not produce itself, such as cotton and semi-precious stone beads. Other goods exchanged between West African peoples included fish, salt, yams, and cattle, to name a few. Such was the well-established nature of these trade relations that there is evidence of native currencies being used that took the form of manillas (heavy horseshoe-shaped bracelets), wiring, and rods all made from metals like copper, brass, and bronze. There is also evidence that cowrie shells—which came via Persia and the Maldives—were used as a currency in Benin before direct European contact, a fact that points to trade with northern African savanna kingdoms who would have acquired them via land trade routes.

The kings of Benin had the title of *oba* and were considered to have a divine right to rule. The king not only controlled all trade with outsiders but also personally owned the vast majority of high-value goods in the kingdom, such as leopard skins, pepper, coral, and ivory. Many rulers are commemorated in Benin art. Ivory masks, intended to be worn at the hip of rulers, show kings with crowns and necklaces of human heads, perhaps Europeans, and signifying either the *oba's* monopoly over trade or his dominance over foreigners. Kings often feature in the brass plaques that adorned the palace of Benin, where they appear as warrior leaders. They can be identified by symbols of their rank, such as leopard-spot scarification marks and leopard-tooth necklaces. The leopard was an appropriate symbol for the *oba* since the animal was considered the 'King of the Bush' and only the king was permitted to kill one, typically done in an annual sacrifice by the king for his own honor. Other royal symbols seen in depictions of Benin kings are a helmet with coral embellishments and mask ornaments worn around their waists (which are white, a color symbolic of both purity and the king's counterpart in rule), and Olokun, the god of the sea and source of wealth and fertility. Just like gods and the spirits of ancestors, the kings received offerings and sacrifices, including human ones, after their death.

Benin, the capital of the kingdom, is located some 30 kilometers (19 miles) from the coast and to the west of the Niger River. Excavations at the city have revealed that it was once surrounded by high earthworks but, as there are many gaps, it is not thought that these were for a defensive purpose. The walls may have served to demarcate different kin groups within the capital, all loyal to the king but each having their own outlying farmland. The city would have been further divided into districts for craftworkers who belonged to guilds.

The king, his court, and the palace were both the political and spiritual heart of the kingdom of Benin. The palace had many courtyards and several galleries with wooden pillars to support the roof. Attached to these pillars were the brass plaques that are considered one of the high points of West African art from any period.

The sculptures produced in Benin using brass (although often termed 'bronzes') have become world famous for their execution and artistry. Originally attached to wooden pillars in the royal palace of Benin, many of the plaques commemorate historical conflicts, show scenes of life at court, and depict Benin religious rituals. Besides plaques, Benin artists produced life-size brass sculptures of heads, small but full human and animal figures, and ceremonial bells. Ivory was another medium that Benin craftworkers favored, carving it into the hip masks mentioned above and also into extremely ornate and intricate boxes, combs, and armlets. It is likely, too, that many Benin sculptors worked with wood, but this material rarely survives very long in Africa due to the ravages of climate and insects.

Bibliography

Anonymous. *Chambers Dictionary of World History.* Larousse Kingfisher Chambers, 2000.

Bullis, D. "The Journeys of Ibn Battuta." Accessed 19 Mar 2020. https://archive.aramcoworld.com/issue/200004/the.longest.hajj.the.journeys.of.ibn.battuta-editor.s.note.htm

Chikumbirike, J. et al. "A Study of Archaeological Charcoal from Great Zimbabwe." *The South African Archaeological Bulletin* 71, no. 204 (December 2016): 107-118.

Chugtai, A.S. "Ibn Battuta: The Great Traveller." Accessed 3 Feb 2019. http://www.silkroadfoundation.org/artl/ibn_battuta.shtml

Curtin, P. *African History.* Pearson, 1995.

de Villiers, M. *Timbuktu.* Walker Books, 2007.

Desmond Clark, J. (ed). *The Cambridge History of Africa, Vol. 1.* Cambridge University Press, 2001.

Dunn, R.E. *The Adventures of Ibn Battuta.* University of California Press, 2012.

El Bailūnī, M.I.F.A. *The Rihla of Ibn Battuta.* Accessed 19 Mar 2020. https://englishattheuniversity.weebly.com/uploads/1/0/5/3/10532852/ibn_battutas_travels.pdf

Fage, J.D. (ed). *The Cambridge History of Africa, Vol. 2.* Cambridge University Press, 2001.

Fage, J.D. (ed). *The Cambridge History of Africa, Vol. 3.* Cambridge University Press, 2001.

Garlake, P. *Early Art and Architecture of Africa.* Oxford University Press, 2002.

Gibb, H.A.R. (translator). *The Travels of Ibn Battuta*. Dover Publications, 2004.

Gordon, S. *When Asia Was the World*. Da Capo Press, 2009.

Green, T. *The Gold Companion*. Rosendale Press Ltd, 1992.

Grillo, L.S. "Ironic Reversals: Gender, Power, and Sacrality." *The Journal of Africana Religions* 2, no. 4 (2014): 465-76.

Hrbek, I. (ed). *UNESCO General History of Africa, Vol. III, Abridged Edition*. University of California Press, 1992.

Huffman, T.N. "Debating Great Zimbabwe." *The South African Archaeological Bulletin* 66, no. 193 (June 2011): 27-40.

Innocent, P. "Great Zimbabwe in Historical Archaeology: Reconceptualizing Decline, Abandonment, and Reoccupation of an Ancient Polity, A.D. 1450-1900." *Historical Archaeology* 47, no. 1, Globalization, Immigration, Transformation (2013): 26-37.

Insoll, T. "The Archaeology of Islam in Sub-Saharan Africa." *Journal of World Prehistory* 10, no. 4 (December 1996): 439-504.

Ki-Zerbo, J. (ed). *UNESCO General History of Africa, Vol. IV, Abridged Edition*. University of California Press, 1998.

Latham, R. (translator). *The Travels of Marco Polo*. Penguin Classics, 1958.

McDougall, E.A. "Salts of the Western Sahara: Myths, Mysteries, and Historical Significance." *The International Journal of African Historical Studies* 23, no. 2 (1990): 231-257.

McDougall, E.A. "The Sahara Reconsidered: Pastoralism, Politics and Salt from the Ninth through the Twelfth Centuries." *African Economic History*, no. 12, Business Empires in Equatorial Africa (1983): 263-286.

McEvedy, C. *The Penguin Atlas of African History*. Penguin Books, 1996.

Mokhtar, G. (ed). *UNESCO General History of Africa, Vol. II, Abridged Edition.* University of California Press, 1990.

Ogot, B.A. (ed). *UNESCO General History of Africa, Vol. V, Abridged Edition.* University of California Press, 1999.

Oliver, R. (ed). *Cambridge Encyclopedia of Africa.* Cambridge University Press, 1981.

Oliver, R. (ed). *The Cambridge History of Africa, Vol. 3.* Cambridge University Press, 1977.

Plankensteiner, B. "Benin: Kings and Rituals: Court Arts from Nigeria." *African Arts* 40, no. 4 (Winter 2007): 74-87.

Preston Blier, S. "Art in Ancient Ife, Birthplace of the Yoruba." *African Arts* 45, no. 4, Gender and South African Art (Winter 2012): 70-85.

Spielvogel, J.J. *Glencoe World History.* McGraw-Hill Education, 2004.

Webber, N. "Great Zimbabwe." *Scientific American* 277, no. 5 (November 1997): 94-99.

Wise, B.S. *The History of the Medieval World.* W. W. Norton & Company, 2010.

Image Credits

5.1 The Mali Empire. Map © Simeon Netchev

5.2 Ibn Battuta's Travels. Map © Simeon Netchev

5.3 Great Mosque of Kilwa Kisiwani, 11th - 18th cents (16). Photo by Richard Mortel, CC BY 2.0, https://www.flickr.com/photos/prof_richard/28991362821/

5.4 Human head, Ife people. Photo by FA2010, Ethnological Museum, Berlin, Wikimedia, public domain, https://

commons.wikimedia.org/wiki/File:Kopf_Ife_EthnM_III_IIIC 27527.jpg

Europe

By Mark Cartwright and Joshua J. Mark

In the Middle Ages, most European societies had a social hierarchy based on local administrative control and the distribution of land into units (fiefs). In this feudal system, a landowner (lord) gave a fief, along with a promise of military and legal protection, in return for a payment of some kind from the person who received it (vassal). The payment of the vassal to the lord typically came in the form of feudal service, which could mean military service or the regular payment of produce or money. Both lord and vassal were freemen, and the term feudalism is not generally applied to the relationship between the unfree peasantry (serfs or villeins) and the person of higher social rank on whose land they labored.

The Feudal System

The word 'feudalism' derives from the medieval Latin terms *feudalis*, meaning fee, and feodum, meaning fief. The feudal system proper became widespread in Western Europe from the 11th century onwards, largely thanks to the Normans, as their rulers carved up and dished out lands wherever their armies conquered. Starting from the top of society's pyramid, the monarch could give a parcel of land (of no fixed size) to a noble who, in return, would be that monarch's vassal, that is, he would promise loyalty and service when required. Thus, a personal bond was created. The most common and needed service was military service. Military obligations included fighting in that monarch's army or protecting assets of the Crown, such as castles. In some cases, a monetary payment (known as scutage), which the monarch then used to pay mercenary soldiers, might be offered instead of military service. The vassal received any income from the land, had authority over its inhabitants, and could pass the same rights on to his heirs.

The nobles who had received land, often called suzerain vassals, could have much more than they either needed or could manage themselves, and so they often sublet parts of it to tenant vassals. Once again, the person was given the right to use and profit from this land, and in return, in one form or another, then owed a service to the landowner. This service could again take the form of military service (typical in the case of a knight) or, as tenants might be of a lower social class (but still be freemen) and they might not have had the necessary military skills or equipment, more usually they offered a percentage of their revenue from the land they rented (either in money or produce) or made a fixed payment of rent.

The arrangement that created a vassal was known as 'homage' as they often knelt before their particular feudal lord and swore an oath of loyalty, for which, in return, they not only received the land but also their lord's protection if and when required. The promise of protection was no small matter in times of war, when there were frequent raids from hostile neighboring states, and a perpetual danger of general banditry.

6.1 Feudal society in medieval Europe

Protection also came in the form of legal support and representation if a vassal found himself in a civil or church court. A tenant usually handed down their tenancy to their heir, although it was sometimes possible to sell the right of tenancy to a third party, provided the lord who owned the land agreed. Another type of relationship in feudal societies, especially in Germany and France, involved the allod, an inalienable property, one that could not be taken back. Holders of an allod still owed some form of allegiance to a superior local lord, but the relationship was not based on land ownership, and so that allegiance was harder to enforce.

The feudal system perpetuated itself as a status quo because the control of land required the ability to perform military service, and, because of the costs involved (of weapons, armor, and horses), land was required to fund military service. Thus, there was a perpetual divide between the landed aristocracy (monarchs, lords, and some tenants) and those who worked the land for them, who could be free or unfree laborers. Unfree laborers were serfs, also known as villeins, who were at the bottom of the social pyramid. Serfs made up 75% of the medieval population but were not slaves, as only their labor could be bought, not their person. The peasantry worked, without pay, on the land owned or rented by others to produce food for themselves and, just as importantly, food and profit for their masters.

Serfs might not have been slaves, but they were subject to certain fees and restrictions of movement, which varied according to local custom. The hub of the medieval rural community and reason for a serf's existence was the manor or castle—the estate owner's private residence and place of communal gatherings for purposes of administration and legal matters. The relationship of the peasantry to these manors and their lords is known as manorialism.

Manors or large country houses (called villae or curtes in medieval Continental Europe) have been built since villages started to be formed in the Neolithic period. As centers of a communal life, such buildings eventually evolved into the private residences that landowners built on their estates for their own use and in order to provide such spaces as the great hall, where feasts, audiences with the peasantry, and local courts of justice could be held. The estates of the richer nobles had their own castle (which could protect several manor estates), but, in time, the greater comfort of a smaller building purpose-built for domestic use became fashionable—the manor. Those landowners without the means or permission to build an expensive stone castle could always make their manor as close to one as possible in terms of defensive features. Thus, manors could be fortified with sections of stone walls, crenellations, wall walks, and sometimes a moat, while semi-fortified manors had only some of these features (or had them without a proper license). In most cases, then, the estate owner was able to make good on their promise of physical protection for those who lived and worked on the immediate lands around them.

The manor estate, besides a manor or castle, might also include a small river or stream running through it, a church, mill, barns, and an area of woodland. The land of the estate was divided into two main parts. The first part was the demesne (domain), which was reserved for the exclusive exploitation of the landowner. Typically, the demesne was 35-40% of the total land on the estate. The second part was the land the dependent tenants lived and worked on for their own daily needs (mansus), typically around five hectares (twelve acres) per family.

The laborers on the estate farmed both the land reserved for their use and the demesne. The most important task of serfs was to work on the demesne land of their lord for two or three days each week, and more during busy periods like harvest time. All of the food produced from that land went to the lord. On the other days of the week, serfs could farm the land given to them for their own family's needs. Aside from payment to their lord of a regular percentage of the foodstuffs produced on their own land, the peasantry had to pay a tithe to the local parish church, typically one-tenth of the peasant's harvest. The latter was used to maintain a priest, the church, and provide a small welfare fund for the poor.

The estate was almost entirely economically self-sufficient, with only things like iron, millstones, and salt being brought in from outside. Consequently, there was not much official or commercial contact with the outside world, and its community became similarly self-contained (but not isolated). The relations between its members, besides being governed by the distant law of the crown, were more specifically determined by the unique customs and traditions of that community, with the lord of the manor presiding at its head. A serf inherited the status of their parents; although, in the case of a marriage between free and unfree laborers, the child usually inherited the status of the father if legitimate, and, if illegitimate, the status of the mother. In England and Normandy, the eldest son inherited the actual land worked on by their serf fathers, with daughters inheriting only if they had no brothers. Widows typically inherited around one-third of their late husbands' land. In contrast, in central and Southern France, Germany, and Scandinavia, inheritance was equal between sons and daughters of serfs.

Men did the heavy agricultural work, with women also doing lighter farm work and helping out at harvest time. Throughout the year, women had their own extensive traditional duties such as milking, making butter and cheese, brewing ale (from malted grains), baking bread, tending fruit trees, cooking in general, making wool and producing wool and linen cloth, looking after poultry, household cleaning, and (probably) looking after any children.

Typical peasant food consisted of coarse bread made from wheat and rye, or barley and rye; porridge made from barley or rye; and thick soup made from any of the following: cereals, peas, cabbage, leeks, spinach, onions, beans, parsley, and garlic. The better-off peasants had milk, cheese, and eggs; meat was another rare luxury, as farm animals were much more valuable alive, the most common meat being salted pork or bacon. Dried and salted fish and eels were available at a price. Fruit, usually cooked, included apples, pears, and cherries, and wild berries and nuts were collected, too. The main drinks were weak ale or water with honey added. Few peasants would have had access to all the food just listed, and most had diets lacking in fats, proteins, calcium, and vitamins A, C, and D.

A serf had leisure time on Sundays and on holidays when the most popular pastimes were drinking, singing, and group dancing to music from pipes, flutes, and drums. There were games like dice, board games, and sports such as hockey and medieval football, where the goal was to move the ball to a predetermined destination, and there were few, if any, rules. Serfs did get to live it up a little once a year when, by tradition, they were invited to the manor on Christmas Day for a meal.

The institution of serfdom was gradually weakened by several developments in the 14th century. The increase in the use of coinage in the late Middle Ages meant that many serfs made a payment to their lord instead of labor, or paid a fee to be absolved from some of the labor expected of them, or even bought their freedom. Free laborers often left the countryside to seek their fortunes in the growing number of towns and cities. Runaway serfs could similarly try their luck, and there was even a custom that by living for one year and a day in a town, a serf earned his freedom. The sudden population declines caused by wars and plagues, particularly the Black Death, meant that labor was in short supply and thus expensive. Without sufficient labor, many estates were abandoned. This situation gave serfs leverage to negotiate a better deal for themselves, even to receive a payment for their work. Serfs increased their political power by acting collectively in village communities, which began to hold their own courts and acted as a counterweight to those of the landed gentry. Finally, there were sometimes serious revolts by the peasantry against their masters. Across Europe, all of these factors conspired to weaken the traditional setup of unfree laborers being tied to the land and working for the rich, so that by the end of the 14th century, more agricultural labor was done by paid workers than by unpaid serfs.

Black Death

The severe depopulation caused by the outbreak of plague in Europe between 1347 and 1352—known as the Black Death—not only upset the feudal system but completely changed the world of medieval Europe. Disease on an epidemic scale was simply part of life in the Middle Ages, but a pandemic of the severity of the Black Death had never been experienced before, and, afterward, there was no way for the people to resume life as they had previously known it.

The plague, caused by bacterium *Yersinia pestis*, carried by fleas on rodents, came to Europe from the East, most probably via the Silk Road over land, and certainly by ship over sea. The Black Death—a combination of bubonic, septicemic, and pneumonic plague (and also possibly a strain of murrain)—had been gaining momentum in the East since at least 1322.

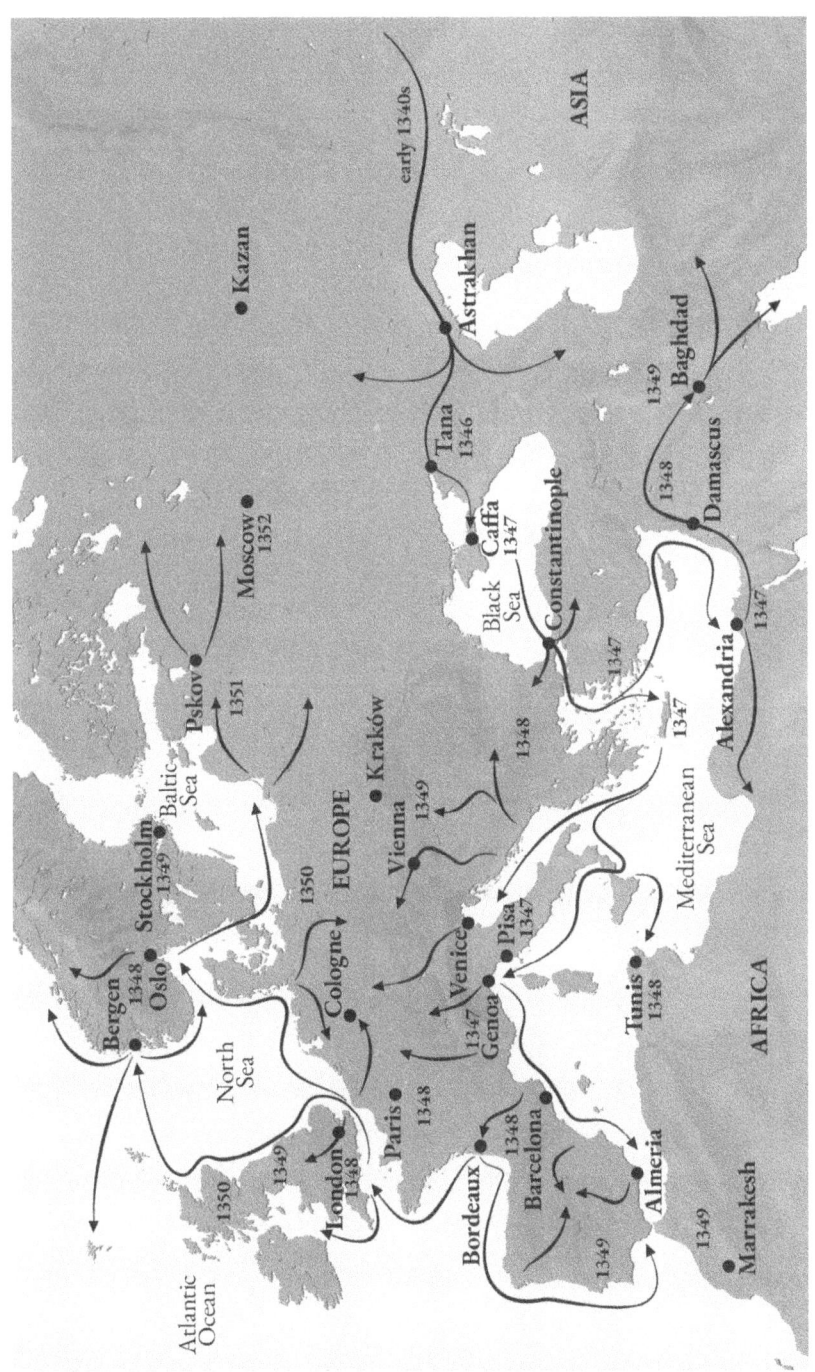

6.2 Spread of the Black Death

By circa 1343, it had infected the troops of the Mongol Golden Horde under the command of Khan Janibeg (aka Djanibek, reign 1342-1357) who was besieging the Italian-held city of Caffa (modern-day Feodosia in Crimea) on the Black Sea. The Italian notary Gabriele de Mussi (circa 1280 to circa 1356) was either an eyewitness to the siege or received a firsthand account and wrote of it in 1348/9. He reports how, as the Mongol warriors died and their corpses filled the camp, the people of Caffa rejoiced that God was striking down their enemies. Janibeg, however, ordered the corpses of his dead soldiers catapulted over the city's walls, and soon the plague erupted in the city.

Eventually, a number of the city's inhabitants fled the city by ship, first arriving at Sicilian ports and then at Marseilles, and others from whence the plague spread inland. Those infected usually died within three days of showing symptoms, and the death toll rose so quickly that the people of Europe had no time to grasp what was happening, why, or what they should do about the situation. The physicians of the day had no idea how to cope with the outbreak. Based on the medical knowledge of the time, folk cures that had been passed down for generations, Christian belief, superstition, and prejudice, the people tried any suggestion offered to defeat death.

One of the most popular 'cures' was the Vicary method, where a healthy chicken's back and rear were plucked clean and the chicken was strapped to the swollen nodes of the sick person. When the chicken showed signs of illness, it was thought to be drawing the disease from the person. Another attempt at a cure was to chop a snake into pieces and rub the various parts over swollen buboes. The snake, synonymous in Europe with Satan, was thought to draw the disease out. Drinking a powder made of the ground-up 'unicorn horn' mixed in water was also thought to be an effective remedy and was also among the most expensive. Another expensive remedy was eating or drinking a small quantity of crushed emeralds. Those who could not afford to consume emeralds drank arsenic or mercury, which killed them faster than the plague. There were also potions, the best-known of which was Four Thieves Vinegar, a combination of cider, vinegar, or wine with spices such as sage, clove, rosemary, and wormwood (among others). The most popular potion among the wealthy was known as theriac. Clearing the air was considered another effective remedy, and people carried bouquets of flowers that they held to their faces, not only to ward off the stench of decomposing bodies but also because it was thought this would fumigate one's lungs.

The only effective means of stopping the spread of the plague—though not curing it—was separating the sick from the well through quarantine. The port city of Ragusa (modern-day Dubrovnik, Croatia), at that time under the control of Venice, was the first to initiate this practice through a 30-day isolation period imposed on arriving ships. Ragusa's policy was effective and was adopted by other cities and extended to 40 days under the law of *quarantino* (40 days), which gives English its word quarantine. However, people broke quarantine and continued the spread of the disease.

Since the plague was thought to have been sent by God as a punishment, processions would wind their way through cities from a given point—say the town square or a certain gate—to the church or a shrine, usually dedicated to the Virgin Mary. Participants would fast, pray, and purchase amulets or charms to keep them safe. Even after European Christians understood that the plague was contagious, these processions and gatherings continued because there seemed to be no other way to appease God's wrath.

As the plague raged and traditional religious responses failed, however, the flagellant movement emerged in 1348 in Austria (possibly Hungary also) and spread to Germany and Flanders by 1349. The flagellants roamed from town to city to countryside whipping themselves for their sins and the sins of humanity, falling to the ground in penitential frenzy, and leading communities in the persecution and slaughter of Jews, Romani ('gypsies'), and other minority groups until they were banned by Pope Clement VI as ineffectual, disruptive, and upsetting. Persecutions of Jews by the Christian community did not start with the Black Death or end there, but it certainly increased in Europe between 1347 and 1352. In 1348, Jews in Languedoc and Catalonia were massacred and, in Savoy, were arrested on charges of poisoning the wells. In 1349, Jews were burned en masse in Germany and France, but also elsewhere in spite of papal bulls issued expressly forbidding these types of actions. Large migrations of Jewish communities fled the scenes of these massacres, many of them finally settling in Poland and Eastern Europe.

By the time the disease had run its course in 1352, an estimated 30 million people were dead, and the social structure of Europe was as unrecognizable as much of the landscape, since "many flourishing cities became virtual ghost towns for a time" (Cantor, *Civilization*, 482) and crops lay rotting in the fields with no one to harvest them.

Depopulation greatly reduced the workforce, and the serf's labor suddenly became an important—and increasingly rare—asset, and survivors could negotiate for pay and better treatment. The lives of the members of the lowest class vastly improved as they were able to afford better living conditions and clothing as well as luxury items.

Once the plague had passed, the improved lot of the serf was challenged by the upper class, who were concerned that the lower classes were forgetting their place. Fashion changed dramatically as the elite demanded more extravagant clothing and accessories to distance themselves from the poor, who could now afford to dress more finely. Efforts of the wealthy to return serfs to their previous condition resulted in uprisings such as the peasant revolt in France in 1358, the guild revolts of 1378, and the famous Peasants' Revolt of London in 1381. There was no turning back, however, and the efforts of the elite were futile. Class struggle would continue, but the authority of the feudal system was broken.

The challenge to authority also affected medical knowledge and practice. Doctors and other caregivers were seen dying at an alarming rate as they tried to cure plague victims using their traditional understanding, and, further, nothing they prescribed did anything for their patients. It became clear, by as early as 1349, that people recovered from the plague or died from it for seemingly no reason at all. After the plague, doctors began to question their former practice of accepting the knowledge of the past without adapting it to present circumstances. The death of so many scribes and theoreticians, who formerly wrote or translated medical treatises in Latin, resulted in new works being written in the vernacular languages. This allowed common people to read medical texts, which broadened the base of medical knowledge. Further, hospitals developed into institutions more closely resembling those in the modern day.

The plague also dramatically affected medieval art and architecture. Artistic pieces tended to be more realistic than before and, almost uniformly, focused on death. The most famous motif was the Dance of Death (also known as *Danse Macabre*), an allegorical representation of death claiming people from all walks of life to come with him. Architecture was similarly influenced. Since peasants could now demand a higher wage, the kinds of elaborate building projects that were commissioned before the plague were no longer as easily affordable, resulting in more austere and cost-effective structures. Scholars have noted, however, that post-plague architecture also clearly resonated with the pervasive pessimism of the time and a preoccupation with sin and death.

In literature, the medieval view of woman-as-property had been largely replaced by the novel concept of woman-as-individual, famously exemplified by Geoffrey Chaucer (circa 1343-1400) in the character of the Wife of Bath in *The Canterbury Tales*. The elevation of womanhood reached its apex in the poetry of Petrarch (1304-1374), whose sonnets to the persona of Laura continue to resonate in the modern day. Petrarch's work was so popular in his time that it influenced social perceptions not only of women but of humanity in general, which is why he is often cited as the first humanist author.

While the romances entertained and edified, another genre sought to elevate and console: the high medieval dream vision, poems featuring a first-person narrator who relates a dream that corresponds to some difficulty they are experiencing. The most famous of these is "The Pearl" by an unknown author, *Piers Plowman* by William Langland, and Chaucer's *The Book of the Duchess* (circa 1370). The genre usually relies on a framing device by which the reader is presented with the narrator's problem, is then taken into the dream, and is then brought back again to the narrator's waking life. Although Dante Alighieri's *Divine Comedy* (circa 1319), in which the poet is taken on a journey through hell, purgatory, and paradise in order to correct the path he was on and assure him of the truth of the Christian vision, is not an actual dream vision, contemporaries interpreted the piece as a dream.

Although poetry continued as a popular medium in the late Middle Ages, more writers began working in prose, and among these were a number of notable women. Female Christian mystics such as Julian of Norwich (1342-1416) and Catherine of Siena (1347-1380) both related their visions in prose. One of the most famous writers of the Middle Ages, Christine de Pizan (1364 to circa 1430), wrote her highly influential works in prose, as did the great Italian artist Giovanni Boccaccio (1313-1375), best known for his masterpiece *The Decameron* (written 1349-1353) in which he describes the flight of ten affluent young people from Florence to a countryside villa during the plague. The characters tell each other stories to pass the time while the plague rages on in the city.

The Black Death was also a dramatic blow to the authority of the Church as people began to doubt the power of God's instruments, who could do nothing to stop people from dying or the plague from spreading. Since no one knew the cause of the plague, it was attributed to the supernatural and, specifically, to God's fury over human sin. Those who died of the plague were suspected of some personal failing of faith, and yet it was clear that the same clergy who condemned them died of the same disease in the same way. Scandals within the Church, and the extravagant lifestyle of many of the clergy, combined with the mounting deaths from the plague, generated widespread distrust of the Church's vision and authority.

The Church

While it is true that the Church focused on regulating and defining an individual's life in the Middle Ages, even if one rejected its teachings, and the clergy were often not the most qualified, it was still recognized as the manifestation of God's will and presence on earth. The dictates of the Church were not to be questioned, even when it seemed apparent that many of the clergy were working more in their own interests than those of God, because, even if God's instruments were flawed, it was understood that the Creator of the universe was still in control.

6.3 Pope Boniface VIII, statue by Arnolfo di Cambio, circa 1298, Italy

By the time of the Middle Ages, the Church had an established hierarchy.

Pope: the head of the Church

Cardinals: advisors to the Pope; administrators of the Church

Bishops/Archbishops: ecclesiastical superiors over a cathedral or region

Priests: ecclesiastical authorities over a parish, village, or town church

Monastic orders: religious adherents in monasteries supervised by an abbot/abbess

The Church maintained the belief that Jesus Christ was the only begotten son of the one true God, and the Christian Bible—considered the word of God and the oldest book in the world—was understood as a handbook on how to live according to divine will and gain everlasting life in heaven upon one's death. Interpretation of the Bible, however, was too great a responsibility for the average person, according to the Church's teachings, and so the clergy was a spiritual necessity. In order to talk to God or understand the Bible correctly, one relied on one's priest as that priest was ordained by his superior, who was, in turn, ordained by another, all under the authority of the pope, God's representative on earth.

The Church hierarchy reflected the social hierarchy. Social mobility was a rarity since the Church taught that it was God's will that one had been born into a certain set of circumstances, and attempting to improve one's life was tantamount to claiming God had made a mistake. The Church paid no taxes and was supported by the people of a town or city. Between 1296 and 1302, one king, Philip IV of France (reign 1285-1314), decided to tax the clergy in defiance of traditional policy. Pope Boniface VIII (served 1294-1303) reacted with a papal bull forbidding the clergy from paying the king anything without papal approval. Philip IV responded with an embargo, which effectively cut the papacy off from significant sources of revenue.

The feud between the pope and the king continued until Boniface VIII issued the *Unam Sanctam* on 18 November 1302, which required the complete submission of all people, including kings, to the authority and dictates of the pope. The response to it was almost universal rejection among the European nobility. Philip IV had the renowned and controversial theologian, philosopher, and Dominican friar John of Paris write a refutation arguing that the Church did indeed have spiritual authority but not over temporal matters, and certainly not over kings who ruled by divine right and so had clearly already been installed in power by God and required no further submission to papal whims. Philip IV then accused Boniface of various crimes and demanded that he step down as pope. Boniface responded by drafting the excommunication of Philip IV, but before he could issue it, Philip IV sent 1,000 knights to attack Boniface in his palace and drag him back to Lyon for trial in September 1303. Boniface was rescued, but he died a month later of fever in October 1303. His successor, Clement V (served 1305-1314), a Frenchman, sided with Philip IV and even moved his court to Avignon to please the king. The excommunication of Philip IV was dropped, and the *Unam Sanctam* was then ignored by the European nobility.

In the same way the papacy dealt with the monarchy, the Church in general operated with the common folk of the Middle Ages, claiming the Church alone had the power to unlock the gates of heaven for a soul, consign it to the suffering of purgatory, or condemn it to hell. Citizens were responsible for supporting the parish priest and the Church overall through a tithe of 10% of their income. Tithes paid for baptism ceremonies, confirmations, funerals, and festivals such as Easter celebrations. Further, they supported social institutions, including poor houses, orphanages, schools, and religious orders that could not support themselves. The lower class bore the brunt of the Church's expenses, but the nobility was also required to donate large sums to the Church to ensure a place for themselves in heaven or to lessen their time in purgatory.

The Church's teachings on purgatory—an afterlife realm between heaven and hell where souls remained until they had paid for their sins—generated enormous wealth for various clergy who sold writs known as indulgences, promising a shorter stay in purgatory for a price. A lord could also safeguard his soul in the next life by helping to establish a monastery, both through the action of his donation and the quota of prayers said in his name as a result of it. Monasteries and other religious institutions, such as priories and nunneries, were a quintessential part of the medieval landscape and an important component of a community's social fabric. A monastery provided local communities with spiritual guidance; very often its church was for wider public use. It gave employment, and its monks provided education, entertained pilgrims who came to visit, looked after orphans, the sick, and the aged, and daily gave out food, drink, and alms to the poor. Monks produced and copied countless invaluable historical documents such as religious treatises, biographies of saints, and regional histories. Monasteries, as institutions full of educators and scholars, also proved useful tools to the state. Monarchs frequently used monks, with their skills in Latin and document-making, in their royal writing offices, or a monastery itself performed that function.

A large monastery was much like a medieval castle or manor house in that it controlled a surrounding area of land and essentially contained all the elements one would find in a small village of the period. A monastery acquired manors through donations and so could end up managing many disparate estates with their income all flowing into the monastery's coffers. Other donations might include properties in towns or even churches, and so more cash came from rents and tithes. Added to their income from donations, land rents, and the sale of goods produced from such land, many monasteries raked in money from holding markets and producing craft goods, while some even had the right to mint their own coinage.

Relics were another source of income, and it was common for unscrupulous clerics to sell fake splinters of Christ's cross, a saint's finger or toe, a vial of water from the Holy Land, or any number of objects that would allegedly bring luck or ward off misfortune.

The teachings of the Church were a certainty to the people of the Middle Ages. There was no room for doubt, and questions were not tolerated. A citizen of Europe who did not belong to Judaism or Islam had to adhere to the orthodox vision of the Church in order to interact with family, community, and make a living. If one found one could not do so (or at least appear to do so), the only option was a so-called heretical sect.

The heretical sects of the Middle Ages were uniformly responses to perceived corruption of the Church. The immense wealth of the Church, accrued through tithes and lavish gifts, only inspired a desire for even greater wealth, which translated as power. An archbishop could, and frequently did, threaten a noble, a town, or even a monastery with excommunication—by which one was exiled from the Church and so from the grace of God and commerce with fellow citizens—for any reason. The priests were often corrupt and, in many cases, only held their position due to family influence and favor.

Some of those who objected to the policies of the Church joined alternative religious sects and attempted to live peacefully in their own communities. The best known of these were the Cathars of Southern France. These kinds of communities were routinely condemned by the Church and destroyed, their members massacred, and whatever lands they had confiscated as church property. Even an orthodox community such as the Beguines was condemned because it was initiated spontaneously as a response to the needs of the people, rather than by the Church. The Beguines were laywomen who lived as nuns and served their community, holding all possessions in common and living a life of poverty and service to others, but they were not approved by the Church and were disbanded along with their male counterparts, the Beghards, in the 14th century.

All dissent was condemned as heresy and silenced, but as one movement was crushed, another would take its place. In England, John Wycliffe objected to the Church's abuses, challenged the hierarchy, and claimed the Christian scriptures were the supreme authority, not the pope. He developed the theology of two domains, an earthly Church and an idealized Church, and claimed the earthly Church had strayed far from what it should have been. He was protected from persecution by powerful political allies in England and by the distractions caused by the Western Schism (1378-1417), during which there were two popes, one in Rome and another in Avignon, France, with different factions of clergy supporting one or the other. Wycliffe's ideas were spread by his followers, known as Lollards, who also assisted him in translating the Bible from Latin into Middle English. Although he came into conflict with church authorities between 1377 and 1382 and was deprived of his teaching position at Oxford, he was not excommunicated nor officially branded a heretic. Although the Church eventually condemned him after his death and burned his works, many of them had already been copied and made their way to Bohemia, where Jan Hus (circa 1369-1415) began his own challenge to the Church's policies, especially condemning the sale of indulgences.

While the Church suffered from the loss of authority, women gained higher status following the plague. Prior to the outbreak, women had few rights. Neither the medieval Church nor the aristocracy had held women in very high regard. Women of the lower classes could work as bakers, milkmaids, barmaids, weavers, and, of course, as laborers with their family on the estate of the lord, but had no say in directing their own fate. After the plague, with so many men dead, women were allowed to own their own land, cultivate businesses formerly run by their husband or son, and had greater liberty in choosing a partner. Women joined guilds, ran shipping and textile businesses, and could own taverns and farmlands. Although many of these rights would be diminished later as the aristocracy and the Church tried to assert their former control, women would still be better off after the plague than they were beforehand.

Trade & Guilds

Guilds treated women unequally, but a widow could carry on a deceased master's business and have the full rights of guild membership if she had once worked alongside her husband and she did not remarry. There were, however, almost no specific guilds for women, and the institutions were always dominated by men (there were a few exceptions, such as the women's silk guilds in Paris and the gold spinners of Genoa). Even a profession dominated by women, such as midwives, did not have its own guild but belonged to that of the surgeons. From the 12th century, guilds were organized according to types of merchants and professionals before the idea expanded to include skilled artisans. Accordingly, there were over 100 guilds in Britain, for example, representing first merchants and traders, and then any skilled craft industry, from weaving to metalworkers. Italy was another country where guilds were popular; the city of Florence alone boasted 21 guilds in the mid-14th century, and the clothmakers' guild there controlled some 30,000 workers. Flanders, France (Paris alone had 120 guilds), and Germany were other places where guilds rose to prominence.

Guilds ensured production standards were maintained and that competition was reduced. In addition, by members acting collectively, guilds achieved political influence. Guilds, especially the merchant guilds, also helped produce a rich middle class in medieval society as merchants prospered and began to buy what has always been regarded as a badge of the aristocratic elite: land and property. These nouveaux riches may not have been fully accepted into high society, but they themselves began to carve out their own unique place in the social order by distancing themselves from everyone below them. Many guilds, even craft guilds, only accepted new members if they were the sons of existing ones or if one could gain the sponsorship of a master who would take them on as an apprentice. Masters were often biased toward relatives, and membership fees were higher for those outside the community, so that many guilds, in effect, produced hereditary professions. Further, by stipulating that masters owned their own means of production in the form of their workshop and tools, guilds thus created a permanent class divide between owners and laborers. However, it is important to remember that in medieval societies, there was less of a conflict between wealth and labor than there was between rival industries and towns. In this sense, guilds may well have actually helped make medieval society, at least in larger towns, more cohesive and stable. Finally, one aspect of society that sprang from educational guilds and helped, at least eventually, to allow some people a means to climb the social ladder was the 22 universities of medieval Western Europe. Merchant guilds did give back to their communities, too, prescribing from their members charitable gifts of food, wine, and money for the clergy and the poor and needy. The political class of a town typically came from the merchant guilds and, with a charter also establishing local courts, a new and powerful middle class sprang up. A similar pattern of development had occurred and was ongoing in other European countries.

Trade of common, low-value goods remained a largely local affair because of the costs of transportation. Merchants had to pay tolls at certain points along the road and at key points like bridges or mountain passes so that only luxury goods were worth transportation over long distances. Consequently, local markets were supplied by the farmed estates that surrounded them, and those who wanted non-everyday items like clothing, cloth, or wine had to be prepared to walk half a day or more to the nearest town. In towns, the consumer had, besides markets, the additional option of shops. Tradespeople usually lived above their shop, which presented a large window onto the street with a stall projecting out from under a wooden canopy. In cities, shops selling the same type of goods were often clustered together in the same neighborhoods to increase competition and make the lives of city and guild inspectors easier. Towns also had banks and money-lenders, many of which were Jews, as usury was forbidden to Christians by the Church.

Trade fairs were large-scale sales events typically held annually in large towns where people could find a greater range of goods than they might find in their more local market, and traders could buy goods wholesale. Prices also tended to be cheaper because there was more competition between sellers of specific items. Fairs boomed in France, England, Flanders, and Germany in the 12th and 13th centuries. For many ordinary people, fairs anywhere were a great highlight of the year. People usually had to travel more than a day to reach their nearest fair, and so they would stay one or two days in the many taverns and inns that developed around them. By the 15th century, trade fairs had gone into decline as the possibilities for people to buy goods everywhere and at any time had greatly increased.

From the 9th century, the Italian city-states, under the nominal rulership of the Byzantine Empire, began to take over the trade networks of the Mediterranean, particularly Venice and Amalfi, who would later be joined by Pisa and Genoa, and suitable ports in Southern Italy. Goods traded between the Arab world and Europe included spices, perfumes, gold, jewels, leather goods, animal skins, and luxury textiles, especially silk. Enslaved people were also bought and sold like goods. Italian cities specialized in the exports of cloths like linen, unspun cotton, and salt (goods that originally came from Spain, Germany, Northern Italy, and the Adriatic). Important inland trading centers developed, like Milan, which then passed on goods to the coastal cities for further export or to more northern cities. By the 13th century, international business was booming as many city ports established international trading posts where foreign merchants were allowed to live temporarily and trade their goods. Genoa, for example, had 198 resident merchants, of which 95 were Flemish and 51 French. There were German traders on the famous (and still standing) Rialto Bridge of Venice, in the Steelyard area of London, and the *Tyske Brygge* quarter of Bergen in Norway. Traders from Marseille and Barcelona established permanent camps in the ports of North Africa. Economic migration reached such numbers that these ports developed their own consulates to protect the rights of their nationals, and shops and services sprang up to meet their particular tastes in food, clothing, and religion.

With this growth, trade relations became more complex between states and rulers, with intermediaries and agents added to the mix. Trading expeditions were financed by wealthy investors who, if they put up all the initial capital, often got 75% of the profits, the rest going to the merchants who amassed the goods and then shipped them to wherever they were in demand. This arrangement, used for example by the Genoese, was called a *commenda*. An alternative setup, the *societas maris*, was for the investor to provide two-thirds of the capital and the merchant the rest. The profits would then be split 50-50. Behind these major investors, there developed consortiums of smaller investors who put up their money for a future return but who could not afford to pay for a whole expedition. Thus, sophisticated mechanisms of borrowing and lending developed, which involved a very large number of families in the Italian cities, in particular. There were more and more financial instruments to tempt investors and extend credit, such as credit notes, bills of exchange, maritime insurance, and shares in companies.

Trade was now assuming the guise we would recognize today, with well-established businesses run by generations of merchants from the same family (for example, the Medici of Florence). There were increased efforts at standardization in product quality, and helpful treatises on how to compare weights, measurements, and coins across different cultures. State control increased with a codification of customary trade laws and regulations, as did the now all-too-familiar imposition of taxes, duties, and protectionist quotas.

Finally, there was also advice on how to best get around these regulations, as mentioned in this extract on Constantinople's trade officials, taken from the 14th-century Florentine trader Francesco Balducci Pegolotti's guide to world trade, *La Practica della Mercatura*: "Remember well that if you show respect to customs officials, their clerks and 'turkmen' [sergeants], and slip them a little something or some money, they will also behave very courteously and will tax the goods that you later bring by them lower than their real value" (Blockmans, 244). By the mid-14th century, the Italian city-states were even trading with as distant partners as the Mongols.

Meanwhile, in Northern Europe, the Hanseatic League (also known as *Hansa*, and *Hanse*, 1356-1862) was formally founded as a multi-city trade league in 1356. Initially, a federation of North German towns and cities formed in the 12th century to facilitate trade and protect mutual interests, the league was centered in the German town of Lübeck and included other German principalities, which established trade centers ranging from Kievan Rus through the Netherlands, Scandinavia, and Britain. By the time of its formal founding, it had already established a monopoly on trade in the Baltic region through its center on Gotland, Sweden's largest island. From Gotland, the Hanseatic League was able to make firm trade alliances and secure even more lucrative arrangements with other nations.

Precisely how early the league was formed is unknown, but it was most likely during the reign of Henry the Lion, Duke of Saxony and Bavaria (reign 1142-1180), who mandated laws for the protection of foreign traders in the Baltic region, specifically those from Gotland. Henry's laws encouraged freer trade but may have also threatened the security of the merchants of Northern Germany. Whenever the league first formed, it was already in operation by 1241, when Hamburg and Lübeck formed an official partnership that monopolized trade in salt and fish. Prior to the rise of the Hanseatic League, the nobility and the Church held so much power that the merchant class was essentially at their mercy, and their economic status was little better than that of a landlocked serf. The league was powerful enough to challenge the social structure by establishing *kontors* (counting houses or offices) in cities ranging from Bruges to London, Novgorod, and beyond, all of which brought them incredible wealth.

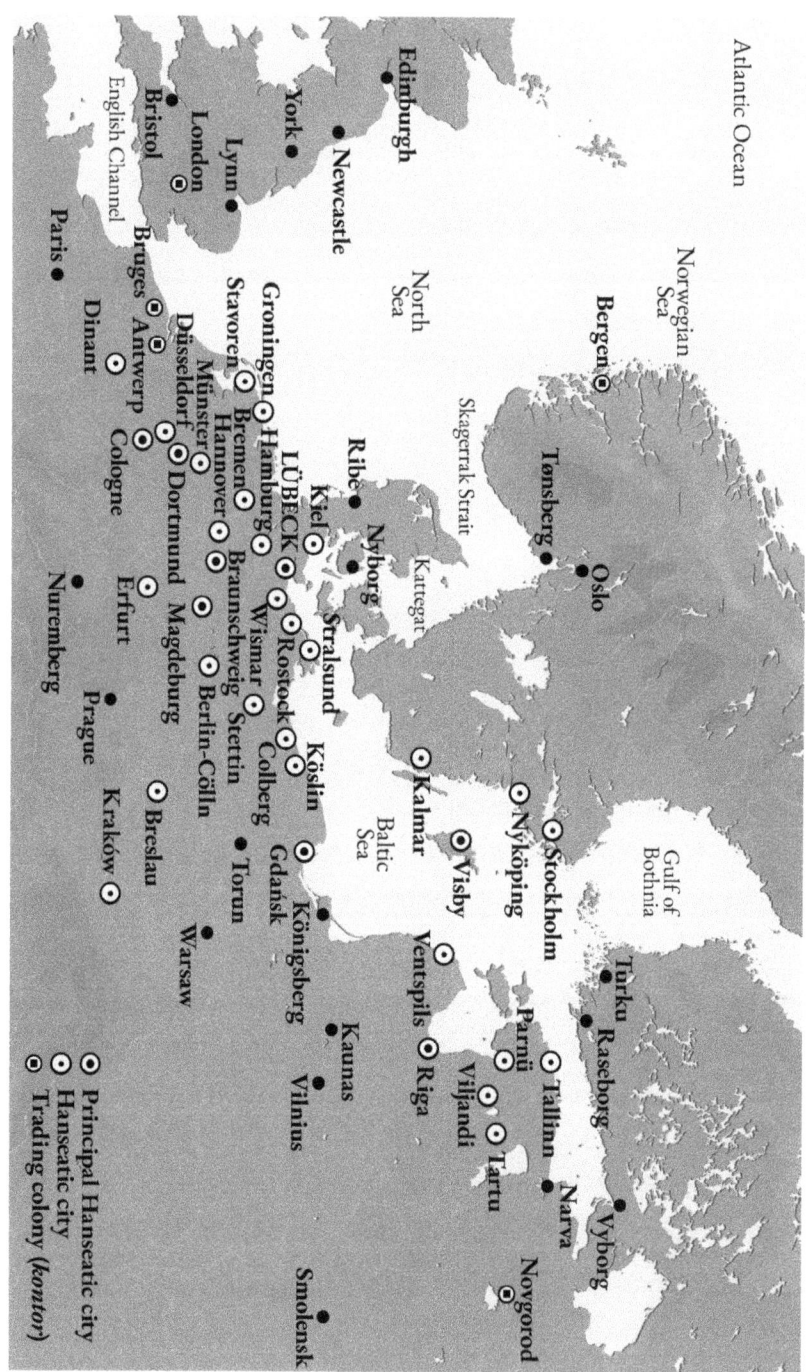

6.4 *The Hanseatic League: Trade in the North and Baltic Seas circa 1400*

The league was able to give a voice to the merchant class via financial success. In the 14th century, the league had approximately 80 members, trading in copper, fish, flax, furs, grain, honey, iron, resin, salt, and textiles, among other goods. Members swore to abide by the Lübeck Law, which stipulated that each would protect and defend another in the league, placing their personal armies at each other's disposal.

Warfare

In medieval warfare, sieges of fortified cities and castles were more common than field battles. Castles and fortified cities offered protection to both the local population and armed forces, presenting an array of defensive features, which, in turn, led to innovations in weapons, siege engine technology, and strategies. From the 12th to 15th century, medieval warfare became very much a case of 'win the siege, win the war,' especially when targets were administrative centers or occupied a position of particular strategic importance.

The particular weak point of any defensive fortification was its main access door, but this came to be protected by a tower on either side with additional safety measures such as a drawbridge, portcullis, and 'murder holes' (holes above the doorway through which missiles and burning liquid could be thrown down). The gate might also receive extra protection with a barbican—a short piece of fortified wall built in front of it.

City gates were such substantial structures that many still stand today across Europe, from York to Florence. The outer walls of a castle (and sometimes even smaller cities) were protected by a moat (dry or wet) and, wherever possible, built on a rise in the land. In the Low Countries, where this was often not possible, the moat was made extremely wide. Walls were given towers at regular intervals to provide more scathing fire from archers, and the construction of wooden hoardings, which overhung the top of the wall, was for the same purpose. Round towers were better than square ones because they eliminated the firing blind spot of the corners and made them more stable and more difficult to dismantle from the base by enemy sappers or miners (who preferred easy corners to swing their picks at). Walls and towers were given a protective covering of stone at their bases (a talus) to impede the enemy climbing them, make undermining more difficult, and give objects thrown down an unpredictable bounce into the enemy ranks.

Safe behind the walls were archers and crossbowmen who could fire missiles through narrow window slits. The defenders also had catapults to hurl large boulders into the besiegers and damage their siege engines and catapults. When all the conventional weapons ran out, the defenders then resorted to whatever they could hurl down on the attackers, such as burning oil, flaming logs, spikes, and rocks. Faced with all of these defenses, the attackers had to consider carefully how to best go about besieging a castle or city. The simplest method was to encircle the target, cutting off its supply of food and reinforcements, and then wait for thirst and starvation to drive the defenders to a surrender. Torching any surrounding farmland and villages was a wise move, too, just in case the defenders were able to smuggle in supplies. Naturally, with a large castle or a city, this could take several months to have its desired effect. Sieges were expensive, and troops might be on a fixed term of service (40 days in English armies, for example), so time was also a factor to consider. In addition, the campaign season was typically limited to spring and summer, and the longer the attackers remained cooped up in their own camp, the more prone they were to attack from a relief force, disease, or even starvation themselves from lack of supplies in a hostile territory.

A more active approach than permanent encirclement was to try to destroy a particular part of the defensive walls. One attack strategy was to pound the wall with huge boulders fired by catapults (or mangonels, which used the torsion of twisted ropes and were based on ancient designs) and trebuchets. Flaming missiles that had been covered in pitch could set fire to the wooden buildings of a town or those within a castle's bailey. Some catapult missiles were containers made from wood, terracotta, or glass containing a flammable liquid such as animal fat, which were designed to smash on impact like Molotov cocktails. Another artillery device was the ballista, a very large crossbow, which fired thick wooden arrows or heavy iron bolts with great accuracy. Not much use at penetrating stone, it was used more by the defenders, as it had the advantage of being more compact than a catapult, and so three could fit into a single floor of a tower. The earliest depiction of gunpowder artillery is a 1326 English manuscript, which shows a cannon on a wooden stand ready to fire a metal bolt. Such early firearms, sometimes known as bombards, were usually more lethal to the people firing them, such was the lack of knowledge and design know-how of the medieval period in this area.

If a castle or city did fall, then it was common practice to sack, pillage, burn, rape, and murder. Acts of clemency toward defenders who had not surrendered when they had had the chance at the start of the proceedings were the exception, not the rule. Churches and members of religious orders were, though, expected to be left unharmed. Some slaughters were deliberate to send a strong message to the enemy during a wider war, such as the massacre ordered by Edward III of England after the fall of the French city of Caen in 1346.

The battle was part of the Hundred Years' War (1337-1453), an intermittent conflict between England and France lasting 116 years. It began principally because Edward III (reign 1327-1377) and Philip VI (reign 1328-1350) escalated a dispute over feudal rights in Gascony to a battle for the French crown. The Hundred Years' War is traditionally divided into three phases.

The Edwardian War: 1337-1360
The Caroline War: 1369-1389
The Lancastrian War: 1415-1453

Edward III was able to make a strong claim to the French crown via his mother, Isabella. Whether or not this claim was a serious one or merely an excuse for invading France is debatable. Certainly, on paper, Edward did have a point. The current French king was Philip VI, who had succeeded his cousin Charles IV (reign 1322-1328), even if, when Charles had died, it was Edward who was his closest male relative, being Charles's nephew and the eldest surviving grandson of Philip IV (reign 1285-1314). The English king had not pressed his claim at the time because he was a minor, and the French nobility, discounting the legitimacy of inheritance through the female line, had naturally preferred a Frenchman as their ruler. However, by the mid-1330s, Edward changed his strategy, perhaps irked by the technicality that, as the Duke of Gascony, the English king was actually a vassal of the French king. Gascony was a useful trade partner of England's, with wool and grain being exported and wine imported. When the French king confiscated Gascony to the French crown in 1337 and raided the south coast of England the year after—an attack that included the destruction of Southampton—Edward was presented with the perfect excuse to start a war.

6.5 The Hundred Years' War in 1360

Edward got the ball rolling by declaring himself King of France in a ceremony in Ghent in January 1340. In addition, the king showed off his newly quartered coat of arms—the three lions of the Plantagenets—to now include the golden fleur-de-lis of France. The Low Countries were important trading partners with England while other allies included rivals to Philip VI, such as Charles II, king of Navarre (reign 1349-1387), and the Gascon counts of Armagnac.

One of the first major actions of the war was in June 1340, when a French invasion fleet was sunk by an English fleet at Sluys in the Scheldt estuary (Low Countries). This was followed up in 1345 with the capture of Gascony and invasion of Normandy, where the strategy of *chevauchées* was employed, that is striking terror into local populations by burning crops, raiding stocks, and permitting general looting in the hope of drawing the French king into open battle. The strategy worked, and the French army, unable to find a response to the combination of English archers and knights fighting on foot, suffered a heavy defeat at the Battle of Crécy in August 1346. Philip was far from beaten, though, and cleverly called on his Scottish allies to invade Northern England in the hope that this would force Edward to withdraw from France. David II of Scotland (reign 1329-1371) duly obliged and invaded England in October 1346, but he was defeated by an English army at the Battle of Neville's Cross (17 October 1346). As an extra bonus, King David was captured and only released in 1357 as part of the Treaty of Berwick, where the Scots paid a ransom and a 10-year truce was agreed between the two countries.

In 1347, Calais was captured, but the arrival of the Black Death interrupted the hostilities. The next major victory was another English one, once again against a much larger French army, this time at the Battle of Poitiers in September 1356. Here, the English army was led by Edward's able son, Edward the Black Prince (1330-1376).

The defeated King John II of France (reign 1350-1364) was captured at Poitiers and was detained for four years. The 1360 Treaty of Brétigny was then signed between England and France, which recognized Edward's claim to 25% of France (mostly in the north and southwest) in return for Edward renouncing his claim to the French crown.

The Peace of Brétigny ended in 1369 when the new French king, Charles the Wise (reign 1364-1380), began to grab back in earnest what his predecessors had lost. Charles did this by avoiding open battle, concentrating on harassment, and relying on the safety of his castles when required. Charles also had a superior navy to the English and so was able to make frequent raids on the south coast of England. Most of Aquitaine was grabbed in 1372, an English fleet was defeated off La Rochelle in the same year, and, by 1375, the only lands left in France belonging to the English Crown were Calais and a slice of Gascony.

In 1389, a truce was declared once again, and relations further improved when, on 12 March 1396, Richard II of England married Isabella of France, the daughter of Charles VI of France. The union cemented a two-decade truce between the two countries.

Bibliography

Allmand, C. *The Hundred Years War.* Cambridge University Press, 1988.

Anonymous. *Chambers Dictionary of World History.* Chambers Harrap, 2018.

Bennett, J. *The Oxford Handbook of Women and Gender in Medieval Europe.* Oxford University Press, 2016.

Blockmans, W. *Introduction to Medieval Europe 300-1500.* Routledge, 2017.

Boccaccio, G. *The Decameron.* Translated by M. Musa and P. Bondanella. Penguin Books, 2003.

Bossy, J. *Christianity in the West 1400-1700.* Oxford University Press, 2010.

Brooke, R. and C. *Popular Religion in the Middle Ages.* Barnes & Noble Books, 1996.

Cannon, J. *The Kings and Queens of Britain.* Oxford University Press, 2009.

Cantor, N.F. *In the Wake of the Plague: The Black Death and the World it Made.* Simon & Schuster, 2015.

Cantor, N.F. *The Civilization of the Middle Ages.* Harper Perennial, 1994.

Charles River Editors. *John Wycliffe and Jan Hus.* Independently published, 2020.

Chaucer, G. *The Riverside Chaucer.* Edited by L.D. Benson. Houghton Mifflin, 1986.

Cohn, S., Jr. "Plague violence and abandonment from the Black Death to the early modern period." Accessed 13 Apr 2020. https://shs.cairn.info/article/E_ADH_134_0039?lang=en

Creighton, O.H. *Castles and Landscapes.* Equinox Publishing Limited, 2004.

Crouch, D. *Medieval Britain, c.1000-1500.* Cambridge University Press, 2017.

Curry, A. *The Hundred Years' War.* Osprey Publishing, 2002.

Dante Alighieri. *The Divine Comedy.* Translated by J. Ciardi. W.W. Norton, 1977.

Davies, N. *Europe: A History.* Oxford University Press, 2014.

Deanesley, M. *A History of the Medieval Church 590-1500.* Obscure Press, 2010.

De Rougemont, D. *Love in the Western World.* Princeton University Press, 1983.

DesOrmeaux, A.L. "The Black Death and its Effect on 14th and 15th Century Art." *Louisiana State University Master's Thesis* (2007).

Dols, M.W. "The Comparative Communal Responses to the Black Death in Muslim and Christian Societies." *Department of History, California State University*: 1-22.

Geary, P.J. "Peasant Religion in Medieval Europe." *Cahiers d'Extrême-Asie*, 12 (2001): 185-209.

Gies, F. *Life in a Medieval City.* Harper Perennial, 2016.

Gies, F. *Life in a Medieval Village.* Harper Perennial, 2016.

Gies, J. *Life in a Medieval Castle.* Harper Perennial, 2015.

Gies, F. and J. *Women in the Middle Ages.* Harper Perennial, 1978.

Gravett, C. *Medieval Siege Warfare.* Osprey Publishing, 1990.

Holmes, G. (ed). *The Oxford History of Medieval Europe.* Oxford University Press, 2002.

Jackson, W. "The Use of Unicorn Horn in Medicine." Accessed 11 Apr 2020. https://www.pharmaceutical-journal.com/news-and-analysis/features/the-use-of-unicorn-horn-in-medicine/20013625.article?firstPass=false

Jones, D. *The Plantagenets.* Penguin Books, 2014.

Keen, M. *The Penguin History of Medieval Europe.* Penguin Books, 1991.

Kohn, G.C. *Encyclopedia of Plague and Pestilence.* Facts on File, 2007.

Legan, J.A. "The Medical Response to the Black Death." *James Madison University Scholarly Commons* (Spring 2015): 1-77.

Leyser, H. *Medieval Women.* Orion Pub Co, 2002.

Loyn, H.R. *The Middle Ages: A Concise Encyclopedia.* Thames & Hudson, 1991.

Lynch, K. *The High Medieval Dream Vision.* Stanford University Press, 1988.

MacCulloch, D. *The Reformation: A History.* Penguin Books, 2005.

Matthews, W. *Later Medieval English Prose.* Goldentree Books, 1963.

McDowall, D. *An Illustrated History of Britain.* Pearson Education Ltd, 1989.

Mayer, J. "The Origin Of The Word 'Quarantine.'" Accessed 11 Apr 2020. https://www.sciencefriday.com/articles/the-origin-of-the-word-quarantine/

Nardo, D. *Living in the Middle Ages.* Thompson/Gale Publishers, 2004.

Nicolle, D. *Medieval Siege Weapons (1): Western Europe AD 585–1385.* Osprey Publishing, 2002.

Nutton, V. *Ancient Medicine.* Routledge, 2012.

OED. "Feudalism." Accessed 19 Mar 2020. Oxford Dictionaries Online, now archived. https://en.oxforddictionaries.com/definition/feudalism

Papal Encyclicals Online. "The Unam Sanctum." Complete Text. Accessed 20 Jun 2019. https://www.papalencyclicals.net/bon08/b8unam.htm

Phillips, C. *The Complete Illustrated Guide to the Kings & Queens of Britain.* Lorenz Books, 2006.

Phillips, C. *The Complete Illustrated History of Knights & The Golden Age of Chivalry.* Southwater, 2017.

Phillips, C. *The Medieval Castle Manual.* Haynes Publishing UK, 2018.

Pounds, N.J.G. *The Medieval Castle in England and Wales.* Cambridge University Press, 1993.

Power, E. *Medieval Women.* Cambridge University Press, 1996.

Rollason, D. *Early Medieval Europe 300-1050.* Routledge, 2012.

Ross, J.B. and M.M. McLaughlin. *The Portable Medieval Reader.* Penguin Classics, 1990.

Rothero, C. *Armies of Crécy and Poitiers.* Osprey Publishing, 1981.

Rublack, U. *The Oxford Handbook of the Protestant Reformations.* Oxford University Press, 2019.

Saul, N. *The Oxford Illustrated History of Medieval England.* Oxford University Press, 2001.

Schevill, F. *Medieval and Renaissance Florence.* Harper Torch Books, 1991.

Singman, J.L. *The Middle Ages: Everyday Life in Medieval Europe.* Sterling, 2013.

Stadtbund Die Hanse. "The Story of the Hanseatic League." Accessed 19 Mar 2020. hanse.org/en/hanse-historic/the-history-of-the-hanseatic-league/

Starkey, D. *Crown and Country.* HarperPress, 2011.

Stewart, C. et al. *The Reformers: Biographical Sketches of Twelve of the Greatest Men in the History of the Church.* Millennial Word Publications, 2018.

Trachtenberg, J. *The Devil and the Jews.* Harper Torchbooks, 2002. Trapp, J.B. *Medieval English Literature.* Oxford University Press, 2002.

Tuchman, B.W. *A Distant Mirror: The Calamitous 14th Century*. Random House Trade Paperbacks, 1987.

Willard, C.C. *Christine de Pizan: Her Life and Works*. Persea, 1990.

Wilson, D. *The Plantagenet Chronicles 1154-1485*. Metro Books, 2020.

Wise Bauer, S. *The History of the Medieval World*. W. W. Norton & Company, 2010.

Wheelis, M. "Biological Warfare at the 1346 Siege of Caffa." Accessed 15 Apr 2020. https://wwwnc.cdc.gov/eid/article/8/9/01-0536_article

Image Credits

6.1 Feudal Society in Medieval Europe. Infographic © Simeon Netchev

6.2 Spread of the Black Death. Map © Simeon Netchev

6.3 Pope Boniface VIII, statue by Arnolfo di Cambio. Photo by Sailko, Opera del Duomo Museum, Italy CC BY 2.5, https://commons.wikimedia.org/wiki/File:Opera_del_duomo_(FI),_arnolfo_di_cambio,_Bonifacio_VIII_,_1298_circa,_03.JPG

6.4 The Hanseatic League: Trade in the North and Baltic Seas Circa 1400. Map © Simeon Netchev

6.5 The Hundred Years' War in 1360. Map © Simeon Netchev

NORTH AMERICA

BY JOSHUA J. MARK AND JAMES B. WIENER

PRIOR TO THE ARRIVAL of Europeans, the Native Americans lived as autonomous nations (also known as tribes) across the continent. They are believed to have migrated into the region between 40,000 and 14,000 years ago, developing into separate nations with distinct and sophisticated cultures and spreading from Alaska through modern-day Canada and the lower United States. The earliest periods of migration, settlement, and development are defined by archaeological evidence (spearheads, tools, monumental structures) from sites throughout North America and are most often referred to by the following terms.

Paleoindian-Clovis culture: circa 40,000 to circa 14,000 BCE
Dalton-Folsom culture: circa 8500-7900 BCE
Archaic period: circa 8000-1000 BCE
Woodland period: circa 500 BCE to circa 1100 CE
Mississippian culture: circa 1100-1540 CE

The cultures that developed by the 14th century were distinct from one another but shared a worldview that included belief in a higher power and disembodied spirits, the value of community over individual needs, reciprocity in interaction with the environment and each other, the importance of ritual and tradition, the practice of warfare and slavery, and conservation of resources. Women were highly respected in the communities and frequently served as leaders or advisors in government.

There was no uniform development of every Native culture at the same time everywhere. Some nations continued to use the technology and adhere to the traditions associated with the Woodland period, while others had developed in ways that characterize the Mississippian culture. Some of the nations were nomadic or semi-nomadic hunter-gatherers for longer than others, who built large urban complexes and engaged in agricultural pursuits and trade, but the latter should not be regarded as more 'highly developed' than the former. The people of the Great Plains continued the hunter-gatherer lifestyle longer than those on the East Coast simply because the terrain and game were better suited in that region.

Mississippian Culture

The Mississippian culture is so called because the people primarily lived in the Mississippi River Valley, but they also established cities and villages in the Ohio River Valley, Tennessee River Valley, and elsewhere, ranging from the northeast down to modern-day Louisiana and out toward Indiana. The Mississippian culture is often cited as though it were the beginning of monumental mound-building, but mounds were built thousands of years before in North America. Watson Brake Mounds date to circa 3500 BCE, and Poverty Point to circa 1700-1100 BCE, with the Mississippian culture's mounds following.

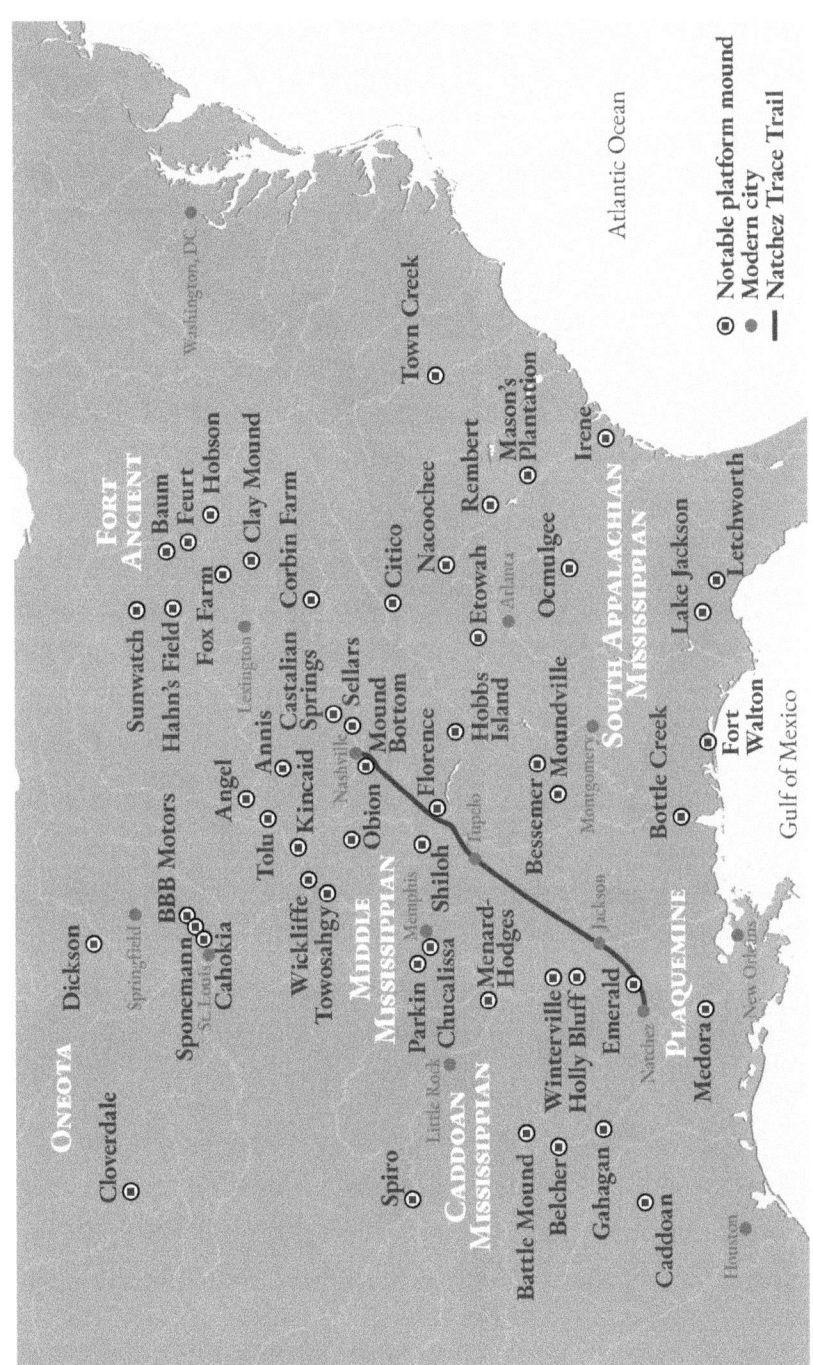

7.1 Mississippian cultures

The Mississippian culture has become the best known and most closely associated with mound-building, however, this is owing to the proliferation of mounds prior to that period and the skill of the people of the Adena culture (circa 800 BCE to 1 CE) and the Hopewell culture (circa 100 BCE to 500 CE) who perfected mound-building and provided the model for later works such as the famous Mississippian Cahokia Mounds and Moundville. Many mounds were constructed during the Archaic period and the Woodland period, but these differed from the later Mississippian culture sites, such as Etowah, in that those of the Adena were conical, while those of the Hopewell were either effigy or flat-topped mounds. The Mississippian culture borrowed from both traditions in the creation of their mounds, which were influenced, at least in part, by the religious beliefs spread throughout the region by the Hopewell culture.

Native American religion took the form of animism—the belief that everything is animated by a spirit that lives on after the physical body has died, and that all things are connected in an intricate web of reciprocity—and it is thought the construction of the mounds, at Etowah and elsewhere, was an expression of this belief. The people devoted themselves to the systematic removal of soil from one place to another for the greater good of the community in honoring the spirits of a given place and raising their chief and priests to a higher level, closer to the sun, which was considered a god. This could be considered an act of reciprocity in that the people were providing a 'home' for the spirits, focusing the energy of those spirits for the good of the community, and then giving back to the spirits through ritualistic ceremonies.

It is thought that the Mississippian peoples built their mounds to focus spiritual power in a central location in their communities. The priests or priest-kings who performed rituals on these mounds were believed to be able to harness this power to protect the people and ensure regular rainfall and bountiful harvests. To commune with the spirits and gods, the people needed to alter how they experienced the world around them, and this was accomplished through rituals, which might have included the act of mound-building, but certainly involved the mounds themselves, which elevated participants. Hallucinogens in the form of especially strong tobacco are also thought to have played a part in this communion. Tobacco was one of the crops raised, along with corn, beans, and squash, which were used in paying laborers for building mounds and other tasks, as well as in trade with other communities, often across vast distances.

Etowah Mounds

Etowah Mounds, near Cartersville, Georgia, USA, are among the best representations of the work of the Mississippian culture, featuring three flat-topped mounds surrounding the central plaza. The original name of the city is unknown; the present designation of Etowah means 'town' in the language of the Muscogee Creek Native Americans. The city was built in three phases, during the different periods of the Mississippian culture.

Early Mississippian: circa 1000-1200
Middle Mississippian: circa 1200-1375
Late Mississippian: circa 1375-1540

The city is thought to have developed from an earlier village on the site associated with the Swift Creek culture, who were mound builders of the Middle Woodland period and created the Leake Mounds three kilometres (two miles) west of Etowah. The Swift Creek peoples, like many early mound builders, were hunter-gatherers who devoted a significant amount of time to constructing their mounds and then abandoned them and moved on. This certainly seems to be the case with the Leake Mounds and at Etowah as well, since artifacts found on-site suggest the earlier Swift Creek village was abandoned circa 600. Whether the Swift Creek people began any of the mounds currently at Etowah is unknown, as only one mound has been excavated to any significant degree, but this is a possibility. The location and height of the mounds seem to honor the chief, religious ceremonies, and the departed in descending order of largest-to-smallest mounds, although this claim is speculative, and the size may have nothing to do with the significance.

Mound A: site of the chief's residence, 19 meters (63 feet) tall and once topped by four buildings surrounding a courtyard.

Mound B: site of religious rituals, 7.6 meters (25 feet) tall and seems to have had temples on it.

Mound C: a burial mound, rises 3 meters (10 feet) tall and also had a temple or chapel at the top.

Mound A is situated directly before the central plaza of the city, with the other two mounds off to the side. The chief of the community was early on known by the title 'Brother of the Sun' and was thought to be able to commune directly with the sun god. His mound at Etowah is the highest to elevate him closer to his 'brother' in the sky and enable more direct communication. The ceremonies enacted on Mound B may have been funerary rituals associated with Mound C, but this is unclear.

The lower class lived in wood and thatch homes surrounding the plaza and the mounds, and there seem to have been industrial and commercial structures in that area as well. To date, 140 structures have been identified at the site. A palisade, a wooden stockade fence, and a moat encircled the site on three sides, while the fourth side was open to the Etowah River. The palisade featured watchtowers spaced at intervals of 24 meters (80 feet) from the opening on the river in a semicircle ending back at the river on the far side.

The people engaged in long-distance trade, which brought raw materials not sourced locally, such as marble, which was used to create the famous Etowah Statues, paired figures of a man and woman thought to have been used as effigies in religious rituals honoring the peoples' ancestors. Daily life centered around hunting, fishing, and tending crops, as well as working on the mounds, religious ceremonies, and leisure activities.

Among the most popular of the latter were ball games, one of which resembled modern-day lacrosse and the other a game called 'chunkey' in which players would throw carved sticks toward a rolling disk, trying to have their sticks land as close to the disk's final resting place as possible; the player whose stick was closet scored the point and the first to reach twelve points was the winner.

7.2 Etowah stone statues, 1250-1375, Georgia

Cahokia

Another nation, considered distinct from both the Adena and Hopewell, built the city of Cahokia (in modern-day Collinsville, Illinois), the largest urban center in North America prior to the 18th century, which flourished between circa 650 and circa 1350. Cahokia may have developed through an appeal by the priestly class to neighboring communities to come and participate in the construction of the city's enormous ritualistic mound—known as Monks Mound today—as well as the other 119 mounds used for other purposes.

The original name of this city has been lost, but at its height, it had a population of over 15,000 people. Cahokia was a grand city with a wide central plaza, shops, ball fields, a solar calendar, residences for the lower class and others for the elite, and long fields of corn and other crops. The city seems to have initially grown organically as more people moved into the region, but the central structures—the great mounds which characterize the site—were carefully planned and executed and would have involved a large work force laboring daily for at least ten years to create even the smallest of the 120 that once rose above the city (of which 80 are still extant). It was most likely the construction of Monks Mound that brought people from other communities to the new city. Since the Cahokians had no beasts of burden and no carts, all of the earth had to be hand-carried. As the mound contains approximately 814,000 cubic yards (622,348 cubic meters) of earth, this would have been a monumental building project requiring a large labor force. After Monks Mound was completed, or while it was ongoing (as it is thought to have been built in stages), other mounds were constructed as well as temples such as the one that once topped Monks Mound. Some of these mounds had residences of the upper class built on their flat tops, others served as burial sites (as in the case of the famous tomb of the ruler known as Birdman, buried with 50 sacrificial victims), and the purpose of still others is unknown.

The city flourished through long-distance trade routes running in every direction, which allowed for urban development. There would have been workers on the mounds, merchants in the plaza, copper workers making plates, bowls, and pipes, basket weavers at work, women tending the children and the crops, and loggers going back and forth between the city and the forest harvesting trees for lumber for the construction of homes, temples, other structures, and the stockade that ran around the city, presumably to protect it from floods. Astrologer-priests would have been at work at the solar calendar near Monks Mound, known as Woodhenge, a wooden circle of 48 posts with a single post in the center, which was used to chart the heavens and, as at many ancient sites, mark the sunrise at the vernal and autumnal equinoxes as well as the summer and winter solstice.

The success of Cahokia led to its eventual downfall and abandonment, however, as overpopulation depleted resources and efforts to improve the peoples' lives wound up making them worse. The city's water supply was a creek (Canteen Creek) that the Cahokians diverted so it joined another (modern-day Cahokia Creek), bringing more water to the city to supply the growing population. The merging of the two streams also allowed woodcutters to send their logs downstream to the city instead of having to carry them further and further distances as the forest receded due to harvesting. With tree cover and root systems dwindling upland from the city, heavy rains had nothing to absorb them and so ran into the creeks and streams, causing flooding, especially of the now-merged creeks, which destroyed crops. The stockade built to protect the city from floods was useless since the merged creeks brought the water directly into the city, and so homes were also damaged. Recognizing their mistake, the Cahokians began replanting the forest, but it was too little too late. The clergy, who were held responsible for the peoples' misfortunes as they had obviously failed to interpret the will of the gods and placate them, initiated reforms, abandoning the secretive rituals on top of Monks Mound for full transparency in front of the populace on the plateau, but this effort also came too late and was an ineffective gesture. The clergy, who were all of the upper class and had established a hereditary system of control, seem to have tried to save face and retain power instead of admitting they had somehow failed and seeking forgiveness, and this, coupled with the other difficulties, seems to have led to civil unrest.

An earthquake at some point in the 13th century toppled buildings, and, at the same time, overpopulation led to unsanitary conditions and the spread of disease. Some scholars now believe that people were repeatedly invited to take up residence in the city to replace those who had died, and graves containing obvious victims of human sacrifice suggest that the people were becoming desperate for help from their gods. Evidence of civil war or at least large-scale social unrest suggests some sort of violent clash circa 1250, and although attempts were made to repair the damage done by floods and the earthquake, whatever central authority had maintained order previously seems to have fallen apart; by circa 1350, the city had been abandoned.

Moundville

The second largest 'mound builder' site preserved in the USA after Cahokia is known today as Moundville in Hale County, Alabama, which flourished between circa 1100 and circa 1450. Both cities had a large mound (Mound A at Moundville and Monks Mound at Cahokia) dedicated to religious/political purposes, and the two cities may have traded with each other but are thought to have been founded and developed by two different cultures. One of the major differences between them is that the elite of the Moundville people lived and buried their dead on the mounds they created as a matter of course, while, at Cahokia, only some mounds were used as graves or to support residences. Other differences include the types of crafts produced and how Moundville, unlike Cahokia, was designed to specifically reflect the highly stratified social hierarchy of the community.

Moundville was a carefully designed and executed urban center in which the upper class lived in wood homes on the flat tops of the mounds overlooking a central plaza, while the lower classes lived in thatch huts below. The residential mounds alternated with burial mounds, although the deceased of the upper class were also buried on their home mound (which is how archaeologists have determined the mounds' purposes, through grave goods and types of burial). In the center of the plaza rose a large mound, now known as Mound A, which served as the site for religious rituals, and the whole city was surrounded by a wooden palisade on three sides, with the fourth side open to the river.

Mound A was built with a direct view of the river from its top, suggesting a connection between all four elements of earth, air, fire, and water in religious rituals. The homes of the upper class were then built on the tops of the other mounds, facing Mound A. The middle and lower classes were buried in simple graves near their homes around the plaza with grave goods such as tools and rough ceramics. The upper and ruling class deceased were interred on the mounds with valuables such as shells, smoothed stones, copper implements, high-grade ceramics, and copper axes. These axes are thought to have been symbols of authority, rank, and political power used in rituals, as they appear unused and, made of copper, are too soft to have been used effectively in warfare or lumber harvesting. The grave goods of the elite came from long-distance trade with other communities, but some of the copper artifacts were most likely made on-site.

The plaza was artificially created, filled, and leveled before the construction of the mounds, which were built in stages and range in height from under 3 meters (10 feet) to over 15 meters (50 feet). The small ponds and lakes one finds at the modern-day site are the pits the Natives harvested soil from to build the mounds that drew people of neighboring communities to settle there as laborers, adding to the population of over 1,000 (which eventually may have reached over 3,000). Moundville's extensive corn crop created a surplus food supply, which was used not only in trade but to pay laborers' wages.

In time, more people seem to have come to the city for spiritual purposes as it became known as a religious and cultural center. This is evidenced by finds suggesting a population increase, and artifacts such as stone pipes, associated with religious ritual. Moundville seems to have been thriving until circa 1300 when the mounds began going unused and rituals on Mound A between circa 1300-1450 slowed and then ceased. No reason for the abandonment of Moundville has been universally agreed upon, and it is possible that it was due to a perceived failure of the priestly class to propitiate the spirits and provide good harvests, health, and prosperity. It is also possible that, as at Cahokia, overpopulation resulted in the depletion of resources.

Spiro Mounds

The 14th century also saw the population decline at the Spiro Mounds in modern-day Oklahoma. The mounds, twelve of which are extant today, were constructed in four phases and completed prior to circa 1250. Nine of the mounds surround a central plaza with a larger mound (Brown Mound) in the center, which served a religious/ceremonial purpose. These ceremonies seem to have centered on the funerary rituals of the community leaders and members of the clergy (who were often, though not always, the same).

The two other extant mounds (Craig Mound and the Great Mortuary) were used for burial and had internal cavities built purposefully for the preservation of various artifacts such as feather bonnets and headdresses, fur and feather coats, and statuary of wood or copper, as well as other pieces. Craig Mound was looted and partially destroyed between 1933 and 1935 by a group who purchased temporary rights from the landowner to excavate and then, when they had finished, purposefully blew up the central chamber of the mound for unknown reasons. Artifacts looted at that time have largely been lost to the antiquities market.

Natchez Trace

There is ample evidence that the Mississippian cultures engaged in local and long-distance trade with each other, establishing well-worn routes between the cities, acceptable forms of barter, and production and distribution methods. The path now known as the Natchez Trace Trail was only one of a network of such routes through the woodlands that different Native American communities used in trade. Like the famous Silk Road between Asia and Europe, the Natchez Trace, stretching 715 kilometers (444 miles) from Natchez, Mississippi, through northern Alabama, to Nashville, Tennessee, was never a single path (nor was it known as a 'trace' until the 18th century), but a series of trails. It is thought to have been formed thousands of years ago by wild animals moving through the woodlands. Bison are often cited as the prime agents in blazing these trails as they are thought to have traveled from modern-day Mississippi in a general northeasterly direction toward grazing areas and salt licks in Tennessee. The paths they made through the forests were then widened and smoothed by Native American hunting and trading parties.

Long-distance trade routes were initially enlarged and extended by the people of the Hopewell culture. They also spread their religious beliefs and practices, whether intentionally or simply through contact in trade, and the mounds that are found today along the Natchez Trace are understood as evidence of this. The Natchez were agriculturalists, growing corn, beans, and squash (among other crops) as well as hunting, fishing, and gathering their food supplies. They used their surplus in trade and used the Natchez Trace as their primary route, as evidenced by artifacts and the mounds still extant along that track today.

The early Natchez Native Americans built their central village (known today as Grand Village) in present-day Natchez, Mississippi, with the Great Sun's Mound in the center. This flat-topped mound provided the elevated area for the residence of the chief, known as the Great Sun, and believed to be the brother of the sun, giver of life. The chief's mound was created here, as at other mound sites, to elevate the chief closer to the sun for clearer communication and communion. Other mounds were built to the northeast along the trace, such as Emerald Mound (built circa 1250-1600). The mound sites were not all residences of chiefs or burial mounds, but also served as sacred ceremonial sites where rituals were performed, either on their tops or in plazas built at their bases. The rituals were informed by the Native American belief in animism—that all things have a soul and are dependent upon each other in a great web of interconnected reciprocity—and at the heart of animism was the concept of spiritual power. Everything was imbued with the energy of the Great Spirit (whatever name a given tribe knew this being as), who had breathed life into the world. As the people gave thanks and participated in rituals at the mound site, they gave energy to the spirit of the place (and, by extension, the Great Spirit) and received energy back in the form of plentiful harvests, abundant game, and nets overflowing with fish.

The Haudenosaunee Confederacy

Native American culture all over the continent was informed by the spiritual beliefs of the people, which held that all things were imbued with the same life force and deserved one's respect. Iroquois spirituality, just as other cultures, maintains the existence of a Great Spirit, the Creator God, who is assisted by other spirits, including Thunder (who brings rainstorms), the Four Thunders (who right wrongs), and the Three Sisters, who are the spirits of corn (maize), beans, and squash. Like other nations, the Iroquois saw life on earth as only one plane of existence, with higher realms above, which are just as real, if not more real, than this one. Each separate nation understood itself as part of every other, but this did not mean they always lived in peace or respected each other's territory. Wars were fought over water rights, to prevent outsiders from hunting in one's territory, for tribal prestige and power, and for captives who could be ransomed or enslaved. Common weapons were the bow and arrow (first developed during the Woodland period), spears, knives, and tomahawks. Some warriors also carried shields made of animal hide and wore breastplate armor of hide and animal bone. Scalps were taken from enemies killed in battle as trophies that encouraged personal prestige, respect, and social standing.

The nations that would form the Haudenosaunee Confederacy (the League of Peace and Power, also known as the Iroquois Confederacy) were constantly at war with each other until the Great Peacemaker, Dekanawida (De-Ka-Nah-Wi-Da), met Chief Hiawatha and established peace between the nations. The oral history was written down in the late 19th century and approved by the Council of the Confederacy in 1900. Although Dekanawida and Hiawatha are commonly cited as the ones who established the Haudenosaunee Confederacy, there was a third, Jigonhsasee, who appears in the history as the Chief Mother and became known as the Mother of Nations for the part she played. Jigonhsasee was an Iroquoian woman living near the path warriors used when going to and coming from battle. She became well-known among them for her hospitality and counsel, and so Dekanawida asked for her help in convincing the different nations to lay down their arms and unite in peace, living together in the same way a family would in a longhouse. After Dekanawida had taught Hiawatha and Jigonhsasee his precepts of peace, he left them to teach others.

The Haudenosaunee (meaning 'People of the Longhouse') Confederacy was formed in either 1142, 1390, or the 15th century (primary sources do not agree on a fixed date) and united the five nations of the Cayuga, Mohawk, Oneida, Onondaga, and Seneca.

After 1715 (conditionally), and then after 1722, the Tuscarora joined as the sixth nation. These six came to be called Iroquois by French traders and explorers, though they continue to refer to themselves as Haudenosaunee. The Haudenosaunee Confederacy's government is the Grand Council of 50 chiefs who represent the bands (clans) that make up each nation, all of whom are Iroquoian-speaking and so united by language and culture, though the various nations have different stories, myths, and legends.

The Iroquois lived in longhouses sided with tree bark, which could be as long as 45 meters (150 feet) and 8 meters (25 feet) across. As with many Native peoples of North America, the men were responsible for hunting, making war, defending the village, making tools, and sitting on the governmental council. The Iroquois follow a matriarchal system, and so the family line passes through the women. Women sat in their own councils whose decisions influenced those of the Grand Council, raised the children, tended to crops, made clothing, managed trade, and built the longhouses. While the people of the Northeastern Woodlands lived in longhouses, homes differed by region and the needs of the people. The hunter-gatherers of the Great Plains favored portable homes, the teepee, made of buffalo skin; the Inuit built igloos and large tents of animal hide, and the Pueblos made their homes of sun-dried brick.

Homolovi

Homolovi or Homolovi State Park contains the ruins of eight pre-Columbian Ancestral Puebloan (Anasazi) and Hopi pueblos in addition to some 300 other remains and petroglyphs. Homolovi lies within sight of the Little Colorado River in a floodplain, northeast of Winslow, Arizona, in the United States. Archaeologists believe that Ancestral Puebloan peoples and the ancestors of the Hopi Tribe once occupied these settlements, which spread out along a 32-kilometer (20-mile) corridor on the Little Colorado River, at different intervals of time from circa 1250 to 1425. Two pueblos—Homolovi I and Homolovi II—each contained more than 1,000 rooms in ancient times, and 40 ceremonial kivas are scattered throughout the park.

There were two periods of inhabitation of Homolovi prior to the construction of the pueblos in the 13th and 14th centuries: an early period from circa 600 to 900 and a middle period from 1000 to 1225. When favorable climatic conditions existed in the 11th and 12th centuries, Indigenous peoples built small pit houses as opposed to large-scale constructions made of adobe. These earlier occupations of the area around Homolovi appear short-lived and sporadic, lasting around a decade or two. This pattern of periodic settlement and abandonment is likely due to changing local environmental conditions and the Little Colorado River. Depending on the year, the river could be bone-dry due to lack of rain or prone to flooding due to heavy snowfalls near the river's headwaters. It is known that the Little Colorado River was flooded regularly in the early 1200s and that the decades leading up to the 13th century were wet.

It is clear from archaeological excavations that there is no overlap in terms of ceramics or stratigraphy between these periods and the period in which the Ancestral Puebloans dwelt at Homolovi. Homolovi had no human population by the middle of the 1200s, and the newcomers who entered Homolovi at the end of the 13th century were migrants from what is now the Hopi Mesas in Arizona. These newcomers settled the Homolovi's floodplain on the Little Colorado River, eking a living based on farming. It is not exactly known why they came to farm and settle at Homolovi, but it is probable that they did so because of a population influx at the Hopi

Mesas, as a result of human migration stemming from the collapse of larger Ancestral Puebloan settlements like Wupatki, Hovenweep, and Mesa Verde. Some anthropologists and archaeologists have suggested that the settlements at Homolovi were of high strategic value to the Ancestral Puebloans of the Hopi Mesas, hence their subsequent settlement and development.

Because Homolovi lay at a crossroads of cultural exchange between the Ancestral Puebloans, the Mogollon culture, and the Hohokam culture, trade stimulated community growth and brought wealth to Homolovi. The remains of ceramics, obsidian, and shells at Homolovi demonstrate that the ancient pueblos traded with members of the Sinagua culture, the Hohokam culture, and other Ancestral Puebloan peoples. Homolovi's Indigenous population cultivated cotton, which enriched the pueblos as this crop was grown primarily for the purposes of trade with surrounding communities. Beginning circa 1300-1350, the Ancestral Puebloans began to build pueblos, supporting a population numbering about 2,500 people by the late 1300s. Homolovi Pueblos II had over 1,200 rooms, making it the largest.

Excavations at Homolovi have shown that the Ancestral Puebloans hunted and perhaps sacrificed certain animals for ceremonial usage and that their placement in ritual spaces created a robust archaeological pattern. Archaeologists believe that changes in ritual animal use over time reflect the rise of the Kachina (also Katsina) religion around 1350.

The kachina is a spiritual entity and divine messenger of the Puebloan peoples, as well as the Hopi, Zuni, Tewa, and Keresan Tribes in what is the present-day Southwestern United States, but the genesis of the Kachina cult is shrouded in mystery. Various theories tie the Kachina cult and kachina dolls to ancient religious practices and rituals in Mesoamerica, while other ethnologists and anthropologists believe that the Kachina cult arose organically in the desert Southwest as a reaction against older Ancestral Puebloan traditions and religious beliefs in an epoch marked by extreme drought and subsequent population displacement.

The kachinas (plural also 'katsinam') function as spiritual guides or intermediaries between people and their gods within Puebloan religion. The word 'kachina' means 'life-bringer,' and various kachina rituals and ceremonies are believed to be essential in securing the growth of crops, the summer rains, and good health in an extreme climate. To survive in such harsh terrain, the Puebloan peoples and their neighbors developed elaborate rituals designed to garner spiritual assistance in achieving life's necessities. The kachinas, in turn, can be viewed as those divine entities that regulate the phases of their terrestrial existence. Kachinas are thus not gods, per se, but rather animistic and ancestral spirits. The Hopi, Zuni, and other Puebloan peoples venerate nearly a thousand different kinds of kachinas, which represent everything from wild animals and food to insects, plants, and even death itself.

Although settlement at Homolovi occurred during an era of considerable upheaval and migration in the ancient Southwest, there is a paucity of evidence for open conflict and social chaos at Homolovi as well as the region near the ruins. The relationship between the various pueblos at Homolovi appears to be peaceful, and unlike at other Ancestral Puebloan sites, archaeologists have not found burned remains, desecrated skeletal remains, but instead open plazas and accessible pueblos. This has led some scholars to theorize that Homolovi's settlement and subsequent abandonment had more to do with climatic change, economics, and new social habits. Homolovi's inhabitants appear to have quietly left their pueblos sometime around 1400 and returned to the communities at the Hopi Mesas.

7.3 Hopi kachina doll, wood and pigment, 1868-1900, Arizona

Pottery designs dating to the 14th century from Homolovi show definitive kachina-like imagery. Perishable materials found in caves in southern Arizona and New Mexico's Rio Grande Valley point to early evidence for the Kachina cult, and archaeologists have also discovered murals of supernatural figures on several kiva walls and blocks with images similar to kachinas as well. It seems probable that Mesoamerican beliefs and ritual practices came to the Southwest via Casas Grandes through trade.

Casas Grandes

Casas Grandes or Paquimé flourished due to its extensive trading networks between circa 1150/1200 and 1450 in the northwest of present-day Chihuahua, Mexico. The region had been inhabited by Indigenous peoples for thousands of years before the community at Casas Grandes began to coalesce into a sizable, organized community in the latter half of the 12th century. The early inhabitants were sedentary agriculturalists who built pithouses around open plazas, hunting wild game for food. Maize was the staple crop, but agave, mesquite beans, piñon, squash, and walnuts were also cultivated. Casas Grandes emerges as a dynamic polity and cultural center in a period immediately following a massive decline and dispersion in the populations of the Anasazi, Mogollon, and Hohokam between 1150 and 1300. While some scholars explain Casas Grandes' rapid rise to prominence via a series of migrations southward by inhabitants belonging to those cultures, others see a more localized origin for Casas Grandes' spectacular rise.

Casas Grandes maintained much stronger ties to Mesoamerica than either the Anasazi or Hohokam cultures—copper bells, beads, the shells of marine mollusks, and the skeletons and feathers of scarlet and soldier macaws all point to a network of close trading relationships between the inhabitants of Casas Grandes and the great cities of Mesoamerica. However, it should be noted that the inhabitants of Casas Grandes, in ways reminiscent of the Hohokam culture that flourished in what is now the US state of Arizona, utilized advanced irrigation techniques and underground reservoirs to ensure the flow of freshwater to the city's inhabitants. Architectural and artistic motifs reminiscent of the Anasazi and Mogollon cultures were also commonly employed.

Casas Grandes, in its heyday, contained 2,000 rooms, making it one of the largest prehistoric pueblo settlements. Its huge room blocks still rise to about 10-12 meters (33-39 feet) in height, and several structures are multiple stories in height. Inhabitants later erected carefully planned, sophisticated structures in a complex layout built from adobe; stonework is apparent as well in the lining of pits, which might have been introduced to Casas Grandes by Mesoamericans. The city includes platform mounds, vast plazas for public and mercantile use, specialized pens for the raising of macaws and turkeys, and two I-shaped ball courts constructed in a style similar to those found in Mesoamerica. There are also effigy mounds and ceremonial mounds at Casas Grandes. One ceremonial mound is shaped like a feathered serpent, and this sacred space might have been devoted to the Mesoamerican god Quetzalcóatl. Another is shaped like a turkey or some other kind of bird. One finds a sweat bath, private courtyards, graveyards, and multiple ceremonial storage spaces throughout Casas Grandes as well. Casas Grandes has T-shaped doorways and square colonnades just like the Anasazi sites in Chaco Canyon. However, unlike other sites in the desert Southwest, there are no kivas (ceremonial chambers built underground).

Casas Grandes was a rich and likely cosmopolitan city ruled by a priestly elite, in which it can be presumed that many inhabitants spoke several languages, worshipping in turn Mesoamerican deities like Tlaloc, Xipe Totec, and Quetzalcóatl in addition to local indigenous deities. It is estimated that Casas Grandes served a population of roughly 2,000-4,000 inhabitants, many of whom built their livelihood on trade, commerce, and artisan production. While other Southwestern cultures—like the Anasazi or Ancestral Puebloan peoples—suffered drought, famines, and widespread violence in the 12th and 13th centuries, the area around Casas Grandes remained rich in natural resources, by virtue of being positioned in a fertile valley and surrounded by rivers, and in a strategic location lying at the crossroads of trade between Mesoamerica and Oasisamerica.

It is believed that around the year 1340, Casas Grandes was burned and subsequently rebuilt. The period between 1350 and 1450 was a period of social and structural decline despite continued population growth. Evidence for this decline is found in the hasty alteration of former public spaces into living spaces for new residences and the burial of the dead in the irrigation system.

The ultimate collapse of Casas Grandes is just as mysterious as its foundation. Several decades ago, some scholars theorized that the interruption of trade routes by the bellicose Tarascan (Purépecha) Empire could have precipitated the decline of Casas Grandes. While it is entirely possible that a prolonged drought or even an earthquake could have contributed to its abandonment, archaeologists see the signs of human violence in Casas Grandes' ruins. Burned plaster along Casas Grandes' walls and the unearthing of hundreds of skeletons around the city point to something entirely more macabre. Ritual items and public plazas seem to have been desecrated, and animals seemingly starved to death within their own pens. When the

Spanish arrived in the region a century after the abandonment of Casas Grandes, they inquired as to the fate of the city's inhabitants. According to Baltasar Obregón (born 1534), the first Spaniard to visit Casas Grandes after the conquest of the Aztecs in 1521, local Indigenous people told him that the former inhabitants had traveled on a six-day journey north after a brutal war, never to return to the region again.

Casas Grandes is renowned for a particular type of ceramic style utilized on pottery, bowls, and effigies: Ramos Polychrome. This style is defined by a white to light-gray colored paste and surface work with fine line work in black and red colors. Striking motifs—often triangular—are combined with other shapes like circles and rectangles, which are rendered in a geometric style in black design. The artisans of Casas Grandes regularly rendered life forms, including macaws, snakes, and humans, in Ramos Polychrome, giving many vessels a stunning sculptural appearance. Salado pottery, demonstrating a striking combination of white, black, and red colors in geometrical shapes and lines with additional compositional characteristics, was also imported and highly prized.

Salado Culture

The Salado culture flourished from circa 1200 to 1450 in the Tonto Basin of what is now the southern parts of the present-day US states of Arizona and New Mexico. The lands that the Salado culture came to occupy witnessed human inhabitation long before the emergence of the Salado. Humans have inhabited the Tonto Basin since circa 5000 BCE, but permanent occupation dates to circa 100-600, when the peoples belonging to the Mogollon settled the eastern parts of this region. The Hohokam moved into the Tonto Basin from around what is now the vicinity of the modern city of Phoenix, Arizona, between circa 600 and 750, and occupied the Tonto Basin for at least 300 years. Archaeologists and historians are divided on whether or not the Hohokam people eventually left the region to return to the Phoenix Basin sometime around 1150. The 12th and 13th centuries were pivotal in the formation and subsequent cultural development of the Indigenous peoples of the ancient Southwest. Deprivation caused by environmental stresses combined with social chaos and political disorder likely prompted the migration of many peoples, but especially the Ancestral Puebloans, to seek fertile lands near the Little Colorado River (in Arizona), the Rio Grande (in New Mexico), and the Tonto Basin (in Arizona). Between circa 1200 and 1300, Ancestral Puebloan peoples (and probably some Mogollon peoples as well) entered the Tonto Basin, encountering other Mogollon and Hohokam communities. Here, the three cultures intermixed socially and intermarried, adopting or adapting new cultural practices in turn based on utility and necessity.

Members of the Salado culture constructed small villages or hamlets as well as shallow pit structures. They also built small, ceremonial platform mounds, irrigation canals, multi-storied pueblo made of adobe, and cliff dwellings by circa 1300. One does find T-shaped doorways, which suggests strong Ancestral Puebloan and Mogollon influence in Salado architecture. Interestingly, one does not find kivas at sites associated with the Salado culture, and Salado structures were often surrounded by stone walls, a prominent feature in Hohokam architectural traditions. It is worth noting, too, that many Salado constructions sit on top of former Hohokam residences in the Tonto Basin. Storage spaces were set aside for agricultural and artisan goods, and space was generally allocated by purpose.

The largest Salado towns once contained as many as 1,500 people, and other settlements included impressive compounds that contained 30-100 rooms. At Tonto National Monument in Arizona, one can still see the Upper and Lower Cliff Dwellings, which encompass over 50 rooms in two-story complexes. Originally occupied from circa 1225 to 1400 and located near what is present-day Globe, Arizona, Besh-Ba-Gowah contained a 200-room multi-storied pueblo. The Tonto Basin may have supported up to 10,000 people during its occupation by the Salado culture, although a more precise figure is difficult to estimate.

Those who belonged to the Salado cultural group grew corn, cotton, squash, and amaranth, as well as beans. They also cultivated agave and used yucca to weave sandals, mats, and baskets. They traded extensively with their neighbors in the Southwest, and their pottery—commonly referred to as Roosevelt Red Ware, Salado Red Ware, or Salado Polychrome—became the most widely traded.

After circa 1350, climatic changes adversely affected Salado settlements in Arizona and New Mexico. The area in and around the Tonto Basin became drier in the 14th century, but there were also periods of devastating floods and famine. It is credible that some inhabitants began to relocate to larger Salado settlements or elsewhere beginning in the late 14th century, and this pattern of outwards migration continued or even accelerated in the 15th century. Some archaeologists have speculated that many communities collapsed when irrigation fields were destroyed by floods and salinization, which hampered agricultural production at Salado farms. This is exactly what happened at Pillar Mound in Arizona, which was deserted after a torrential flood destroyed its irrigation canals. There is some evidence of intercommunal strife at Besh-Ba-Gowah, and violence may have encouraged migration en masse as well. Native American oral traditions tell us that some members of the Salado cultural group migrated north and northeast to join the Hopi and Zuni communities, some joined the pueblos along the Rio Grande in what is modern New Mexico, and others moved south toward Casas Grandes.

Bibliography

Adams, E.C. and C. Hedberg. "Driftwood Use at Homol'ovi and Implications for Interpreting the Archaeological Record." *Kiva* 67, no. 4 (Summer 2002): 363-384.

Adams, E.C. et al. "Homolovi: An Ancestral Hopi Flace." *Archaeology Southwest* 14, no. 4 (Fall 2000): 1-13.

Adams, E.C. "Homol'ovi III: A Pueblo Hamlet in the Middle Little Colorado River Valley." *Kiva* 54, no. 3 (1989): 217-230.

Adams, E.C. *Homol'ovi*. University of Arizona Press, 2002.

Adams, E.C. "The Homol'ovi Research Program: Investigations into the Prehistory of the Middle Little Colorado River Valley." *Kiva* 54, no. 3 (1989): 297-311.

Anwar, Y. "New Study Debunks Myth of Cahokia's Native American Lost Civilization." UC Berkley News. Accessed 25 Apr 2021. https://news.berkeley.edu/2020/01/27/new-study-debunks-myth-of-cahokias-native-american-lost-civilization/

Archaeology Southwest. "Who or what is Salado?" Accessed 19 Mar 2020. https://www.archaeologysouthwest.org/pdf/salado_fact_sheet.pdf

ASU Museum of Anthropology. "The Mystery Beneath The Lake: Who Were The Salado?" Accessed 11 Oct 2018. https://web.archive.org/web/20100613011240/http:/archaeology.asu.edu/vm/Southwest/Salado_Mystery/index.html

Atkins, A. "The Katsina Cult and Pueblo IV Religious and Political Organization." *Lambda Alpha Journal* 37 (2007): 51-55.

Barnett, J. "The Natchez Indians." Accessed 8 May 2021. http://www.mshistorynow.mdah.ms.gov/articles/4/the-natchez-indians

Blitz, J.H. "Moundville Archaeological Park: A History." University of Alabama. Accessed 26 Apr 2021. https://encyclopediaofalabama.org/article/moundville-archaeological-park/

Cabrillo College. "The Salado: A Crossroads in Cultures." Accessed 19 Mar 2020. https://www.cabrillo.edu/~crsmith/salado.html

Cahokia Mounds Museum Society. Official Historical Park Site. Accessed 25 Apr 2021. https://cahokiamounds.org/

Charles, C. *Casas Grandes*. Edited by G.J. Fenner; illustrated by A.W. Di Peso. Northland Press, 1974.

Cheek, L.W. *A.D. 1250: Ancient Peoples of the Southwest*. Arizona Highways, 1994.

Cordell, L.S. *Archaeology of the Southwest*. Routledge, 2012.

Deeds, S.M. "Legacies of Resistance, Adaptation and Tenacity: History of the Native Peoples of Northwest Mexico." *The Cambridge History of the Native Peoples of the Americas, Vol. 2*. Edited by R.E.W. Adams and M.J. Macleod. Cambridge University Press (2000): 44-88.

Desert USA. "Paquime – Casas Grandes: The Great Puebloan Abandonments and Migrations." Accessed 9 Jul 2020. https:// www.desertusa.com/ind1/ind_new/ind13.html

Dennis, Y.W. et al. *Native American Almanac*. Visible Ink Press, 2016.

Diel, S. "What's really old is new again after renovation at Alabama's Moundville Archeological Park." Accessed 26 Apr 2021. https://www.al.com/birmingham-news-stories/2010/04/whats_really_old_is_new_again.html

Doyel, D.E. "Salado Cultural Development in the Tonto Basin and Globe-Miami Areas, Central Arizona." *Kiva* 42, no. 1 (1976): 5-16.

Dunbar-Ortiz, R. and D. Gilio-Whitaker. *"All the Real Indians Died Off" And 20 Other Myths About Native Americans.* Beacon Press, 2016.

Dunbar-Ortiz, R. *An Indigenous Peoples' History of the United States.* Beacon Press, 2015.

Edmonds, M. and E. Clark. *Voices of the Winds: Native American Legends.* Chartwell Books, 2021.

Elliot, J.D., Jr. "Paving the Trace." Accessed 8 May 2021. http://mshistorynow.mdah.state.ms.us/articles/311/paving-the-trace

Elson, M.D. "Highlights of Tonto Basin Prehistory: Results of the Roosevelt Community Development Study." *Newsletter of the Center for Desert Archaeology* 9, no. 3 (Summer 1995): 1-7.

Etowah Indian Mounds State Historic Site. Accessed 5 May 2021. https://gastateparks.org/EtowahIndianMounds

Etowah Valley Historical Society. "Native American." Accessed 5 May 2021. https://evhsonline.org/native-american

Fagan, B.M. *Ancient North America: The Archaeology of a Continent.* Thames & Hudson, 2018.

Fisher, R. *America A.D. 1000: The Land and the Legends.* National Geographic Society, 1999.

Forbes, J.D. "Indigenous Americans: Spirituality and Ecos." American Academy of Arts & Sciences. Accessed 19 Aug 2023. https://www.amacad.org/publication/indigenous-americans-spirituality-and-ecos

Franklin, H.H. "The San Pedro Salado: A Case of Prehistoric Migration." *Kiva* 75, no. 2 (Winter 2009): 219-228.

Gilpin-Hays, K.A. "Commercialization before Capitalists: Hopi Ceramic Production and Trade in the Fourteenth Century." *Journal of the Southwest*, 38, no. 4 (Winter 1996): 395-414.

Glowacki, D.M. and S. Van Keuren (eds). *Religious Transformation in the Late Pre-Hispanic Pueblo World.* University of Arizona Press, 2012.

Green, S.M. *Rock Art.* Falcon Guides, 2018.

Gumerman, G.J. and S.A. Skinner. "A Synthesis of the Prehistory of the Central Little Colorado Valley, Arizona." *American Antiquity* 33, no. 2 (April 1968): 185-199.

Gutierrez, R.A. *When Jesus Came, the Corn Mothers Went Away.* Stanford University Press, 1991.

Harry, K.G. "The Obsidian Assemblage from Homol'ovi III: Social and Economic Implications." *Kiva* 54, no. 3 (1989): 285-296.

Hays, K.A. "Katsina Depictions on Homol'ovi Ceramics: Toward a Fourteenth-Century Pueblo Iconography." *Kiva* 54, no. 3 (1989) 297–311

Health & Fitness History. "Native American Chunkey." Accessed 25 Apr 2021. https://healthandfitnesshistory.com/ancient-sports/native-american-chunkey/

Homolovi State Park. Accessed 19 Mar 2020. https://azstateparks.com/homolovi/

Hoxie, F.E. *The Oxford Handbook of American Indian History.* Oxford University Press, 2021.

James, S.E. "Some Aspects of the Aztec Religion in the Hopi Kachina Cult." *Journal of the Southwest* 42, no. 4 (Winter 2000): 897-926.

Jameson, J.H.J. *The Reconstructed Past.* AltaMira Press, 2003.

Johnson, M.G. *Encyclopedia of Native Tribes of North America.* Firefly Books, 2022.

Kachina Resource. Accessed 16 Jan 2019. http://www.popflock.com/learn?s=Kachina

Lawrence, D. *Contesting the Borderlands*. University of Oklahoma Press, 2016.

Leblanc, S. and B. Nelson. "The Salado in Southwestern New Mexico." *Kiva* 42, no. 1 (1976): 71-79.

Legends of America. "Mound Builders of Mississippi." Accessed 8 May 2021. https://www.legendsofamerica.com/ms-moundbuilders/

Mann, C.C. *1491: New Revelations of the Americas Before Columbus*. Vintage Books, 2006.

Marriott, A. and C.K. Rachlin. *American Indian Mythology*. Apollo Editions, 1970.

Minear, T. *Discover Native America*. Hippocrene Books, 2008.

Minnis, P.E. and M.E. Whalen (eds). *Ancient Paquimé and the Casas Grandes World*. The University of Arizona Press, 2015.

Minnis, P.E. "The Casas Grandes Community." *Archaeology Southwest* 17, no. 2 (Spring 2003): 2-3.

Minnis, P.E. and M.E. Whalen. *Discovering Paquimé*. University of Arizona Press, 2016.

Moundville Archaeological Park. "About Moundville." University of Alabama. Accessed 26 Apr 2021. https://moundville.museums.ua.edu/about/

NatchezTraceTravel.com. "Chickasaw Agency Natchez Trace." Accessed 8 May 2021. https://www.natcheztracetravel.com/natchez-trace-mississippi/houston-mantee-ms/150-chickasaw-agency.html

Nozedar, A. *The Element Encyclopedia of Native Americans*. HarperCollins Publishers Ltd, 2023.

Page, J. *In the Hands of the Great Spirit*. Free Press, 2004.

Peregrine, P.N. et al. *Encyclopedia of Prehistory*. Springer, 2001.

Phillips, D.A., Jr. "The End of Casas Grandes." *73rd annual meeting of the Society for American Archaeology, Vancouver, Canada* (27 March 2008): 1-30.

Pottery Typology Project. "Ramos Polychrome." Accessed 9 Jul 2020. http://ceramics.nmarchaeology.org/typology/type?p=328

Rakita, G.F.M. and G.R. Raymond. "The Temporal Sensitivity of Casas Grandes Polychrome Ceramics." *Kiva* 68, no. 3 (2003): 153-184.

Rakita, G.F.M. *Ancestors and Elites.* AltaMira Press, 2009.

Reid, J. *The Archaeology of Ancient Arizona.* University of Arizona Press, 1997.

Roediger, V.M. *Ceremonial Costumes of the Pueblo Indians.* University of California Press, 1991.

Sapp, R. *Native Americans State by State.* Chartwell Books, 2010.

Senior, L.M.S. and L.J. Pierce. "Turkeys and Domestication in the Southwest: Implications from Homol'ovi III." *Kiva* 54, no. 3 (1989): 245-259.

Sharp, J.W. The Mysteries of Paquime Collapsed in the Mid-fifteenth Century. Accessed 19 Mar 2020. https://www.desertusa.com/desert-people/paquime.html

Silverman, D.J. *This Land Is Their Land.* Bloomsbury Publishing, 2020.

Smithsonian. "The National Museum of the American Indian: Object Collections." Accessed 26 Apr 2021. https://americanindian.si.edu/explore/collections/object-collections

Sublette, M. "Deciphering Katsina: How to Identify Vintage Katsina Dolls." *Native American Art* (February/March 2018): 58-65.

"The Origin and Development of the Pueblo Kachina Cult." Accessed 16 Jan 2019. http://jur.byu.edu/?p=3914

UNESCO. "Archaeological Zone of Paquimé, Casas Grandes." Accessed 9 Jul 2020. https://whc.unesco.org/en/list/560

US National Park Service. "The Salado Culture." Accessed 19 Mar 2020. https://www.nps.gov/tont/learn/historyculture/salado_culture.htm

US National Park Service. "The Salado: People of the Salt River." Accessed 19 Mar 2020. https://www.nps.gov/tont/planyourvisit/upload/brochure.pdf

US National Park Service. "What Does Salado Mean?" Accessed 19 Mar 2020. https://www.nps.gov/tont/learn/historyculture/upload/Salado_Overview-3.pdf

Weaver, D.E. "Salado Influences In The Lower Salt River Valley." *Kiva* 75, no. 2 (Winter 2009): 209-218.

Weber, D.J. *What Caused the Pueblo Revolt of 1680?*. Bedford/St. Martin's, 1999.

Whalen, M.E. *Casas Grandes and Its Hinterlands.* University of Arizona Press, 2001.

WHC Nomination Documentation. "Archaeological Zone of Paquimé, Casas Grandes." Accessed 9 Jul 2020. https://whc.unesco.org/uploads/nominations/560rev.pdf

Wilson, J. *The Earth Shall Weep: A History of Native America.* Grove Press, 2000.

Wright, B. *Hopi Kachinas.* Northland Press, 1977.

Zimmerman, L.J. *The Sacred Wisdom of the Native Americans.* Chartwell Books, 2016.

Image Credits

7.1 Mississippian Cultures. Map © Simeon Netchev

7.2 Etowah Statues. Photo by Heironymous Rowe, CC BY-SA 3.0, https://commons.wikimedia.org/wiki/File:Etowah_statues_H Roe_2007.jpg

7.3 Kachina Doll (Angaktsina). Photo by Brooklyn Museum Collection, CC BY, https://www.brooklynmuseum.org/en-GB/objects/121320

SOUTH AND MESOAMERICA

BY MARK CARTWRIGHT AND JOSHUA J. MARK

Mesoamerica

THE HISTORY OF MESOAMERICA is usually divided into specific periods, which, taken together, reveal the development of culture in the region.

The Archaic period, 7000-2000 BCE: During this time, a hunter-gatherer culture began to cultivate crops such as maize, beans, and other vegetables, and the domestication of animals (most notably dogs and turkeys) and plants became widely practiced.

The Olmec period, 1500-200 BCE: This era is also known as the Preclassic or Formative Period, when the Olmecs, the oldest culture in Mesoamerica, thrived. The Olmecs settled along the Gulf of Mexico and began building great cities of stone and brick.

The Zapotec period, 600 BCE-800 CE: In the region surrounding modern-day Oaxaca, the cultural center now known as Monte

Albán was founded, which became the capital of the Zapotec kingdom.

The Teotihuacán period, 200-900 CE: During this era, the great city of Teotihuacán grew from a small village to a metropolis of enormous size and influence. Teotihuacán was an important religious center devoted to the worship of a Great Mother Goddess and her consort, the Plumed Serpent. Teotihuacán was abandoned sometime around 900.

The Classic Maya period, 250-950 CE: This is the era that saw the consolidation of power in the great cities of the Yucatec Maya, such as Chichén Itzá and Uxmal. It was the height of the Maya civilization, in which they perfected mathematics, astronomy, architecture, and the visual arts, and also refined and perfected the calendar.

The Postclassic period, 950-1524 CE: At this time, the great cities of the Maya were abandoned. Thus far, no explanation for the mass exodus from the cities to outlying rural areas has been determined, but climate change and overpopulation have been strongly suggested, among other possibilities. The Toltecs, a new tribe in the region, took over the vacant urban centers and repopulated them. Tula and Chichén Itzá became dominant cities in the region.

Purépecha Civilization

In the Postclassic period, the Purépecha civilization (named the Tarascan Empire by the Spanish) dominated western Mexico and built an empire, with its capital at Tzintzuntzan on Lake Pátzcuaro, which controlled over 75,000 square kilometers (30,000 square miles), second in size only to the Aztec Empire.

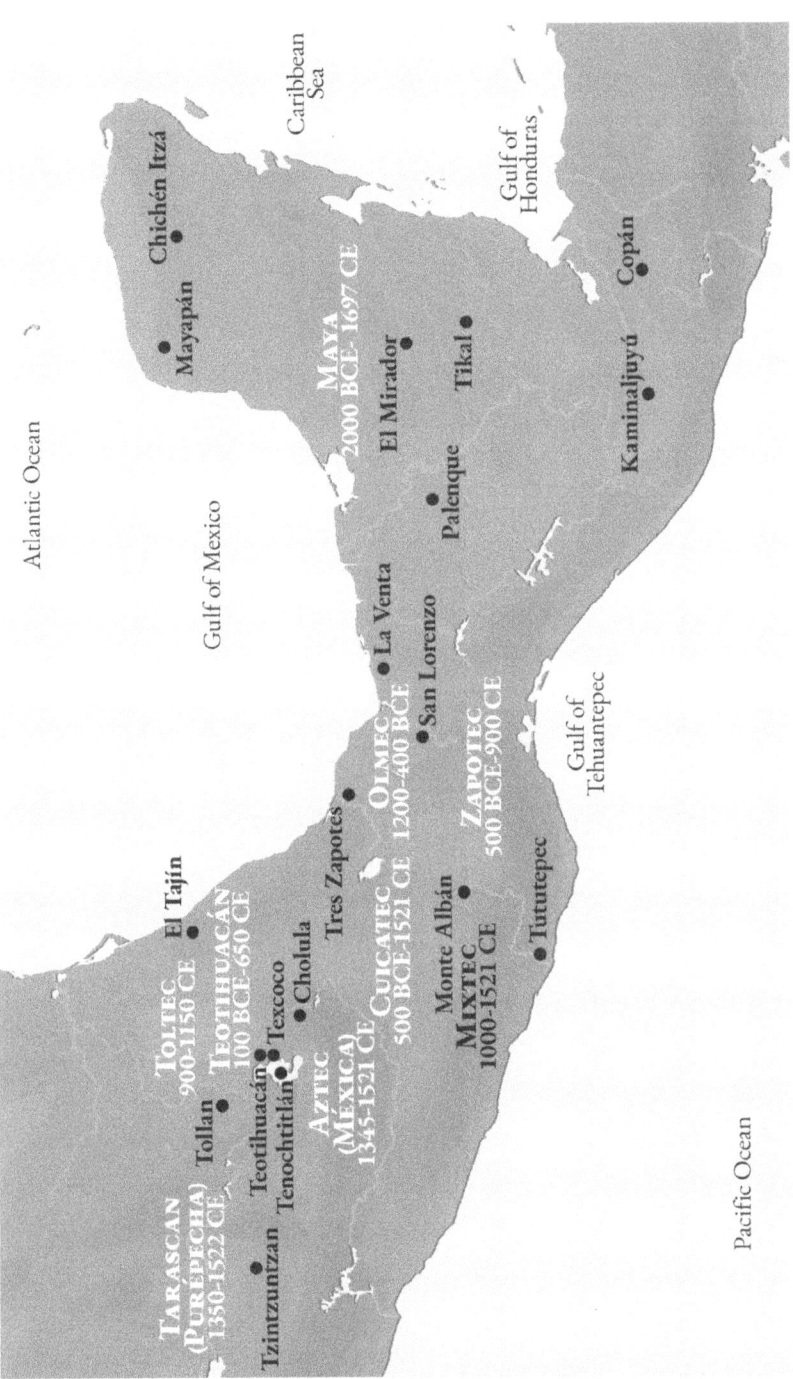

8.1 Mesoamerican civilizations

The Purépecha were based in the central and northern Michoacán (meaning 'place of the fish masters') around the lake basins of Zacapu, Cuitzeo, and Pátzcuaro (modern western Mexico). From as early as the late Preclassic period, Purépecha society developed into a more sophisticated culture with a high degree of political centralization and social stratification by the middle Postclassic period. According to the *Relación de Michoacán*, written by the Franciscan friar Jerónimo de Alcalá in the mid-16th century, the most important tribe was the Wakúsecha (from the Chichimec ethnic group), whose chief, Taríakuri, established the first capital at Pátzcuaro around 1325.

The territory controlled by the Purépecha state was now double the extent of previous generations, and the production and trade of maize, obsidian, basalt, and pottery correspondingly increased. The rising level of the lake in the Pátzcuaro basin also meant many low-lying sites were abandoned, and the competition for resources became ever more fierce. So, too, in the higher lands of the Zacapu, population concentration greatly increased so that 20,000 people inhabited just 13 sites. This period was marked by an increase in local state rivalries and a general instability among the ruling elite, but the foundations of the great Tarascan (Purépecha) Empire were now in place.

From the late Postclassic period, the Purépecha capital and largest settlement was at Tzintzuntzan on the northeast arm of Lake Pátzcuaro. Ultimately, the Purépecha also came to control a highly centralized and hierarchical political system, with some 90-plus cities around the lake. Extensive irrigation and terracing projects were carried out in order to make such a large population sustainable on local agriculture, but significant imports of goods and materials remained a necessity.

A network of local markets and a system of tributes ensured there was a sufficient quantity of basic goods, but there was also a ready supply of pottery, shells, and metals (particularly gold and silver ingots), and also labor to meet demand. At these busy marketplaces, fruit, vegetables, flowers, tobacco, prepared food, craft goods, and raw materials such as obsidian, copper, and bronze alloys were bought and sold. The state controlled the mining and smelting of silver and gold (in the Balsas Basin and Jalisco), and the production of goods made from these precious materials came via skilled craftsmen who probably resided in the palace complex of Tzintzuntzan. There is some evidence of independent gold and silver production in the southeast and western regions, compatible with evidence of secondary and tertiary administrative centers. In addition, the Purépecha imported turquoise, rock crystal, and green stones, while from local tribute they acquired cotton, cacao, salt, and exotic feathers. The Purépecha were themselves the most important producers of tin-bronze, copper, and copper-alloy bells (used in ceremonial dances) in Mesoamerica.

The Purépecha state also controlled land allocation, copper and obsidian mines, forests, the fishing industry, and craft workshops in general. However, the degree of control is unclear, and local communities and traditional tribal leaders may well have granted royal access to these resources. These diverse ethnic groups within the empire, although subject politically to Tzintzuntzan, also maintained their own language and local identities, but in times of war, their regular tribute to their Purépecha overlords was augmented by the supply of warriors.

According to the *Relación de Michoacán,* the Purépecha nobility was divided into three groups: royalty, upper nobility, and lower nobility (the Wakúsecha elite). Royalty resided at the capital and the sacred site of Ihuátzio, which had been the previous

Purépecha capital. The funeral of one Purépecha king is described in the *Relación* where the dead ruler's entourage are sacrificed to accompany him in the land of the dead—40 male slaves, his 7 favorite female slaves, his cook, wine bearer, toilet attendant, and finally, the doctor who had failed to prevent his death.

The Purépecha religion was led by a supreme high priest, who was the head of a multi-layered priestly class. Priests were easily identified by the tobacco gourd they wore around their necks. An interesting feature of the Purépecha religion was the absence of such common Mesoamerican gods as a rain god and a feathered serpent god. Neither did the Purépecha use the 260-day calendar, but they did employ the 18-month solar year with 20-day months. Purépecha religion claimed the Pátzcuaro basin as the center of the cosmos, or at least its power center. The universe had three parts: the sky, the earth, and the underworld. The sky was ruled by the most important deity, the sun god Kurikaweri, whose wife was Kwerawáperi, the earth-mother goddess. Their most important child was Xarátenga, the moon and sea goddess. The Purépecha also seem to have taken earlier local divinities and metamorphosed or combined these with wholly original Purépecha gods. In addition, the gods of conquered tribes were usually incorporated into the official Purépecha pantheon. Kurikaweri was worshipped by burning wood and offering human sacrifice and bloodletting, and pyramids were built in honor of the Purépecha gods, five at Tzintzuntzan and five at Ihuátzio.

A unique feature of Purépecha late Postclassic architecture is the monumental structures that combine rectangular and circular stepped pyramids known as yacata. These are shaped like keyholes, but there were also regular rectangular pyramids. At Tzintzuntzan, five such structures rest on an enormous platform 440 meters (1,444 feet) long. The yacata were originally faced with close-fitting slabs of volcanic stone, and excavations inside them have revealed tombs rich in artifacts. In front of the yacata, sculptures were placed for receiving sacrificial offerings (Chacmools) as in many other Mesoamerican cultures. At Ihuátzio, there is also an example of a court for the Mesoamerican ball game.

The ball game was played by all the major Mesoamerican civilizations, and the impressive stone courts became a feature of many cities. More than just a game, it could have a religious significance and featured in episodes of mythology. The game was invented sometime in the Preclassic period, probably by the Olmec, and became a common Mesoamerican-wide feature of the urban landscape by the Classic period. Eventually, the game was even exported to other cultures in North America and the Caribbean. Courts were usually a part of a city's sacred precinct, a fact that suggests the ball game was more than just a game. The exact rules of the game are not known for certain, and in all probability, there were variations across the various cultures and different periods. However, the main aim was to get a solid rubber (latex) ball through one of the rings on the walls around the ball court. This was more difficult than it seems, as players could not use their hands. Players could be professionals or amateurs, and there is evidence of betting on the outcome of important games. The game also had a strong association with warriors, and war captives were often forced to play the game.

Games often had a religious significance in choosing sacrifices to the gods. Such scenes are depicted in the decorative sculpture on the courts themselves, perhaps most famously on the South Ball Court at El Tajín and at Chichén Itzá, where one relief panel shows two teams of seven players with one player having been decapitated. Another ominous indicator of the macabre turn that this sporting event could take is the presence of *tzompantli* (the skull racks where severed heads from sacrifices were displayed) rendered in stone carvings near the ball courts. The Classic Maya even invented a parallel game where captives, once defeated in the real game, were tied up and used as balls themselves and unceremoniously rolled down a flight of steps.

Maya Civilization

The Maya have continuously inhabited the lands comprising modern-day Yucatan, Quintana Roo, Campeche, Tabasco, and Chiapas in Mexico, and southward through Guatemala, Belize, El Salvador, and Honduras. The designation 'Maya' comes from the ancient Yucatan city of Mayapán, the last capital of a Maya kingdom in the Postclassic period.

The Maya believed deeply in the cyclical nature of life—nothing was ever born and nothing ever died—and this belief inspired their view of the gods and the cosmos. Their cosmological views, in turn, encouraged their imaginative efforts in architecture, mathematics, and astronomy. Beneath the earth was the dark realm of Xibalba (pronounced 'shee-Bal-ba' and translated as 'place of fear') from whence grew the great Tree of Life, which came up through the earth and towered into the heavens, through thirteen levels, to reach the paradise of Tamoanchan ('place of the misty sky') where beautiful flowers bloomed. In Maya belief, however, one did not die and go to a 'heaven' or a 'hell' but, rather, embarked on a journey toward Tamoanchan. This journey began in the dark and treacherous underworld of Xibalba, where the Xibalbans who lived there were more apt to trick and destroy a soul than help one.

If one could navigate through Xibalba, however, one could then find the way to ascend through the nine levels of the underworld, and the thirteen levels of the higher world, to paradise. The only ways in which a soul could bypass Xibalba and travel instantly to Tamoanchan were through death in childbirth, as a sacrificial victim, in warfare, on the ball court, or by suicide (the Maya had a special goddess of suicide named Ixtab, who was depicted as the rotting corpse of a woman hanging by a noose in the heavens). Once one reached Tamoanchan, there was eternal happiness; however, it must be noted that this paradise was not thought to actually exist in the sky but on the earth.

After ascending through the thirteen levels, one did not live in the air but, rather, on a mystical mountain back on the planet. Those people who were offered to the gods did not 'die' but simply moved on. This cosmological belief influenced every aspect of the Maya civilization, and rituals were performed regularly in caves, evoking the darkness of Xibalba, and on hills or high temples.

The ball game also symbolized the human struggle and reflected the way the Maya viewed existence. It has long been believed that the losing team (or the captain of the losing team) would be killed at the end of the match, but recent advances in deciphering the Maya glyphs, together with archaeological evidence, suggest it may have been the winning team or the winning captain who was given the honor of a quick death and instant passage to paradise. Whoever was chosen, the game is thought to have been symbolic of the cyclical nature of life. It was because of this cyclical view that the Maya did not believe there was anything wrong with human sacrifice.

The Aztecs

However, the culture that has gained the most infamous reputation for bloodthirsty human sacrifice with lurid tales of the beating heart being ripped from the still-conscious victim, decapitation, skinning, and dismemberment was the Aztec civilization, which flourished in Mesoamerica from 1345 to 1521. All of these things did happen, but it is important to remember that for the Aztecs, like other Mesoamerican cultures, the act of sacrifice—of which human sacrifice was only a part—was a strictly ritualized process, which gave the highest possible honor to the gods and was regarded as a necessity to ensure humanity's continued prosperity.

Sacrifices were viewed as a repayment for the sacrifices the gods had themselves made in creating the world and the sun. The great gods Quetzalcóatl and Tezcatlipoca ripped the reptilian monster Cipactli (or Tlaltecuhtli) into pieces to create the earth and sky, and all other things, such as mountains, rivers, and springs, came from her various body parts. To console the spirit of Cipactli, the gods promised her human hearts and blood in appeasement. According to another story, Ehecatl-Quetzalcóatl stole bones from the underworld and used them to make the first humans, and so sacrifices were a necessary apology to the gods. Gods then were 'fed' and 'nourished' with the sacrificed blood and flesh, which ensured the continued balance and prosperity of Aztec society.

Bloodletting and self-harm—for example, from the ears and legs using bone or maguey spines—and the burning of blood-soaked paper strips were common forms of sacrifice, as was the burning of tobacco and incense. Other types of sacrifice included the offering of other living creatures, such as deer, butterflies, and snakes. In a certain sense, offerings were given in sacrifice, precious objects that were willingly handed over for the gods to enjoy. In this category were foodstuffs and objects of precious metals, jade, and shells, which could be ritually buried. One of the most interesting such offerings was the dough images of gods (*tzoalli*). These were made from ground amaranth mixed with human blood and honey, with the effigy being burnt or eaten after the ritual.

With human sacrifices, the sacrificial victims were most often selected from captive warriors. Those who had fought the most bravely or were the most handsome were considered the best candidates. Indeed, human sacrifice was particularly reserved for those victims most worthy and was considered a high honor, a direct communion with a god. Another source of sacrificial victims was the ritual ball games. Children, too, could be sacrificed, in particular, to honor the rain god, Tlaloc, in ceremonies held on sacred mountains. It was believed that the very tears of the child victims would propitiate rain. Slaves were another social group from which sacrificial victims were chosen; they could accompany their ruler in death or be given in offering by tradesmen to ensure prosperity in business.

Among the most honored sacrificial victims were the god impersonators. Specially chosen individuals were dressed as a particular god before the sacrifice. In the case of the Tezcatlipoca impersonator in the ritual during Tóxcatl (the 5th or 6th month of the Aztec solar year), the victim was treated like royalty for one year prior to the sacrificial ceremony. Tutored by priests, given a female entourage, and honored with dances and flowers, the victim was the god's manifestation on earth until that final brutal moment when he met his maker. Perhaps even worse off was the impersonator of Xipe Totec, who, at the climax of the festival of Tlacaxipehualiztli, was skinned, most probably in imitation of seeds shedding their husks, to honor the god who was himself known as the 'Flayed One.'

Conducted at specially dedicated temples on the top of large pyramids, sacrifices were most often carried out by stretching the victim over a special stone, cutting open the chest, and removing the heart using an obsidian or flint knife. The heart was then placed in a stone vessel (*cuauhxicalli*) or in a Chacmool (a stone figure carved with a recipient on their midriff) and burnt in offering to the god being sacrificed to. Alternatively, the victim could be decapitated or dismembered, or both. After the sacrifice, the heads of victims could be displayed in racks (*tzompantli*), depictions of which survive in stone architectural decoration, notably at Tenochtitlán. The flesh of those sacrificed was also, on occasion, eaten by the priests conducting the sacrifice and by members of the ruling elite or warriors who had themselves captured the victims.

Besides sacrifices, the gods were honored with festivals, banquets, music, dancing, decoration of statues, burning of incense, and the ritual burial of precious goods. The Aztec pantheon included a mix of older Mesoamerican gods and specifically México deities. The two principal gods worshipped were Huitzilopochtli (the war and sun god) and Tlaloc (the rain god), and both had a temple on top of the Templo Mayor pyramid at the heart of Tenochtitlán. Other important gods were Quetzalcóatl (the feathered serpent god), Tezcatlipoca (supreme god at Texcoco), Xipe Totec (god of spring and agriculture), Xiuhtecuhtli (god of fire), Xochipilli (god of summertime and flowers), Ometeotl (the creator god), Mictlantecuhtli (god of the dead), and Coatlicue (the earth-mother goddess).

This sometimes bewildering array of gods presided over every aspect of the human condition. The timing of ceremonies in honor of these deities was dictated by a variety of calendars. There was the 260-day Aztec calendar, which was divided into 20 weeks, each of 13 days, which carried names such as Crocodile and Wind. There was also a solar calendar consisting of 18 months, each of 20 days. The 584-day period covering the rise of Venus was also important, and there was a 52-year cycle of the sun to be considered. The passing of one 52-year cycle (*xiuhmolpilli*) to another was marked by the most important religious event of the Aztec world, the New Fire Ceremony, also known, appropriately enough, as the 'Binding of the Years' ceremony. This was when a human sacrifice was made to ensure the renewal of the sun. If the gods were displeased, then there would be no new sun and the world would end. The New Fire Ceremony was successfully held in 1351, 1403, 1455, and again in 1507. The last New Fire Ceremony, then, ushered in the 5th sun of the Aztec era, poignantly the last according to Aztec mythology, and, with the arrival of the European invaders, so it turned out to be. The New Fire Ceremony is referred to in various instances of Aztec art. One of the most famous of all Aztec artworks is the turquoise mosaic mask thought to represent Xiuhtecuhtli, now in the British Museum. Perhaps similar to the masks worn by the high priests in the Fire Ceremony, it has conch shell eyes and dates to the 14th century. Although the 52-year periods were important blocks in Aztec history, they were never given an individual name, and all dates started afresh at the beginning of a new cycle. This, no doubt, reflected the Aztec cosmos mythology where the world and humanity were being constantly renewed in perpetual cycles of change.

Mythology and religion, as with most ancient cultures, were closely intertwined for the Aztecs. In Aztec mythology, the founders of Tenochtitlán migrated from the legendary Aztlán cave in the northwest desert, which involved a protracted journey that eventually led to Lake Texcoco. During this migration, priests had carried a huge idol of the god Huitzilopochtli, who whispered directions, gave the Méxica their name, and promised great wealth and prosperity if he was suitably worshipped. Along the way, the Méxica settled at different spots, none of which really suited their purpose. A decisive event in the migration was the rebellion incited by Copil, son of Huitzilopochtli's sister Malinalxochitl. This was in revenge for the goddess's abandonment by the Méxica, but with Huitzilopochtli's help, Copil was killed.

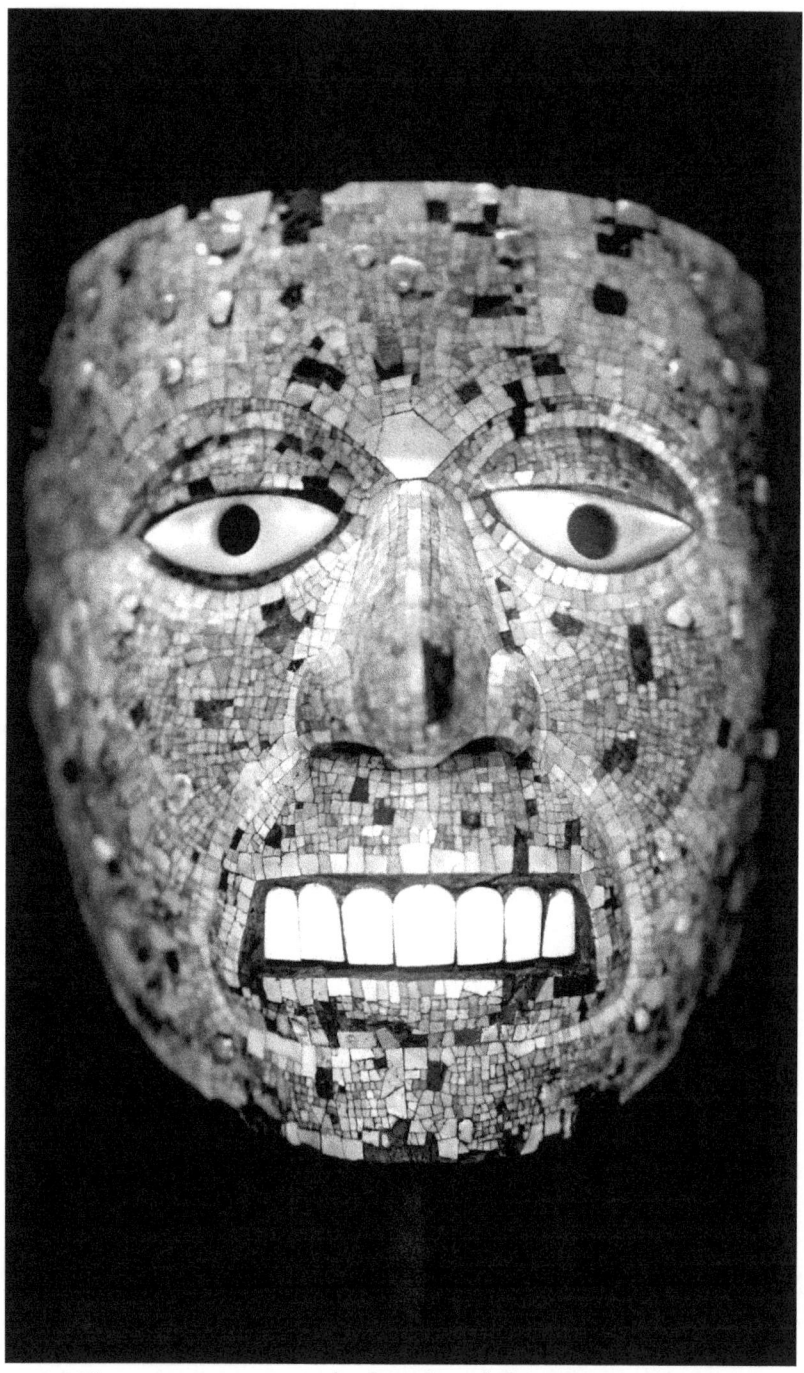

8.2 Turquoise mosaic mask of Xiuhtecuhtli, 1400-1521, Aztec or Mixtec

The great war god instructed that the rebel's heart be thrown as far as possible into Lake Texcoco, and where it landed would indicate the place the México should build their new home, the precise spot being marked by an eagle sitting on a prickly pear cactus (*nopal*) and devouring a snake. This is exactly what came to pass, and the new capital of Tenochtitlán (modern-day Mexico City) was built, the traditional date being 1345.

Tenochtitlán was one of the greatest cities in Mesoamerica and, with over 200,000 residents, certainly the most populous. It covered, at its greatest extent, some 12-14 square kilometers (5 square miles) and was connected to the western shore of the lake and surrounding countryside by three causeways (running north, east, and west), which included gaps traversed by removable bridges to allow boats to pass. There was also a stone aqueduct, which brought fresh water to the city from springs near Chapultepec Hill. The lake provided an important source of food, but good agricultural land was scarce, and this fact would necessitate reclaiming land from the lake and, eventually, military conquest to take land by force from neighboring states.

The Aztec diet was dominated by fruit and vegetables, as domesticated animals were limited to dogs, turkeys (*totolin*), ducks, and honey bees. Game (especially rabbits, deer, and wild pigs), fish, birds, salamanders, algae (used to make cakes), frogs, tadpoles, and insects were also valuable food sources. The most common crops were maize (*centli*, famously used to make tortillas but also tamales and gruel), amaranth (a grain), sage, beans (*etl*), squash, and chili peppers. Red and green tomatoes were cultivated (but were much smaller than the modern variety), as were white sweet potatoes, jicama (a type of turnip), chayote (vegetable pear), the nopal cactus, and peanuts. The Aztecs also grew many types of fruit, including guavas, papayas, custard apples, mamey, sapotes, and cherimoyas.

Snacks included popcorn and the sweet baked leaves of the maguey agave. Not using oils or fats, most dishes were either boiled or grilled, and extra taste was added using condiments, for the Aztecs loved their sauces and seasoning. Chocolate was usually consumed as a warm, frothy drink. Bitter to taste, it could be flavored by adding, for example, maize, vanilla, flowers, herbs, and honey. So esteemed was chocolate that beans were used as money. Other popular drinks were *octli* (*pulque* to the Spanish), a light alcoholic beer made from the fermented sap of the maguey, and *pozolli* made from fermented maize dough.

To maximize crop yields, various measures were taken. For example, terracing to increase the area of farmland and irrigation were widely employed across the Aztec Empire, sometimes in ambitious large-scale projects, but more commonly via artificially flooded fields known as *chinampas*. These covered large areas of the Chalco-Xochimilco basin and greatly increased the agricultural capacity of the land. Their use in Mesoamerica went back centuries, but it was not until the 13th and 14th centuries that they began to spread beyond the lake basin of Chalco-Xochimilco, where they eventually covered up to 9,500 hectares (23,500 acres). The *chinampas* could feed an ever-growing population, which at the capital Tenochtitlán alone was at least 200,000 and perhaps 11,000,000 throughout the empire.

Tenochtitlán itself was laid out in a grid pattern with many canals permeating the city. Most streets and canals were narrow, especially as there were no wheeled vehicles or beasts of burden, so goods were transported by porter or small boats and canoes. The heart of the city was the walled ceremonial precinct with its three entrances, impressive temples, and pyramids, from which the city spread out into four principal residential quarters. These had sometimes vast palaces, smaller flat-roofed stone residences for nobles and officials, huge marketplaces, judicial chambers, treasure houses, storerooms, closely packed areas of workshops, and small adobe brick and reed homes where the lower classes lived.

The sacred precinct contained 78 separate structures. Among the most important were the Templo Mayor of Tlaloc and Huitzilopochtli, which was flanked by the Eagle's House (named after its stone decoration) on one side and the pyramid of Tezcatlipoca on the other. In front of the Templo Mayor stood the gladiator stone (where sacrificial victims were bound and attacked by 'knights'), a stone *tzompantli*, and an I-shaped ball court. In the southwest corner stood the Sun Temple of Tonatiuh and a temple to Quetzalcóatl. There was also a temple to the earth goddess, Tonantzin, and the Coateocalli building, which housed the statues of gods and various other artworks captured from conquered enemies. Finally, on the Tlaloc side of the Templo Mayor, excavations have revealed a man-made mountain of offerings and deposits, which was designed to imitate Tlaloc's sacred mountain.

The city's inhabitants were divided into several social strata, as Aztec society was hierarchical. The nobility dominated the key positions in the military, state administration, judiciary, and priesthood. While traders could become extremely wealthy and powerful, even their prosperity was based on their class, and most citizens remained simple farmers. Within Aztec society, there was a limited opportunity for individuals to better their social position, especially in the military and religious spheres. It is also true that nepotism prevailed, but at the same time, promotions could be obtained on merit as well as demotions for incompetence. In practice, though, the vast majority of the Aztec population would have remained in the social group of their immediate family throughout their lives.

The most important social grouping in Aztec society was the *calpolli*, which was a collection of families connected either by blood or long association. Elders, led by the *calpolec* (a chief elected for life), controlled the landholdings of the *calpolli*, distributing them for members to farm as their own on the condition that they paid a regular tribute in return. Farmers, or *macehualtin*, were by far the largest section of Aztec society, and they were divided into two further groups. First, and lower in status, were the field workers who did the donkey work of hoeing, weeding, planting, irrigating, and so on. The higher group was more supervisory in role and consisted of specialized horticulturalists, who were responsible for seeding and transplanting. They also understood such matters as crop rotation and the best times for planting. Aztec farmers may be further divided into those who worked their own land and those who worked the land of large estates, paying their rent with whatever they farmed. These serfs were the lowest class of all in Aztec society, known as *mayeque*; they owned no land and paid up to 30% of their produce to their overlords. In addition to farming, the *macehualtin* were also expected to perform military service in times of war and assist in state projects such as road and temple building.

Aztec society also contained slaves or *tlacohtin* ('bought ones') who were conquered peoples, those guilty of serious crimes such as theft, or individuals who had gotten themselves into so much debt (most often through gambling) that they were forced to sell themselves as a commodity for a certain period or even for life. If they had the means, slaves could also buy themselves free again. Slaves could be required not only to farm but also to work as general laborers, domestic servants, or concubines. Slaves were generally not resold and were protected by law from any abuse by their masters or anyone else. Talented slaves could gain important positions such as estate managers and were free to marry non-slaves, with any children from such a marriage being born free.

The artisan class, known as *tolteca* after the earlier Toltec civilization, was held in high regard. They often worked in specialized large-scale workshops, and they included carpenters, potters, stonemasons, metalworkers, weavers, feather workers, and scribes. Other important professions were the merchants, traders, and professional hunters. The most prestigious traders were those who conducted their business over extensive territories and were known as *pochteca*, a hereditary position. They often traded for the state and specialized in such precious goods as tropical bird feathers, gold, turquoise, shells, greenstone, cacao beans, and exotic animal skins. The *pochteca* were supervised by the *pochtecatlatoque*, the most experienced traders, who administered trade and justice among the trading class in special courts. One specialized group of traders was the *tlaltlani*, who traded in slaves. As they had the important role of providing the state with sacrificial victims, they were given special privileges and gained great wealth. Two other groups of traders were the *tencunenenque*, who acted as tribute collectors, and the *naualoztomeca*, who disguised themselves and traded in hostile territory, acting as spies for the state as they picked up loose gossip in foreign markets.

The nobility or *pipiltin* (singular, *pilli*) were easily identified by their appearance as they exclusively wore prized feather garments. As owners of private land, they were wealthy thanks to tribute from their tenants and serfs. State administrators were selected from the *pipiltin* class, although commoners might enter this hereditary class by performing deeds of great valor on the battlefield. These social risers were known as *cuauhpipiltin* or 'eagle nobles.' One level above the *pipiltin* was the *teteuhctin,* who held the highest positions in the state apparatus. Living in large palaces, they wore even more splendid clothes and jewelry, and they had the prestigious *-tzin* suffix added to their names. The Aztec king, the *tlatoani*, was a member of this class.

The priestly class not only orchestrated the state religion but also ran the state education system. A male or female from any social class could become a priest, or *tlamacazqui*, but the most powerful ones always came from the *pipiltin* class. At the very top of the religious hierarchy was the king himself, aided by two high priests. Other notable priestly positions included the supervisor of the elite state-run schools and the general supervisors of the priesthood, festivals, and temple sites. Some priests also became experts in other, yet closely related areas such as astronomy and writing. Still others developed a talent for medicine, prophesy, and the interpretation of visions and dreams. Priests could also be warriors, and two important priestly functions in Aztec warfare were to carry into battle effigies of the major Aztec gods and to collect sacrificial victims from the bravest warriors among the vanquished. Finally, a separate but related group was the witchdoctors and magicians who performed strange ceremonies, claimed transformational gifts, and cast spells on the wicked.

As in modern societies, Aztec education could determine one's future social position. Children of commoners went to school, which was compulsory, but only from their early teens. Before that, children were educated by their parents. The *telpochcalli* or 'youth house' for boys gave military training, while the one for girls taught duties to be performed in religious ceremonies. Both sexes would also learn dancing, singing, public speaking and recital skills, and history, as well as take fundamental moral and religious lessons. The *calmecac* school was reserved for children of the nobility who learnt essential skills for a public career in the military, politics, or the state religion. Again, the sexes were separated, and there is some evidence that exceptionally gifted children from the lower classes could also attend. A young person's education ended when they were ready to be married. This was arranged by elders, and partners generally came from the same *calpolli*. Aged in their late teens or early twenties, the couple would marry in a four-day ceremony when the bride would be decked in red feathers and covered in sparkling pyrite powder, fool's gold.

Although women were expected to tend the home, cook, care for children, and practice weaving and basketwork, Aztec women also retained control of their personal property and inherited wealth, and they could participate in public life in the fields of medicine, education, religion, and even commerce. Also unusual for ancient societies, Aztec men were expected to bear the responsibility of bringing up their male offspring.

All males were expected to actively participate in warfare, as battle was regarded as a perpetual religious and political necessity. The military commander-in-chief was the king himself. He was assisted by his second-in-command, who had the title *cihuacoatl*. Joining these two in a war council were four more of the highest-ranking nobles, typically relatives of the king. Aztec symbols of rank included the right to wear certain feather headdresses, cloaks, and jewelry—lip, nose, and ear-plugs. Officers also wore large ensigns of reeds and feathers. The most prestigious units were the *cuauhchique* or 'shaved ones' and the *Otontin* or 'Otomies.' These two elite units could only be joined by warriors who had displayed no fewer than 20 acts of bravery in battle and were already members of the prestigious jaguar and eagle warrior groups. Even the lowest ranks could win privileges through valor.

The Aztecs did not have a permanent or standing army but called up warriors when required. Each town was required to provide a complement of 400 men for campaigns, during which they would march under their own standard but also be a part of a larger group of 8,000 men. As many as 25 such divisions, or 200,000 men, could be mobilized for a large-scale campaign. Aztec warriors were taught from childhood in weapons handling, and they became expert users of clubs, bows, spears, and darts. Protection from the enemy was provided via round shields (*chimalli*), and, more rarely, helmets. Body armor (*ichcahuipilli*) was also worn and made from quilted cotton, which was soaked in saltwater to make the garment stiffer and more resistant to enemy blows. There was no uniform, but ordinary warriors wore a simple tunic over a loincloth and wore war paint. Elite warriors were much more impressively decked out with exotic feathers and animal skins. The jaguar warriors wore jaguar skins and helmets with fangs, while the eagle warriors were dressed for battle in feathered suits complete with talons and a beaked helmet.

On the battlefield, usually a plain, combat was typically preceded by both armies facing each other with much shouting and the beating of drums. Then heavy stones were thrown, followed by a more deadly volley of darts. Then came a bloody hand-to-hand combat. Victory conventionally came when the enemy's main temple had been sacked. Besides the desire for new territory and war booty, the Aztecs very often specifically went on campaign to acquire sacrificial victims. Indeed, both sides agreed to the battle beforehand, agreeing that the losers would provide warriors for sacrifice. These campaigns were known as *xochiyaoyotl* or a 'flowery war' because the victims were defeated warriors who were trussed up, and with their splendid feather war costumes, looked like flowers as they were unceremoniously transported back to Tenochtitlán. The earliest known example of a *xochiyaoyotl* was in 1376 against the Chalca, a conflict that, perhaps unsurprisingly, developed into a full-scale war. Generally speaking, though, the intention was only to take a sufficient number of victims and not to start all-out hostilities.

South America

The Lambayeque Civilization

The Lambayeque civilization (aka Sicán) flourished between circa 750 and circa 1375 on the northern coast of Peru, straddling the Middle Horizon and Late Intermediate period of the ancient Central Andes. The traditional founder of the Lambayeque dynasty was Naymlap, who, with an entourage of warriors, came from the south by sailing balsa boats or rafts and colonized the various valleys of the region, a legend appropriated by the later Chimú civilization. The founding city was Chot (today identified as Huaca Chotuna), and the dynasty traditionally ruled for twelve generations, with the last ruler named as Fempellec, although in reality, the period of Lambayeque culture probably began in the 8th century when it emerged from the shadows of the previously dominant Wari civilization. Rather than a unified empire, the Lambayeque rulers oversaw a loose network of cities linked via blood ties.

One of the most important Lambayeque sites was Batán Grande ('Great Anvil'), which was abandoned circa 1100, probably due to an El Niño climate disaster (floods followed by sustained droughts), although the buildings show signs of deliberate fire destruction. Túcume then became the new religious capital and grew to cover 370 hectares (915 acres), making it the largest ceremonial center ever constructed in the ancient Andes.

The center of Lambayeque metal production was Cerro Huaringa, where smelting furnaces and workshops have been excavated. Metalwork was a Lambayeque speciality, particularly goldwork where the alloy material was engraved, beaten against molds, cut, soldered, or welded, and then inlaid. Some of the most famous art pieces from the Andes are Lambayeque—for example, gold ceremonial knives (*tumi*) with the handle representing a Sicán Lord.

The sheer wealth of the Lambayeque society shouts out from their art and architecture. Palaces were built as massive enclosures of vast areas of land, and gold is the prevalent material for all manner of goods, from body ornaments to masks. Certainly not shy to display their wealth, the elite wore tunics embroidered with panels of gold; one surviving example has 2,000 square gold additions, oversized ear spools in gold and turquoise, magnificent feather headdresses, and even golden gloves.

The Lambayeque rulers seem not to have made any attempts at regional conquest, but eventually they found themselves defeated and assimilated into the Chimú Empire around 1375, and artists were forcibly relocated to Chan Chan, the Chimú capital. In this way, a continuity in Andean art passed through successive cultures, and iconography such as rulers with crescent-shaped headdresses, pottery forms, and techniques in metalwork were perpetuated.

Chimú Civilization

The Chimú civilization, otherwise called the kingdom of Chimor, flourished between the 12th and 15th centuries. The traditional founding ruler of the Chimú was Taycanamo, who was considered to have been born from a golden egg and then arrived from the sea. Other notable rulers include Guacricaur, who expanded into the Moche, Santa, and Zaña valleys, and Nancinpinco, who conquered the Lambayeque (Sicán) culture. The La Leche valley was also brought under control, and by the end of the 14th century, during the reign of Minchançaman, the area of Chimú influence stretched 1,300 kilometers (800 miles) along the coast of northern Peru.

The initial prosperity of the Chimú was largely due to their agricultural skills as they built an extensive irrigation system, using canals. Later, their successful military campaigns and policy of extracting tribute ensured that they became the dominant regional power. Chan Chan came to be the capital of other administrative centers, such as Farfán, Manchan, El Milagro, Quebrado Katuay, and the fortress site of Paramonga. Chan Chan (known as Chimor to its original inhabitants) was built at the mouth of the Rió Moche, covered some 20 square kilometers (8 square miles), and had a population of up to 40,000 at its peak. The city became the hub of a vast trade and tribute network, and no fewer than 26,000 craftspeople resided there, often forcibly removed from conquered cities to mass-produce high-quality goods in a wide range of precious materials.

The city is without a recognizable center and spreads out in a series of blocks interspersed with stone-lined canals and punctuated with small artificial lakes and wells. The architecture at Chan Chan is characterized by buildings constructed using pre-prepared sections of poured mud or adobe. Most impressive are the large rectangular palace compounds (*ciudadelas*), which served multiple functions as royal residence, storage facility, mausoleum, and administrative center.

Ten royal palaces or compounds were constructed over the centuries at Chan Chan. It is possible that the Chimú system of royal inheritance was for each new king to inherit the title but not the wealth of his predecessor. This would result in a late ruler's family taking over the royal palace while the new king was required to build himself a new one, explaining the high number of such palaces at Chan Chan.

8.3 Adobe walls, Chan Chan, Peru

The system has the added benefit of ensuring a new ruler actively engages in expanding the empire in order to fund his reign. The palaces were built in a rectangular layout, each with ten-meter-high double exterior walls, labyrinthine interiors, and with only a single entrance guarded by two standing wooden statues set in niches. Of special note are the U-shaped audience or ritual rooms (*audiencias*), which controlled access to the storerooms. Functional structures within each compound include administrative and storage buildings and burial platforms accessed by a ramp. The large T-shaped tomb within the latter contained the mummified leaders while smaller tombs their family and entourage.

The walls of the compounds, built to restrict access by commoners, were decorated on the outside with bold relief designs, typically repeated geometric shapes, animals, and sea life, especially fish. Similar adobe compounds were built at other Chimú sites—for example, nine at Manchan and six at Farfán. All of the compounds at Chan Chan are in the center of the city, while more modest habitation lies on the city's outskirts. Here were the residences for administrators in smaller versions of the larger compounds, and artisans (metalworkers, woodworkers, and weavers), who lived in more modest dwellings of wattle-and-daub and cane with steep roofs and a single hearth. Finally, on the outskirts of the city, were two large burial pyramid-mounds known as Huaca el Dragon and Huaca Tacaynamo. The city also had an extensive irrigation system, which combined canals, shallow reservoirs, and wells.

Chimú rulers were enthusiastic collectors of art from other cultures, and their palaces were like museums full of niches in which objects and statues were placed for display. Influenced by the Wari and Moche civilizations, the Chimú would continue to expand upon artistic themes that have become staple features of Andean art ever since. Chimú pottery is characterized by mold-made blackware and redware with sculpted decoration, which is given a highly polished finish. The most common shape is double-spouted bulbous jars. Textiles have natural colors, the most precious with exotic feather decoration, where plumes are sewn in rows onto a cotton backing and dyed to create designs. Popular motifs include open-armed figures wearing headdresses—probably representing the ruling class—and double-headed 'rainbow' snakes. Textiles could also be decorated with precious metal additions, and one tunic survives with 7,000 small gold squares individually sewn onto the fabric.

Carved and inlaid spondylus shells, acquired from Ecuador, were another popular medium for Chimú art, with diamond-shaped inlays creating striking jewelry pieces. Precious goods could also be made using gold, silver, and imported amber and emeralds from Colombia.

Muisca Civilization

Colombia was the home of the Muisca (or Chibcha) civilization, which flourished between 600 and 1600 and lived in scattered settlements spread across the valleys of the high Andean plains. Important annual ceremonies related to religion, agriculture, and the ruling elite helped unite these various communities. Such ceremonies involved large numbers of participants and included singing, incense burning, and music from trumpets, drums, rattles, bells, and ocarinas (bulbous ceramic flutes). The communities were also linked by trade, and there was even a movement of skilled craftsmen, especially goldsmiths, between Muisca cities.

Founded by the legendary figure of Bochica, who came from the east and taught morality, laws, and crafts, the Muisca were ruled by chieftains aided by spiritual leaders. They controlled and defended their territory with such weapons as clubs, spear-throwers, arrows, and lances. Warriors also had protective helmets, armored breastplates, and shields. The Muisca took trophy heads from their defeated enemies, and they sometimes sacrificed captives to appease their gods. However, warfare was highly ritualized and probably small-scale.

Idolizing the sun, the Muisca also had a special reverence for sacred objects and places such as particular rocks, caves, rivers, and lakes. At these sites, they would leave votive offerings (*tunjos*) as they were considered a portal to other worlds. The most important Muisca gods were Sué (also spelled Zue), the sun god, and Chía (also spelled Chie), the moon goddess. We also know of Chibchacum, the patron of metalworkers and merchants. The most common type of offerings to the gods was foodstuffs, along with typical *tunjo* of snakes, and flat male, female, and animal figures rendered in gold alloy, which were placed at sacred sites. Elite members of society could also be buried at such religiously significant places. First they were dried and then wrapped in many layers of fine textiles, and finally placed in a tomb seated on their seat of office—a small stool or *tianga*—surrounded by the precious goods they had enjoyed in life.

Figures in Muisca art are often transformational—for example, a man with elements of a bird, which may represent the hallucinatory visions of shamans induced by the consumption of coca leaves or crushed yopo tree seeds. Animals such as bats, felines, snakes, alligators, and amphibians were also popular subjects. Gold was the material of choice, as it was valued for its lustrous and transformational properties and its association with the sun. It was not used as a currency, but rather as an artistic medium. The Muisca goldsmiths employed a wide range of techniques in their work, such as lost-wax casting, depletion gilding, which gives a two-tone finish, repoussé, soldering, granulation, and filigree. Gold was also made into thin sheets by hammering on round stone anvils or carved stone molds using an oval hammer of stone or metal. Mined from exposed veins and panned from mountain rivers, gold and its alloy *tumbaga* (a mix of gold and copper with traces of silver) were used to make *tunjos* such as figures and masks, coca containers (*poporos*) with lime dippers, and also exquisite jewelry—typically pectorals, earrings, and nose studs. The most famous example of a *tunjo* is a golden raft with cast figures wearing jewelry standing upon it, the significance of which is discussed below. The raft was found in a clay vessel inside a cave and now resides in the Museo del Oro (Museum of Gold) in Bogotá, Colombia.

The Muisca today are most famous for the legend of El Dorado or 'The Gilded One.' According to the legend, among the Muisca, when it was necessary to crown a new monarch, the man who would be king prepared for his great day with a period of abstinence. Secluded in a cave, he was forbidden chili peppers, salt, and women. When the coronation day finally arrived, the future king traveled to Lake Guatavita, a remote lake formed in an extinct volcanic crater just north of modern-day Bogotá, in order to give offerings to the gods so that they might bless his reign. This he did by going to the centre of the lake on a raft. The raft, made from reeds, was laden with treasures of gold and emeralds, and on it were placed four large incense burners. The incense was *moque,* and the braziers, joined by those set around the shores of the lake, gave off clouds of thick smoke, which must only have added to the mystique of the ceremony.

The most fantastic treasure of all, though, was the royal person himself. He had been stripped naked and entirely covered in a sticky layer of resin on which was blown fine gold dust. The result was a sparkling man of gold; literally a 'gilded man.' Also traveling on the raft were four attendants, less spectacularly attired but still weighed down with heavy gold jewelry on any part of the body it could be hung from. The great moment came when, accompanied by mass trumpets and singing from the shores, the raft arrived in the very centre of the lake. At that moment, silence fell on the crowd, and the attendants threw the fabulous treasure of gold and jewels into the lake, and the people on the shores also threw their golden offerings into the sacred waters. The climax of the ceremony came when the golden king himself leapt into the lake, and when he emerged, cleaned of gold, he had become the king of the Muisca.

The Spanish conquistadors, on hearing this story, allowed their imagination and lust for gold to leap beyond the bounds of reality, and soon a legend arose of a magnificent city built with gold. Naturally, as it never existed in the first place, the city was never found, and even the lake has stubbornly refused to reveal its secrets despite several costly attempts over the centuries.

Bibliography

Alden Mason, J. *Ancient Civilizations of Peru.* Viking Penguin, 1975.

Almere Read, K. *Mesoamerican Mythology.* Oxford University Press, USA, 2002.

Attenborough, D. *The Tribal Eye: Episode 3 Sweat of the Sun.* BBC, 1975.

Coe, M.D. *Mexico.* Thames & Hudson, 2013.

Cosmic Log. "Maya calendar workshop documents time beyond 2012." Accessed 1 Dec 2016. https://cosmiclog.msnbc.msn.com/_news/2012/05/10/11639788-maya-calendar-workshop-documents-time-beyond-2012?lite

D'Altroy, T.N. *The Incas.* Wiley-Blackwell, 2014.

Demarest, A. *Ancient Maya.* Cambridge University Press, 2005.

Gibson, C. *The Hidden Life of the Ancient Maya.* Metro Books, 2012.

Jones, D. *Mythology of Aztec & Maya.* Southwater, 2007.

Jones, D.M. *Mythology of the Incas.* Southwater, 2007.

Jones, D.M. *The Complete Illustrated History of the Inca Empire.* Lorenz Books, 2012.

Kubler, G. *The Art and Architecture of Ancient America, Third Edition.* Yale University Press, 1984.

de Landa, D. "Yucatan Before and After the Conquest Index." Translated by W. Gates. Accessed 1 Dec 2016. http://www.sacred-texts.com/nam/maya/ybac/index.htm

Mann, C.C. *1491: New Revelations of the Americas Before Columbus.* Vintage, 2006.

McEwan, C. *Moctezuma.* British Museum Press, 2009.

Miller, M.E. *The Art of Mesoamerica.* Thames & Hudson, 2019.

Miller, M.E. *The Gods and Symbols of Ancient Mexico and the Maya.* Thames & Hudson, 1993.

Moseley, M.E. *The Incas and Their Ancestors.* Thames & Hudson, 2001.

Nichols, D.L. and C.A. Pool. *The Oxford Handbook of Mesoamerican Archaeology.* Oxford University Press, 2012.

Phillips, C. *The Illustrated Encyclopedia of the Aztec & Maya & Central America.* Lorenz Books, 2007.

Phillips, C. *The Mythology of the Aztec and Maya.* Anness, 2006.

Soustelle, J. *Daily Life of the Aztecs on the Eve of the Spanish Conquest.* Stanford University Press, 1961.

Stephens, J.L. *Incidents of Travel in Central America, Chiapas, and Yucatan, Vols. I and II.* Cosimo Classics, 2008.

Stone, R.R. *Art of the Andes.* Thames & Hudson, 2012.

Stuart, G.E. and G.S. Stuart. *Lost Kingdoms of the Maya.* National Geographic Society, 1993.

Townsend, R.F. *The Aztecs.* Thames & Hudson, 2009.

Vila Llonch, E. *Beyond El Dorado.* British Museum Press, 2013.

Image Credits

8.1 Mesoamerican Civilizations. Map © Simeon Netchev

8.2 British Museum: Turquoise mosaic mask. Photo by Paul Hudson, CC BY 2.0, https://www.flickr.com/photos/pahudson/32032445037/

8.3 Statues Guarding Chan Chan. Photo by Bruno Girin, CC BY-SA 2.0, https://www.flickr.com/photos/brunogirin/66145040/

Oceania and Australia

By Liana Miate

OCEANIA IS A REGION located in the Central and South Pacific Ocean, which is made up of hundreds of different islands, some larger and more well-known than others. Oceania is considered a continent, with Australia being its main landmass; however, in more modern times, the continent is often referred to as Australia, instead of Oceania.

Today, Oceania can be split into four subregions or island groups.

Australasia: Australia and New Zealand

Polynesia: Samoa, American Samoa, French Polynesia, the Cook Islands, Tonga, Niue, Tuvalu, and Tokelau

Melanesia: Papua New Guinea, Fiji, New Caledonia, the Solomon Islands, and Vanuatu

Micronesia: Kiribati, Guam, Marshall Islands, Nauru, Palau, Northern Mariana Islands, and the Federated States of Micronesia

By the end of the 14th century, the people of Oceania had completed their migration and settlement across the different islands. Most cultures saw the Pacific Ocean as a bridge to other lands, rather than a barrier, and they utilized navigational techniques and an understanding of the ever-changing ocean to explore and occupy these new lands.

The settlement of Oceania began in Southeast Asia, with people moving to the islands of Micronesia and Melanesia. During the 1300s, travelers migrated to Tonga, Fiji, and the Samoan Islands. This movement became the birthplace of Polynesian culture.

While the 14th century is well-documented in many cultures around the world, it was vastly different for the civilisations of Oceania due to their lack of a written record. However, that did not mean that their cultures were any less complex or diverse. The islands and people of Oceania have always fascinated historians, academics, and linguists due to their diversity, their sacred connection to the land, their kinship, and the rich collection of languages that can be found across the islands. American linguist William Foley has calculated that there are around 1,200 languages in the Southwest Pacific Ocean alone, making up an impressive 20-25% of the world's total languages.

Australia

Australia, the largest landmass in Oceania and also the smallest continent, has been home to the Indigenous Australians (Aboriginal peoples) for around 60,000-65,000 years, making them the First Australians. There are hundreds of different Indigenous Australian groups, each with its own language, traditions, and cultures. They are considered to have the oldest living culture in the world, which has survived through significant changes and challenges, including British colonization, which began in 1788.

The Dreamtime, or the Dreaming, is the mythology and spirituality of the Aboriginal people. It is a religion, worldview, philosophy, and way of life, and was at the center of Indigenous Australian life, influencing everything they did, setting the rules and structures for society and behavior. The stories of the Dreamtime have been passed down for thousands of years through oral tradition, rock art, song, and dance. The Indigenous Australians believed that their lives had already been predestined by the ancestral and spiritual beings of the Dreamtime, and they lived in accordance with those terms. These ancestral beings traveled across the land and created all living things. They were able to transform into animal or human form and gave humans language, traditions, and law.

The Indigenous Australians formed a deep connection with the land. Every single tree, lake, and rock had a vital significance and was considered sacred. They viewed themselves as the custodians of the land. Certain areas were more sacred to the Indigenous Australians than others. These places include Uluru (Ayers Rock), Kata Tjuta (the Olgas), and the waters of Kununurra.

9.1 Aerial view of Uluru, Australia

Each group of Indigenous Australians had their own unique language, and there was no one common language. However, neighboring groups were often in contact with one another for trade and even marriage between members of different language groups. Most children grew up learning at least two different languages. Social units usually consisted of the immediate family—a man, his wife or wives, and their children. However, children were also surrounded by their extended family, and multiple family groups would sometimes hunt and forage together. Children were educated about their family tree and taught how to address their relatives. They would often refer to their maternal aunts as 'mother,' and paternal uncles were called 'father.' Young men would practice 'bride service' in which they would temporarily move to their wife's tribe.

When it came to health and medicine, healers or medicine men were the holders of knowledge. They had often had a near-death experience themselves and were believed to possess spiritual powers from the Dreaming, offering unique insights and wisdom about treatments and remedies. Older women were exceptionally knowledgeable about bush medicine and foods, midwifery, and herbal remedies. Many illnesses were treated with natural remedies and with what was found in the surrounding environment, including leaves, bark, or roots, and even animals. For example, toothaches were treated with eucalyptus gum, soaked wattlebark was consumed for coughs, goanna fat was used as a salve for burns, stringy bark was used as bandages, and spiderwebs were also used to stop blood loss.

Although the society of the Aboriginal peoples was considered an equal (egalitarian) one without any chiefs, as seen in Polynesian or Melanesian cultures, there were still community leaders, known as 'elders.' To be an elder, one had to be taught the entire work of spiritual knowledge, which could take as long as 40 years. The elders were a link between the past and present and passed on their skills, knowledge, and wisdom to future generations. There could be multiple elders in each community. Important decisions were made by a group of male elders who would sit down and have a long discussion until an agreement was made.

Law and order were dealt with in each group and were derived from the Dreaming. The punishment for smaller, more trivial offenses was dealt with by the immediate family and involved humiliation or threats. The punishment for serious crimes, including incest, murder, and breaking sacred laws, was decided by the elders. Punishments included exile, death, or a spearing in the thigh. If a person died from a snake, spider, or shark bite or even from natural causes, it was believed to have been caused by evil spirits that were sent on behalf of an enemy. Medicine men would identify the person responsible for sending the evil spirits, and revenge was often carried out.

The Indigenous Australians were primarily hunter-gatherers, and their diet was influenced by the land they inhabited; the groups living near water had a fish-heavy diet, while those living in the desert ate a lot of dingo meat. Native plants and berries were also consumed. Animals were hunted and killed with spears, traps, nets, and decoys. Boomerangs were used to bring down birds from the sky, and viscous gum was spread on trees to trap birds, which formed a large part of the Aboriginal peoples' diet. They employed many methods to catch their fish, sharks, and crocodiles, including using fishing lines, harpoons, spears, nooses, trickery, and even their bare hands. When the women fished, they sang to entice the fish to take their bait.

The complexity of cooking methods differed across Australia. Usually, it included ground or earth ovens, which involved digging a hole, lighting a fire, placing green leaves on the embers, laying the meat on the leaves, covering it with hot stones and more leaves, and topping it with earth or sand. Fires were also kindled on clay, sand, or seaweed; fish was steamed in green leaves, and meat was covered in coal and lightly roasted. Indigenous Australians only hunted and produced what they required on a day-to-day basis, so no special roles were assigned; everybody pitched in when needed. The only times roles were assigned and extra food was prepared were during ceremonies and large gatherings.

The main ceremonies of the Indigenous Australians included initiation rites for boys and girls, which marked their transition from child to adult, rain-making ceremonies, which invoked the help of the Rainbow Serpent (a key figure of the Dreamtime who represented the spirit of water) and involved the use of pearls, quartz crystals or calcite, which were placed in waterholes to bring rain. Increase ceremonies were also performed to nurture and give thanks to the ancestral beings.

Indigenous funerals were elaborate celebrations of one's life. There was wailing and even self-harm. The possessions of the deceased were either destroyed or buried with them in log coffins or hollow trees. Cremation and mummification (with the bones being interred in a rock shelter) were also practiced. The Aboriginal peoples believed that death was only the end of the bodily existence of an individual, but that their soul was indestructible. After death, the body and soul return to their 'bone and soul' country, where the spirit would be reincarnated and be reborn. Every group had its own ways to celebrate these ceremonies, with dancing, chanting, singing, headdresses, body decorations, or painting.

The Aboriginal peoples have been described as being an unchanged people living in an unchanged environment. Although there were climate and environmental changes that saw the Indigenous Australians move across the vast landscape of Australia for survival, and make contact with other Indigenous Australian groups, it is recognized and acknowledged that their traditions, culture and beliefs largely remained the same for thousands of years, from when they first arrived in Australia, during the 14th century, and beyond, until the British arrived in 1788 and turned life on its head for the Indigenous Australians.

New Zealand (Aotearoa)

New Zealand (Aotearoa) is the sixth-largest island country in the world, located in the southwestern Pacific Ocean. The Māori were the first human inhabitants of New Zealand, who were descended from the Polynesians of the Eastern Polynesian islands, who discovered and settled much of the Pacific. Archaeological evidence of ivory fishhooks found on Enderby Island (south of mainland New Zealand) proves that Polynesians were already exploring parts of New Zealand as early as 1350. There is also evidence showing that there were visitors to Jackson Bay (southwest of the Southern Island) during the early 14th century.

The discovery and settlement of New Zealand were made popular by the series of Great New Zealand Myths, which begins with the discovery of New Zealand in 950 by the Polynesian navigator Kupe. This was followed by the arrival of the Moriori people (people from the Melanesian islands) between 950 and 1150, and then the first Māori settlement in 1150 after the voyages of Toi and Whātonga. Finally, in the mid-14th century, the 'Great Fleet' arrived in New Zealand from the Polynesian islands.

The Great Fleet of the 14th century is taught to thousands of students across New Zealand. The myth tells of seven canoes setting sail from Island Polynesia to New Zealand to escape tribal wars and seek a more peaceful home in Aotearoa, whose beauty they had heard much about. Once the seven boats had finally reached

Aotearoa, their crews mixed with the people who already inhabited New Zealand and founded the Māori race, who occupied both the North and South Islands. After the arrival of this great fleet, ocean voyages between Polynesia and New Zealand slowed down.

The Great New Zealand Myths have been a contentious topic for years. During the 20th century, historians and academics argued that New Zealand had been settled before the 14th century, and that there was no 'Great Fleet' in 1350, and that there had been no Moriori settlement from Melanesia. However, during the 21st century, people began to look more favorably upon the myths. Although most of New Zealand's original settlers had come from East Polynesia, evidence shows there was early contact with people from the Fiji Islands and West Polynesia. As for the 'Great Fleet,' a large number of canoes had traveled from East Polynesia within a hundred years of 1350. Furthermore, archaeology, carbon dating, genetic analysis, and burnt pollen remains all point toward New Zealand being settled during the 13th-14th century, a time of vast Polynesian exploration and ocean voyaging.

There is very little physical evidence of the type of canoes the Polynesians used for their sea voyage to New Zealand. To date, only one piece of a hull has been discovered at Anaweka River on the Buller coast (the South Island). The hull dates to 1350-1400 and is thought to be from a double canoe, used for long-distance sea trips. However, it does not paint a clear picture of the sailing mechanisms of the canoes used, and without written history or detailed rock art to rely on, European and Māori historians have had to turn to Polynesian traditions and historical observations to gain a better understanding of how the canoes worked. They argued that the settlement of New Zealand involved large and fast double-hulled canoes and astral navigation, and were more sophisticated than first realized. This idea has been heavily debated and is seen as a 'traditionalist' view. Research on the pressure systems surrounding New Zealand over the last 1,300 years argues against the traditionalist theory. From 1100 to 1300, high-pressure systems were found to have moved to the east side of New Zealand, creating northeasterly winds that flowed from the Polynesian islands to New Zealand. If that were the case, then sailing from East Polynesia to New Zealand would not have necessarily been as difficult as first imagined, and the Polynesians would not have required such complex canoes or navigational methods.

The earliest known habitation sites in New Zealand include the North Island (northeast), the South Island (southeast), and the Cook Strait. Archaeologists, including Jack Golson (1926-2023), believe that these areas were where the settlers hunted, grew plants and herbs, and were treated as 'resource islands.' As the population grew, they spread out to cover more of the land and to discover their local resources. The first settlers on New Zealand would have been faced with a vast landscape that ranged from beaches, forests, mountains, and at least six active volcanoes, much different from the small islands and coral atolls of Polynesia. As they adapted to their new home, they transitioned from Polynesian to New Zealand Māori.

The first phase of Māori settlement was known as the 'colonial' period. During this period, the now-extinct flightless bird, the moa, played an essential role in the daily life of the Māori; their meat made up a large part of the Māori diet, their hollow eggs were used as water carriers or collectors, and their bones were turned into ornaments, fishhooks, and harpoon or spear heads. Seals, swans, pelicans, dolphins, and pilot whales were also part of their diet.

9.2 Moa and Haast's eagle recreation

Local minerals such as obsidian and basalt were utilized to make weapons. The movement of these minerals shows that the earliest settlers were in contact with one another and moved freely throughout New Zealand.

Although it is easy to dismiss the first Māori as only a hunter-gatherer society, evidence shows that they transported plants from Eastern Polynesia to New Zealand, which survived due to their nurturing and harvesting. The Māori had a home base but traveled to hunt and collect minerals and other natural resources. During the first 100-150 years of settlement, animals became close to extinction because of heavy hunting and habitat destruction caused by fires that swept through New Zealand during the 14th and 15th centuries. Due to the extinction of many of their food sources, the Māori turned to foraging, fishing, and gardening. Smaller birds, such as pigeons, kiwis, and wekas, were also hunted instead of larger birds.

Like the Indigenous Australians and the other cultures of Oceania, all knowledge and history were passed down from generation to generation through oral tradition. Although they had no words to describe or name their culture, their identity was linked to their families, the land, and tribes. They used songs and chants to proclaim their *whakapapa* (their connection to their family, ancestry, the land, and the spiritual realm). The membership of tribes was determined by descent from a founding member or sometimes a foundational canoe. Marriages between different tribes formed alliances, although only the descendants from a marriage could have full membership of a tribe and the privileges that came with it.

In Māori culture, the land is sacred, and their cosmology was centered on Ranginui (the sky father) and Papatūānuku (the earth mother), whose union resulted in the creation of humans. Every tree, mountain, and river was seen as an ancestor and deepened the Māori connection to the land they lived on. The cosmos was used to guide navigation and as a timekeeping tool. Although the Māori brought their own gods, myths, and place names with them to New Zealand, over time, they were modified to better represent the land, native flora, and fauna of their new home.

Social differences were a big part of Māori culture. Aristocrats or nobles (*rangatira*) had more illustrious ancestors than the commoners (*tūtūā*) and therefore were given authority and leadership. The leaders were seen as intermediaries between the gods and humans and between the ancestors and their descendants. It was easy for an individual to lose their status over crimes or by ignoring their tribal responsibilities. Each tribe had its own land, which was defined by its natural landmarks, such as mountains or forests. Tribes that did not belong to a specific region needed to get permission before entering it and using its resources. The *marae* was a common meeting spot, where tribes would come together to exchange stories, songs (*waiata*), and perform the famous *haka* (a war dance), which strengthened the bonds of identity, family, and community.

Despite the widespread distribution of people living across New Zealand and the different tribes, Māori society shared a common language (*Te Reo Māori*) and the same traditions. Wars or conflicts were rare, and their lives revolved around their families and tribes, hunting, foraging, tool-making, fishing, gardening, and maintaining their homes. Other vital aspects of Māori daily life included the practice of tattoos (*tā moko*), which were created using bone chisels to make marks into the skin and ink made from various materials. These tattoos represented the social status and the personal achievements of an individual, and were much more than just a form of body art.

The 14th and 15th centuries saw changes to art forms and the introduction of art that has become inextricably linked to Māori culture, especially hei-tiki (pendants made from jade or greenstone). It also saw the Māori settle into permanent regions and become less nomadic, due to the loss of big game and the general growth of the population, which made it more difficult for people to travel long distances. By the 16th century, the Māori of New Zealand shared a similar culture and had become a unified society, with the exception of the Māori living on the lower half of the South Island, who remained largely nomadic.

Polynesia

The Polynesians were a diverse group of cultures that inhabited the various islands of the Pacific Ocean, including Samoa, Tonga, the Cook Islands, French Polynesia (Tahiti), Easter Island (Rapa Nui), and Tuvalu. The Polynesian people are believed to be descended from the Austronesians, who originally came from Taiwan circa 3000 BCE, but migrated to the Philippines, and then onto the Pacific Islands. Another theory about the origin of the Polynesian people involves the Lapita cultural complex, a civilization that lived in the southwestern Pacific from 1600 to 500 BCE. They are known for their distinctive pottery, which has unusual shapes and patterns. Archaeologists believe that the Lapita people were expert sea voyagers who played a pivotal role in settling the islands of the Pacific Ocean, notably Vanuatu, the Solomon Islands, and New Caledonia.

Despite cultural differences between the different islands, Polynesians from all over the Pacific Ocean have a lot in common, namely their respect for the land, nature, and their community and ancestry. They also shared common traditions, including tattooing, making canoes, and hula dancing. History and knowledge were passed down through oral tradition, with the exception of Easter Island (Rapa Nui), which had the only known written script in Polynesia. This writing was known as *rongorongo* and looked very similar to hieroglyphs.

As with all Indigenous cultures, their lives revolved around religion and spirituality, shaping their view of the world, society, and the land. They believed that the natural and supernatural coexisted and that the gods, spirits, and ancestors were a part of their daily life, including navigation, agriculture, and social interactions. Each island had its own pantheon of gods; however, there were often common themes or personifications among the deities. Two of the main gods found across the Polynesian islands, Tāne, the god of woods and birds, and Tangaroa, the god of the sea, were believed to have created the world and were worshipped in different ways. The Polynesians knew that the gods could positively or negatively impact their food sources, fishing and voyaging trips, health, and their survival on the battlefield, so they performed offerings and rites led by priests (*tohunga*) to appease the gods.

Mana is a spiritual power that could occur in individuals, nature, and objects. Important figures like priests, warriors, and tribal leaders had more *mana*, which gave them even more power and influence. *Mana* could also be gained or lost based on an individual's actions. The Polynesians held their ancestors in high regard. They believed that their spirits (*'aumakua*) continued to live on and protected their descendants. Religious ceremonies involved chants, singing, and offerings, and were mainly celebrated at special events like weddings, births, and even burials.

In Polynesia, the art of tattoos was known as *tatau*. They were more than a way to decorate a body; they were symbols of status, identity, and religious beliefs. The tattoos were applied by *tufuga* (tattoo artists) with bone, wood, and ink that was collected from plant-based materials. Chants, prayers, and rituals were performed for spiritual protection and guidance. Both men and women received tattoos, and it is a Polynesian tradition that remains important to this day. Carving is another artistic practice the Polynesians are famed for. They used bone, wood, and stone to create beautifully carved objects that featured patterns and designs that symbolized the land, religious beliefs, and genealogies. The most famous example of Polynesian carving is, without a doubt, the moai statues found on Easter Island (Rapa Nui), which honor the ancestors of the inhabitants.

9.3 Moai statues, Easter Island (Rapa Nui)

Music and dance are deeply connected to Polynesian culture and daily life. The voice is the main instrument in Polynesian music; songs and chants were used to praise the gods and ancestors, convey emotions, and pass on histories and stories. Dance was a form of storytelling and consisted of graceful movements and synchronized steps to tell a specific story. Each Polynesian island had its traditional dances. In Tahiti, the *'ori Tahiti* is a fast-paced dance with rhythmic hip movements and high energy levels, which is performed at large celebrations or festivals. In Samoa, the *Siva* dance has slower, more graceful movements. It is mainly performed at weddings, village festivals, and cultural ceremonies. In Tonga, the traditional dance is known as the *lakalaka,* which is performed by large groups of men and women who move in intricate patterns that represent strength and unity. This dance is mainly seen at royal ceremonies.

The Polynesian people are known for their incredible voyaging and navigational skills, which saw them discover and settle new lands, namely New Zealand (Aotearoa), during the 14th century. They used celestial navigation, their knowledge of wind patterns, and the waves to find their way around the ocean. Experienced navigators passed on their knowledge and observations through chants, songs, and stories. Polynesian navigators and sailors also used maps, although not physical maps, but mental ones, which were memorized and easily called upon when they traveled the seas.

Around the 14th-15th centuries, Polynesian exploration of the waters slowed down significantly. This may have been due to a number of factors, including a shift in the climate that resulted in colder, windier weather and rougher waves, or because of changes in cultural priorities or practices. Whatever the reason, the Polynesians had become the most widely dispersed people on the planet during the 14th and 15th centuries.

Fiji

Fiji comprises a large number of islands spread across the South Pacific Ocean. Only 106 of these islands have people living on them. The two largest islands are Viti Levu and Vanua Levu. The first humans to inhabit Fiji were the Lapita people, who traveled from either the Solomon Islands or through Vanuatu and New Caledonia.

The Lapita people brought with them a prosperous agricultural economy and a sophisticated seafaring tradition.

Between 1000 and 1600, Fijian society transformed from a clan-based structure to a more formalized one with clear hierarchies. This transformation in society saw an increase in the power of leaders and chiefs, land expansion, and new alliances. These changes revolved around *vanua* (land, community, and identity), which was all connected under chiefly leadership, and through which authority was given. Chiefs were given the right to rule through their ancestral connections to the land and military prowess. They were seen as a link between the living and the dead, and between the land and the sky. The chiefs would determine land rights and work duties, which would be obeyed through forced loyalty and dependence, and were controlled by a redistributive economy.

Much importance was put on titles, descent terminology, and location names, which defined which bloodlines held ancestral importance and how sacred knowledge was to be passed down. Genealogies were often spoken out loud during community gatherings to promote legitimacy and resolve any conflicts. Marriage was a way to extend kinship connections. New brides would often move between different villages, which would strengthen family ties, political alliances, and social interactions.

Gender roles in Fiji were similar to those found across Oceania; the men hunted, fished, built, cleared land, and engaged in warfare, while women collected shellfish, grew taro and other plants in gardens, and wove mats and barkcloth (*masi*). During times of village feasts, ceremonies, or seasonal requirements, these roles often became less defined. Women sometimes held special roles, such as ritual specialists (*vasu levu*), where they would perform healing rituals or offer *masi* to new chiefs during their installation ceremonies. They also had a say in land ownership rights and were custodians of sacred knowledge. In some particular regions, like Viti Levu, women acted as mediators for enemy clans and settled disputes.

A vital part of pre-colonial Fijian life was conquest and warfare. Warfare was seen as an act of balance and renewal, not necessarily one of violence. War broke out due to rivalries and conflicts over land, insults to honor, or acts of taboo. There was nothing bad about warfare; it was a sacred obligation to defend one's honor or that of one's ancestors. Battles were held near rivers or spirit forests, sacred places where an ancestor could determine the outcome. Hidden trails, stone ramparts, and fortified settlements on hills were utilized as places of ambush and hiding, especially on the island of Viti Levu.

Warriors often had to undertake rigorous training, including fighting skills and rituals. Their initiation rites involved them spending time in seclusion, fasting, and learning war chants. Some warriors were believed to possess powers that allowed them to channel the power of certain spirits or be shielded from spears and other weapons.

Raids were carried out as a controlled form of conflict, where pigs, woven mats, or women were the primary targets. They were permitted by law and were sometimes part of a ritualistic event; however, chiefs first had to consult with priests, elders, and warriors before they could approve a raid; it was not something that was done lightly.

In Fijian culture, the land was not only lived on, but it also had certain power and was considered sacred. One important landmark of the land was burial caves, which were located in elevated or secluded locations. These caves were the final resting places of high-ranking family members and symbolized a portal between the dead and the living world. Ritual platforms were communal spaces that were the social, religious, and political centre of a village. They were foundations for ceremonial halls, the residences of chiefs, or spirit houses. Dense forests with ancient trees, bodies of water, and standing stones were known as spirit forests. They were believed to be the home of gods, guardian deities, and ancestral spirits. These three landmarks were deeply intertwined with spiritual and ancestral power.

The 14th century in Fiji was considered Fiji's pre-contact period. By the 15th and 16th centuries, some Fijian islands were introduced to centralized politics, with certain chiefs in higher positions of authority and larger territorial influence. This change was the result of years of military successes, sacred geography, and strategic marriages.

Papua New Guinea

Papua New Guinea is located in the southwestern Pacific Ocean on the eastern half of the island of New Guinea. The land is rich in rainforests, valleys, and beaches, and its prominent landmark, Mount Wilhelm, is one of the tallest mountains in Oceania. Papua New Guinea has an impressive 800 languages, with every ethnic group having their own distinct language and traditions. The Eastern Highlands of Papua New Guinea show evidence of human occupation dating back 10,000 years, while the Western Highlands show some of the earliest evidence of ditch and drainage systems and crop cultivation, including taro.

The people of Papua New Guinea had a special relationship with the land and were big believers in animism (every aspect of the land had a spiritual power, whether it was a living thing or an inanimate object). The spirits found upon the land could be either evil or friendly and influenced an individual's destiny. They were appeased and honored through religious ceremonies, rituals, and offerings of food and art (carvings). Like in the Indigenous Australian culture, the Papua New Guineans viewed specific landmarks or sites as being more sacred than others. One of these sites was the Sepik River, which was considered a life-giving force and a way to communicate with the spirits. Shamans were seen as holy men who were the messengers between the spirit world and humans.

Besides being a sacred landmark, the Sepik River was a highway of trade, communication between ethnic groups, and an exchange of traditions and beliefs. Archaeological evidence, such as pottery fragments, shows that the Papua New Guineans had contact with Oceania and Southeast Asia via the Sepik River. Southeastern Papua New Guinea has helped to link multiple islands and cultures through a complex and sophisticated *kula* trade network. *Soulava* necklaces (red shell necklaces) were traded for *mwali* armbands or bracelets (shell armbands). The *soulava* moved clockwise through the surrounding islands, which included the Trobriand Islands, the Marshall Bennetts, the Laughlan Islands, and the Louisiade Archipelago, while the *mwali* moved counterclockwise. Traders often maintained contact with each other for life, and would visit each other's tribes with gifts and offerings to renew their pledges of loyalty to the trade network. Specially designed canoes, painted in black, white, and red patterns, were used for the *kula* trade network. The number of *kula* shells traded determined the status of an individual.

The Papua New Guineans had a vibrant oral tradition, with epic myths, heroic tales, histories, and creation stories all being passed down from generation to generation through chanting and singing. Spirits and mysterious mythological creatures often made appearances in stories and songs, symbolizing respect and fear of the unknown. The people who had the honor of passing down these oral traditions were often tribal elders or shamans, and they were viewed with great respect, as they were tasked with a pivotal role in the community.

Life started to change forever in Papua New Guinea when the Spanish and Portuguese first discovered the island in the early 16th century. However, the Papua New Guineans managed to hold on to control of their island until it was colonized by the Europeans in the 19th century.

Author's note: *This author acknowledges the Traditional Owners of the land on which she writes. She would also like to pay her respects to Elders past, emerging, and present.*

Bibliography

Ancient Chronicles. *The History of Polynesian People: Tracing the Migration and Settlement of the Māori Across New Zealand and the Pacific Islands.* Independently published, 2024.

Anderson, A. *The First Migration: Māori Origins, 3000 BCE-AD 1450.* BWB Texts, 2016.

Andrews, M. *Journey Into Dreamtime.* Evolve Communities, 2018.Bashford, A. and S. Macintyre. *The Cambridge History of Australia, Volume 1: Indigenous and Colonial Australia.* Cambridge University Press, 2013.

Blainey, G. *A Shorter History of Australia.* Vintage Books Australia, 1994.

Carson, T. M. *Archaeology of Pacific Oceania: Inhabiting a Sea of Islands.* 2nd ed. Routledge, 2024.

Fields, J. *Origins and Oceania: Volume 1: Fiji Before Empire, 1000 BCE-1800 CE.* Independently published, 2025.

Fischer, R.S. *A History of the Pacific Islands.* 2nd ed. Palgrave Macmillan, 2002.

Flood, J. *The Original Australians: The Story of the Aboriginal People.* Allen & Unwin, 2006.

King, M. *The Penguin History of Aotearoa New Zealand.* Penguin Books, 2003.

Santoso, B.B. *The History of Papua New Guinea: Echoes of the Sepik.* Independently published, 2023.

Strathern, A. et al. *Oceania: An Introduction to the Cultures and Identities of Pacific Islanders.* 2nd ed. Carolina Academic Press, 2017.

Williams, M. *Polynesia, 900-1600.* Arc Humanities Press, 2021.

Williams, T. *Fiji and the Fijians: The Islands and Their Inhabitants.* HardPress, 2017.

Image Credits

9.1 Uluru/Ayers Rock from the Air. Photo by Corey Leopold, CC BY 2.0, https://www.flickr.com/photos/97708873@N00/2562614982/

9.2 Wellington – Te Papa 9. Photo by Alan and Flora Botting, Te Papa Tongarewa, Museum of New Zealand, CC BY-SA 2.0, https://www.flickr.com/photos/alan-flora_botting/24766854685/

9.3 Easter Island: Moai statues. Photo by Mike W., CC BY-SA 2.0, https://www.flickr.com/photos/squeakymarmot/16491363758/

About the Authors

Mark Cartwright is a professional writer, researcher, historian, and editor. His university studies focused on political history, constitutional theory, military history, and political philosophy. He has been a history writer since 2012. He is interested in art and architecture, and especially ancient pottery and what these everyday objects can reveal about past lives and traditions. Other interests include maritime history, exploration, and polar history. Having lived in Italy and the Czech Republic, been a frequent visitor to Greece, and now based in France, he is a great believer in Jacques-Yves Cousteau's maxim: *Il faut aller voir*—we must go and look for ourselves.

Joshua J. Mark is co-founder and content director of World History Encyclopedia. He has lived in Greece and Germany, traveled extensively, especially through Egypt, and currently lives in upstate New York with his dog, Sammie. Mark was a part-time philosophy professor and writing instructor at Marist College, where he received a Faculty of the Year Award and the Special Services Award of Merit, and has also taught history and literature courses at the college level. He has published articles, short fiction, and creative nonfiction through various journals, magazines, and online.

Liana Miate has always been passionate about ancient history—particularly ancient Rome and Greece, and anything to do with mythology, and the study of women in the ancient world. She has completed a Bachelor of Arts degree with a major in Greece, Rome, and Late Antiquity at Macquarie University in Sydney, Australia. She is also interested in writing (screen and creative), and social media, and is currently working as a social media editor and writing articles for World History Encyclopedia. She hopes to attract more people to the fascinating world of ancient history through photos and interesting facts. She believes that many lessons can be learned if people just take the time to look to the past.

Patit Paban Mishra, Professor of History (retired) at Sambalpur University, India, and the Northern University of Malaysia, specializes in world history with particular reference to South Asian and Southeast Asian history. He obtained his MA in History at Delhi University and his MPhil and PhD at JNU, New Delhi. Professor Mishra was awarded the DLit degree from Rabindra Bharati University, Kolkata. He has taught history for almost 38 years and supervised M.Phil, PhD, and DLit scholars in India and abroad. He was the President of the Indian History Congress (Sect. IV) and Odisha History Congress. He is the author of over 8 books and 30 research articles.

James Blake Wiener is a co-founder and the former communications director at World History Encyclopedia. He now heads the advisory board. Originally trained as a world historian, James is a public relations professional who is interested in cross-cultural exchange, world history, and international relations. While committed to fostering increased awareness of the power of the digital humanities and the valorization of cultural heritage, James is also dedicated to excellence in research and open-access education.

INDEX

Aboriginal, 246-251
Abu Bakr Shah, 82
Abu Bakr II, 100
Abu Inan, 108
Abu Sa'id, 48
Abyssinia, 114
Adena culture, 178, 182
agriculture, 16-17, 47, 66, 78, 86, 214, 222, 238, 258
al-Hasan ibn Suleiman, 119
Alauddin Sikandar, 82
Aleppo, 47, 53
animism, 37, 124, 178, 189, 263
Aotearoa (New Zealand), 251-257
arban, 43
archery, 40
art, 18-19, 48, 60, 71, 91, 121, 125-126, 127-128, 147, 223, 234, 237, 239, 247, 256-259, 263-264
Ashikaga Shogunate, 15-23
Ashikaga Takauji, 13-15
Ashikaga Yoshimitsu, 18-19
Austria, 145
Australia, 245-251, 255, 264
Ayers Rock (Uluru), 247

Azuchi-Momoyama period, 1
Aztec, 199, 212, 219-232
Baghdad, 53, 106
Baidu, 47
Bahman Shah, 83-85
Bahmani Sultanate, 83-86, 89
ball game, 181, 217-218, 219
banking, 158
Batán Grande, 233
Battle of Crécy, 168
Battle of Dannoura, 2
Battle of Kauthal, 84
Battle of Kulikovo, 50
Battle of Minatogawa, 14
Battle of Neville's Cross, 168
Battle of Poitiers, 168
Battle of Poyang Lake, 64
Bavaria, 161
Beijing (Daidu), 45, 57, 70, 73
Bhanu Deva II, 91-92
Bhanu Deva III, 92
Beghards, 155
Beguines, 155
Benin, 127-129
Bible, 151, 155
Black Death, 46, 50, 141-149, 168
Boccaccio, Giovanni, 149
Bochica, 238
Bohemia, 155
Boniface VIII, 150-152
bronze, 12, 16, 126-129, 215

Buddha, 11-12
Buddhism, 11, 18-20, 38, 46, 60, 68
Bukka Raya I, 84, 86-89, 92
burial, 69, 180, 183, 185, 187-189, 198, 222, 236-237, 258, 262
Byzantine Empire, 49, 159
Caffa, 144
Caen, 165
Cahokia, 178, 182-184
Cairo, 101, 103, 106, 108
Calais, 168-169
calpolec, 228
caravan, 47, 50, 100, 105, 108-110, 124
Casas Grandes, 196-199
Catalan Atlas, 101
Catherine of Siena, 148
cavalry, 27, 42-43, 84-85, 100, 112
Cerro Huaringa, 233
Chagatai, 44
Chagatai Khanate, 44-46, 50
Chan Chan, 234-236
Charles II, 168
Charles IV, 166
Charles VI, 169
Chaucer, Geoffrey, 148
Chimú, 234-237
China, 22-23, 27, 40-45, 58-74, 89, 105-106, 116
Ch'oe Musŏn, 22
Chot (Huaca Chotuna), 233
Christianity, 38, 46, 114, 149-156
Christmas, 141
Cipactli, 220

Clement V, 152
Clement VI, 146
clothing, 20, 29-32, 114, 120, 146-147, 158-159, 191
Coatlicue, 222
coinage, 6, 16, 46-49, 100, 117, 141, 154, 160
Compendium of Chronicles, 48
Confucian, 58-60, 64, 70
Da Ming lü, 66
Daibutsu, 11
Daidu (Beijing), 45, 57, 70, 73
daimyo, 1, 5, 16
Damascus, 47, 133
Danse Macabre, 147
Dante Alighieri, 148
Daud Shah, 85
David II, 168
Dekanawida, 190
Delhi Sultanate, 53, 77-83, 91
Dibing, 57
Djanibek (Janibeg), 144
Dreamtime, 246-247, 250
Dual Courts, 14
Duanzong, 57
earthquake, 11, 184, 198
Easter Island (Rapa Nui), 257-259
education, 17, 58, 66, 121, 153, 157, 230-231
Edward III, 166-168
Edward the Black Prince, 168
Egypt, 47, 49, 101, 105, 113-114
El Dorado, 239
Emerald Mound, 189

Engaku-ji, 11
England, 140, 155, 158, 165-169
Etowah Mounds, 179-181
Etugen, 38
famine, 16, 45, 63, 198, 201
Fang Xiaoru, 70
feudalism, 1-6, 9, 135-142, 166
Fiji, 245-246, 252, 260-263
Feroz Shah Kotla (fortress ruins), 80
Firuz Shah Bahmani, 86
Firuz Shah Tughluq, 92
flagellant, 145-146
Flanders, 146, 157-158
Florence, 149, 157, 160, 163
food, 8, 20-21, 22-36, 40, 100, 116, 120, 122, 138, 139-141, 153, 158-159, 164, 186, 188, 194, 196, 215, 220, 225-226, 238, 248-250, 255, 258, 264
France, 138, 140, 146-147, 151, 154-158, 166-169
Gaikhatu, 47
Genghis Khan (Temüjin), 27, 39-41, 52-53, 61
Genoa, 49, 100, 156, 159
Germany, 138, 140, 146, 157-163
Ghazan, 47-48
Ghiyasuddin (Ghiyath al-Din Tughluq), 77-79, 91
Go-Daigo, 13-14
Go-Toba, 3
Go-Komatsu, 18
gold, 6, 18, 20, 97-102, 110, 112, 119-122, 124, 156, 159, 215, 229, 234-240
Golden Horde, 44, 48-53, 144
Gongzong, 57

Great Fleet, 251-252
Great Plains, 176, 191
Great Spirit, 189
Guacricaur, 234
Hanseatic League, 161-163
Harihara I, 86, 88
Harihara II, 89-90
Hasan ibn Suleiman al-, 119
Haudenosaunee (Iroquois), 189-191
Hausa, 111-114
Heiankyo (Kyoto), 2, 13, 19
heretic, 154-155
Hikitsukeshu, 4
Hindu, 77-78, 80, 83-90
Hohokam, 193, 196, 199-200
Hōjō Sadatoki, 12
Hōjō Tokimune, 11
Hōjō Tokiyori, 11
Homolovi, 191-196
Hongwu (Zhu Yuanzhang), 45, 63-66, 68-69, 71
Hopewell culture, 178, 188
Hopi, 191-196, 202
Hu Sihui, 35
Hu Weiyong, 68
Huaca el Dragon, 237
Huaca Tacaynamo, 237
Hundred Years' War, 166-169
Hungary, 146
hunter-gatherer, 176, 179, 191, 212, 249, 255
Hus, Jan, 155
Hyojoshu, 4

Ibn Battuta, 105-108
Ibn Juzay al-Kalbi, 105, 108
Ife, 122-126
Ilkhanate, 44, 47-49, 52
Ilyas Khoja, 50
ikki, 17
India, 53, 72, 78-93, 105-106, 116
Iroquois (Haudenosaunee), 189-191
irrigation, 17, 47, 63, 66, 80, 197-198, 200-201, 214, 226, 235, 237
jagun, 43
Jama Masjid, 80, 82
Janibeg (Djanibek), 144
Japan, 1-23, 61
jarquchi, 59
Jean de Joinville, 32
Jew, 146, 158
Jianwen (Zhu Yunwen), 69-71
Jigonhsasee, 190
jitō, 4-6, 16
Jochi, 44
Jōei Shikimoku, 4
John II, 169
Julian of Norwich, 148
kachina, 191-196
Kamakura, 1-15, 17-18
Kamakura period, 1-17
kanrei, 15
Karakorum, 45
Kata Tjuta, 247
Kebek, 46
Keita, Sundiata, 98-100

Kenchō-ji, 11
Kenmu Restoration, 12-14
kesikten, 40
Kievan Rus, 161
Kilwa, 115-119
Kinkaku-ji, 18-19
Kitayama culture, 19
Kōmyō, 14
Korea, 21-23, 27, 58
koshu, 9
Kōtoku-in Temple, 11
Kublai Khan (Shizu), 13, 40, 44, 57-63
kula, 264
Kumonjo, 4
Kununurra, 247
kurultai, 39
Kyoto (Heiankyo), 2, 13, 19
lakalaka, 260
Lambayeque, 233-234
Lapita, 257, 260-261
law, 4-5, 15-16, 29, 32, 39, 58-59, 66-71, 78, 80, 114-115, 140, 145, 160, 161, 163, 228, 238, 247, 249, 262
Leake Mounds, 179
Lin'an, 57
literature, 17, 72-73, 86, 91, 105, 148
Lollards, 155
London, 147, 159, 161
Luo Guanzhong, 72
Mahmud Shah II (Nasiruddin Muhammad Shah), 53, 83
Mali, 97-105, 110, 113
Mamluks, 47-50, 77

Mandokoro, 4
Mansa Maghan I, 104
Mansa Musa (I), 100-104
Mansa Sulayman, 104
Māori, 251-257
market, 8, 73, 101, 119, 121, 154, 158, 187, 215, 227
marriage, 9-10, 28, 60, 114, 121, 231, 140, 156, 229, 248, 255, 263
Maya, 212, 218-219
Mecca, 101, 105-106
medicine, 33-34, 103, 126, 230-231, 248-249
Meiji Restoration, 2
Mexico, 196-199, 212-214, 218, 225
Mictlantecuhtli, 222
migration, 111-146, 159, 175, 193-194, 196, 200-202, 223, 245
Minamoto no Yoritomo, 2-3, 13
Ming dynasty, 16, 65-73
minghan, 40, 43
Mississippian culture, 175-179, 187
Mogadishu, 115-116, 119
Mogollon, 193, 196-197, 199-200
monastery, 8, 11, 63-64, 153-154
Monchujo, 4
Monks Mound, 182-185
Moriori, 251-252
Morocco, 103-104, 108
Moscow, 50, 52
mosque, 53-54, 78-80, 82, 103, 113, 115
mother goddess, 38, 212, 216, 222
mound, 176-189, 197, 200-201, 237
Moundville, 178, 185-187
Muhammad bin Tughluq (Ulugh Khan), 79-80, 82-83, 92

Muhammad Shah I Bahmani, 84
Muhammad Shah II Bahmani, 85
Muisca, 238-241
Mujahid Shah Bahmani, 84-85
Muromachi period, 1, 14, 20
Muslim, 46-48, 50, 52-53, 59, 77-78, 80, 100, 104, 108, 122, 113-115, 117
Mussi, Gabriele de, 144
Nanjing, 45, 64, 66, 69-70
Narasimha Deva II, 91
Narasimha Deva III, 92
Narasimha Deva IV, 92-93
Nasiruddin Muhammad Shah (Mahmud Shah II), 53, 83
Nasiruddin Khusrau Shah, 77
Natchez Trace, 187-189
Naymlap, 233
nerge, 36, 43
New Fire Ceremony, 222-223
New Zealand (Aotearoa), 245, 251-257, 260
Niger, 100-101, 110, 111-112
Nitta Yoshisada, 13-14
Nizamuddin Auliya, Khawaja, 79
Noh theater, 19
Norway, 159
Obon festival, 11
obsidian, 193, 214-215, 221, 255
Öljaitü, 48
Ometeotl, 222
oral history, 111, 126, 190, 201, 247, 255, 258, 264-265
Ottoman Empire, 50-51
Ögedei, 44

Papatūānuku, 255
paper money, 45, 47, 63
Papua New Guinea, 245, 263-265
Paris, 156-157
Pax Mongolica, 45, 48
Peasants' Revolt, 147
Persia, 47, 52, 61, 63, 83, 86, 89, 102, 106, 113, 116, 121, 127
Peru, 233, 234, 236
Petrarch, 148
Philip IV, 151-152, 166
Philip VI, 166, 168
pilgrimage, 103-106
pirate, 22-23, 64
Pizan, Christine de, 149
poetry, 60, 72, 148
Poland, 146
Polo, Marco, 61
Polynesia, 245, 251-253, 255, 257-260
Pope, 146, 149, 150-152
porcelain, 6, 16, 63, 72-74, 116-118, 121
pottery, 8, 73, 110, 116, 124-125, 196, 199, 201, 214-215, 234, 237, 257, 264
Pueblo, 197-201
Pure Land, 11, 18
Purépecha (Tarascan), 198, 212-218
pyramid, 216, 221-222, 226-227, 237
Qarshi, 46
Quetzalcóatl, 197-198, 220, 222, 227
Qutub Minar, 80-81
Rainbow Serpent, 250
Ranginui, 255

Rapa Nui (Easter Island), 257-259
Rashid al-Din Hamadani, 48
Red Turbans, 45, 63-64
rensho, 4
renza, 16
Richard II, 169
Rihla, 105
Rokuon-ji, 18
Romani, 146
rongorongo, 258
Russia, 27, 46, 49-52
sacrifice, 65, 71, 124, 128, 184, 193, 216-223, 232, 238
Sahara, 100-102, 108-114, 124
Salado, 199-202
salt, 32, 64, 100, 102, 109-110, 112, 116, 124, 127, 140-141, 159, 161, 163, 188, 215, 240
Samarkand, 53-54
samurai, 1, 3-6, 9-10, 12-13, 15, 17, 20
Sarai, 49, 52
sculpture, 62, 122-123, 125-126, 129, 217-218
Sengoku period, 1
shaman, 37-38, 239, 264-265
Shari-den, 12
Shinto, 11
Shizu (Kublai Khan), 13, 40, 44, 57-63
shōen, 4
shogun, 2-4, 11-16, 18-19
shugo, 5-6
Shumi Yuan, 58
silk, 6, 16, 19, 29-30, 42, 63, 116, 156, 159
Silk Road, 53, 142, 188

slavery, 23, 28, 40, 49, 80, 98, 102, 108, 110, 112, 116, 124, 159, 190, 216, 221, 228-229

Song dynasty, 57, 60-61, 64-65

Songhai, 98, 104 110

soulava, 264

Spain, 101, 108, 159

Spiro Mounds, 187

Sugimoto, 2

Sultaniyya, 48

Sumiyoshi, 2

Sweden, 161

Syria, 47, 53 106, 108

Swahili Coast, 114-120

Swift Creek culture, 179-180

Tabriz, 48

Tahiti, 257, 259

Taira clan, 2-3

Tamoanchan, 218-219

Tarascan (Purépecha), 198, 212-218

Tarmashirin, 46

Tartar, 33

Taoism, 71

tax, 2-6, 8-9, 16, 45, 59, 61, 66, 68, 79-80, 90, 100-101, 112, 151, 160

Taycanamo, 234

tea, 6, 12, 21, 34

Temüjin (Genghis Khan), 27, 39-41, 52-53, 61

Temür Öljeyitü, 44, 63

Tengri, 38

Tenochtitlán, 222, 225-227, 232

Tezcatlipoca, 220-222, 227

The Secret History of the Mongols, 28

Timur, 46-54, 83
Timbuktu, 102-104, 108, 110
Tlaloc, 198, 221-222, 227
Toghon Temür, 45
Toi, 251
Tokhtamysh, 50
Tokyo, 2
Tolui, 44
Tonga, 245, 257, 260
Toqta, 49
Tuareg, 102, 104
Tughlaqabad, 78, 80
Tughlugh Timur, 46, 50
Tughluq Shah, 82
tutqaul, 59
Tzintzuntzan, 214-216
Ulugh Khan (Muhammad bin Tughluq), 79-80, 82-83, 92
Uluru (Ayers Rock), 247
Unam Sanctam, 152
Uzbeg, 49-50
vassal, 3-6, 9, 78, 135-137, 166
Venice, 49, 100, 145, 159
Vijayanagara, 79, 84-90, 92
Wari, 233, 237
wakō, 22
Western Schism, 155
Whātonga, 251
White Lotus Movement, 45, 64
Woodland period, 175-176, 178-179, 190
Wycliffe, John, 155
Xibalba, 218-219

Xipe Totec, 198, 221-222
Xiuhtecuhtli, 222-224
Xochipilli, 222
yam, 39
Yinshan Zhengyao, 35
Yongle (Zhu Di), 69-70, 72
Yoruba, 111, 122, 124-126
Yuan dynasty, 40, 44-45, 57-66, 73
yurt, 27, 29, 32, 37, 38, 42
Zen, 11-12, 18
Zimbabwe, 119-122
Zheng He, 70, 73
Zhu Biao, 68
Zhu Di (Yongle), 69-70, 72
Zhu Yuanzhang (Hongwu), 45, 63-66, 68-69, 71
Zhu Yunwen (Jianwen), 69-71
Zuni, 193, 194, 202